MAKING
CABINETS & BUILT-INS

Sam Allen

128883

STERLING

New York / London
www.sterlingpublishing.com

STERLING and the distinctive Sterling logo are registered trademarks of
Sterling Publishing Co., Inc.

Library of Congress Cataloging-in-Publication Data

Allen, Sam.
  Making cabinets and built-ins : planning—building—installing / Sam Allen.
      p. cm.
  Includes index.
  ISBN-13: 978-1-4027-3038-2
  ISBN-10: 1-4027-3038-1
  1. Cabinetwork—Amateurs' manuals. 2. Built-in furniture—Design and construction—Amateurs'
manuals. I. Title.

TT197.A45 2007
684'.08—dc22

                                                        2006100785

Published by Sterling Publishing Co., Inc.
387 Park Avenue South, New York, NY 10016
© 2008 by Sam Allen
This edition is based on material found in *Making Cabinets & Built-Ins* ©1986 by Sam Allen
Distributed in Canada by Sterling Publishing
c/o Canadian Manda Group, 165 Dufferin Street
Toronto, Ontario, Canada M6K 3H6
Distributed in the United Kingdom by GMC Distribution Services
Castle Place, 166 High Street, Lewes, East Sussex, England BN7 1XU
Distributed in Australia by Capricorn Link (Australia) Pty. Ltd.
P.O. Box 704, Windsor, NSW 2756, Australia

Interior design: T. Reitzle, S. Williams/Oxygen Design

Sterling ISBN-13: 978-1-4027-3038-2
        ISBN-10: 1-4027-3038-1

For information about custom editions, special sales, premium and
corporate purchases, please contact Sterling Special Sales
Department at 800-805-5489 or specialsales@sterlingpublishing.com.

Acknowledgments

I WOULD LIKE TO THANK my wife, Virginia, for her help in preparing this book. Without her help and encouragement, this book would not have been possible. I also want to thank my mother, Betty Allen, for her help in preparing the manuscript. My brother, John Allen, has always encouraged me, and I want to thank him also. My thanks also go to my sons, Paul and John; their hands appear in some of the photos.

This book is based largely on practical experience I have gained during 35 years of woodworking, so I would like to thank the experienced cabinet-makers with whom I have worked for generously sharing their knowledge with me.

Contents

Introduction

THIS BOOK IS DESIGNED to lead you step-by-step through the fundamentals of making cabinets and built-ins. Beginning with selecting materials, reading plans, and laying out the cuts on the wood, the book progresses through joinery and assembly techniques, plus all the other basic components of cabinetmaking, to a complete set of plans and directions for an entire system of cabinets **(I–1)**. There is also a section on building cabinets to accommodate electronic components for home entertainment and computer systems **(I–2)**. Then, in a separate appendix, you will find a built-in planner, which will help you visualize the completed installation and give you the chance to try various layouts on paper.

I–1. Kitchen cabinets.

I–2. Home entertainment cabinets.

THE TERM *CABINETMAKING* is sometimes used in reference to making all kinds of fine furniture, but in this book it is used in its strictest sense. It simply means making cabinets, including built-ins for kitchens and baths, book-shelves (**I–3**), and freestanding cabinets like chests of drawers (**I–4**).

Recent technology has added many new materials and techniques to the craft of cabinetmaking. Although commercial cabinetmakers use these new products extensively, traditional materials and practices are still important to today's cabinetmaker. This book will give you a firm foundation in traditional methods as well as introduce you to some of the most recent technological developments in the field.

I–3. Bookshelves.

I–4. Freestanding chest of drawers.

Tools

SOME PEOPLE THINK that you must invest a large amount of money into tools before you can build cabinets, but this is not true. With just a few basic tools, you can build all but the most complex cabinets; however, additional tools, especially power equipment, will enable you to tackle more complex projects and get them done faster. **Table I–1** is a list of tools to get you started in cabinetmaking.

I-5. *Hand tools.*

HAND TOOLS (I–5)
One 12" tape measure with $3/4$" blade
One framing square
One combination square
One 16-ounce finishing hammer
One set of screwdrivers
One backsaw and miter box
One set of butt chisels ($1/4$", $1/2$", $3/4$", 1")
One sharpening stone
One four-in-hand file
Two 3" C-clamps or fast-action clamps
Four 54" bar clamps

Table I–1.

I-6. *Power tools.*

POWER TOOLS AND ACCESSORIES (I–6)
Safety glasses or goggles
One $^3/_8$"-chuck electric drill
One set of drill bits ($^1/_{16}$" to $^1/_4$")— brad-point drills are best for woodworking
One set of spade bits ($^3/_8$" to 1")
One $7^1/_4$" portable circular saw
One saw and router guide
One router ($^1/_2$" is best, but $^1/_4$" will do)
Router bits (straight $^1/_4$", $^1/_2$", $^3/_4$")
One jigsaw

Table I–2.

Additional Equipment

Once you have a basic set of tools, there are three more power tools that you may want to consider for your next purchase. An air-powered nail gun takes the work out of nailing, and it is less likely to split the boards or leave hammer marks on the wood (I–7). For cabinet work, a nail gun that will handle 16- or 18-gauge nails is best. You also will need a compressor to provide air for the gun. A biscuit joiner can simplify joinery tasks (I–8). And a power miter saw will speed up the process of cutting face frames and moldings (I–9).

When you are ready to make some larger investments in tools, consider some stationary power equipment. Probably the first piece of stationary power equipment you should buy is a table saw. After that, the rest depends on the type of work you are doing. If you will be working with solid lumber extensively, consider a jointer and a surface planer. They will allow you to use less expensive rough-cut lumber and plane it to the exact thickness you require. A band saw is useful for making curved cuts. A lathe will enable you to make legs, spindles, and other turnings. With a shaper, you can make decorative edges on doors and drawer fronts faster than if you made them with a router.

There are many other pieces of specialized equipment you may want to consider, but keep in mind that these large pieces of equipment are not essential for you to get started in cabinetmaking. You can accomplish a great deal with the basic set of tools, so don't let the high cost of extra equipment keep you from enjoying the craft of cabinetmaking.

I–7. An air-powered nail gun takes the work out of nailing and it is less likely to split the boards or leave hammer marks on the wood.

I–8. A biscuit joiner can simplify joinery tasks.

Safety

IT IS ABSOLUTELY CRUCIAL that you keep your tools sharp and in good working order. A dull tool makes you exert too much force for maintaining good control. When you work with a chisel, clamp the work down and keep your hands behind the blade. Wear eye protection whenever you are doing any operation that sends dust or chips flying. When you are using power equipment, don't wear loose clothing such as a necktie or a shirt with floppy sleeves and remove jewelry such as necklaces and rings. If you have long hair, tie it back when you work. You don't want your clothing, jewelry, or hair to get caught in a piece of equipment.

Always keep your fingers well clear of the cutting part of any piece of power equipment. Use push sticks when necessary. Use the guards provided with power equipment. *If you keep safety in mind while you work, your enjoyment of cabinetmaking won't be marred by an accident.*

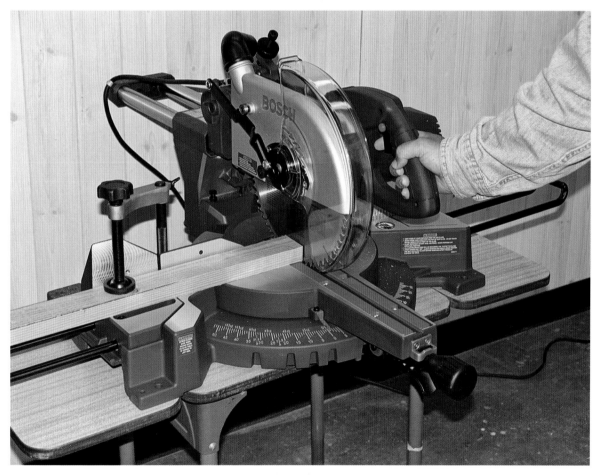

I–9. A power miter saw will speed up the process of cutting face frames and moldings.

① Materials

WOOD IS THE BASIC MATERIAL of the cabinetmaker. Many varieties of wood and several manufactured wood-composite products are used in cabinetmaking. Before you begin building cabinets and built-ins, you should have a basic understanding of these materials so that you can buy your materials intelligently and use them correctly (**1–1** and **1–2**).

1–1. The material you choose for your cabinets will play a large role in the finished look of the project. Here, pine, a softwood, was used to give the cabinets a rustic look.

1–2. These cabinets are made from maple, a hardwood. The clear subtle grain and light color give the cabinets a contemporary look.

Wood Properties

1–3. Tree rings appear as parallel lines in the section of the trunk that has been cut lengthwise. Where the trunk has been cut crosswise, the rings show their true circular outline. The thin dark line between the outer bark and the inner wood is called the cambium; it is the area where all growth occurs. The small removed block shows the size of the enlarged sections in 1–4.

THE DRIED, CUT, AND SURFACED boards you buy at the lumberyard began as part of a living tree (**1–3**). The way that trees grow and the arrangement of their cells give wood its unique properties.

Tree cells are long, thin cylinders; some may be a hundred times longer than they are wide (**1–4**). Ninety percent of these cells run vertically in the standing tree; they are called *longitudinal* cells. It is the direction, density, and structure of these cells that give wood most of the properties that affect cabinetmaking. In addition to the longitudinal cells, all woods have horizontal cells, called *ray cells*. They radiate from just below the bark towards the middle of the tree. In most wood species, these cells are so small that they are not noticed. However, oak and a few other types of wood have very prominent ray cells. Ray cells can affect the way wood shrinks as it dries. The effect this has on cabinetmaking will be discussed later in more detail.

As it grows, a tree adds an additional layer of cells around the outside of the trunk in a layer just below the bark called the *cambium*. This process adds both height and width to the tree. Periods of rapid growth in the spring create cells that are larger and less dense than the cells produced during the slower growth of the summer. The wood produced in the spring is called *earlywood*, and the wood produced in the summer is called *latewood*. Together these two layers produce one *annual ring*. The annual

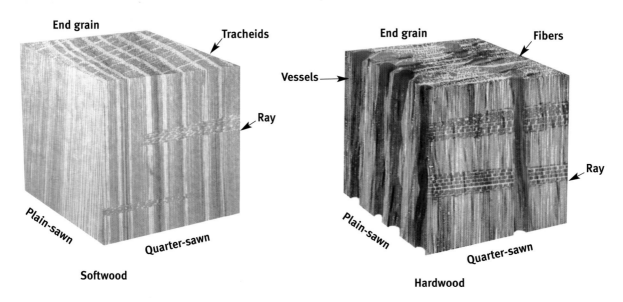

1–4. These enlarged cubes of wood show how the cell structure varies between softwood and hardwood. Notice that softwood is fairly uniform in its structure, whereas hardwood contains specialized vessel and fiber cells.

rings are very important to the cabinetmaker, because they produce the grain pattern that gives wood its character and affects how well the wood can be worked.

Most of the living processes take place in a narrow band around the outside of the tree. This area is composed of the last few annual rings and is called the *sapwood*. The older wood in the middle of the tree is called the *heartwood*. The heartwood no longer conducts sap to various parts of the tree as the sapwood does; it is inactive and essentially dead.

A variety of materials, collectively called *extractives*, collect in the heartwood. These extractives vary from one species to another, and they give the heartwood properties that are different from those of the sapwood. In some species, such as walnut, the extractives contain pigments that give the heartwood a darker color than the sapwood. In species such as redwood, they contain natural preservatives and toxins that make the heartwood resistant to fungus, decay, and insect damage. Resinous extractives in the heartwood make it more durable than the sapwood in some species.

Softwoods and Hardwoods

THERE ARE TWO MAJOR classifications of wood: softwood and hardwood. These classifications do not actually refer to the hardness of the wood; rather, they refer to the wood's cell structure.

Softwoods come from trees that bear needles, such as pines and firs (**1–5**). The cell structure of softwoods is very uniform; almost all of the wood is made from a single type of cell, called a *tracheid* (**1–4**). Tracheids are hollow cells that are filled with fluids while the tree is alive. When the tree is cut, the fluids evaporate, leaving the hollow outer shell of the cell.

In some species of softwood, there is little difference between the tracheids in the earlywood and those in the latewood. These species are highly prized for their easy-working qualities. A few such species are eastern white pine, western white pine, and sugar pine.

In other softwood species, the earlywood tracheids are thin-walled and the

1–5. Trees with needles are classified as softwoods. Softwoods usually have a large central trunk that extends their entire height; small branches are arranged radially around the trunk. This structure makes them ideal for producing the large boards necessary for building construction.

latewood tracheids are thick-walled. The resulting wood tends to have an uneven grain. Uneven-grained woods are usually stronger than even-grained woods, but they are more difficult to shape and have a greater tendency to split when nailed. Two examples of uneven-grained woods are Douglas fir and southern yellow pine.

Hardwoods come from trees that have broad leaves (**1–6**). Their cell structure is more complex than that of softwoods. Instead of a single predominant type of cell, the hardwoods have several specialized cells that perform different functions (refer to **1–4** on page 10). The strength of a hardwood comes from its thick-walled cells, called *fibers*. They have practically no interior cavity and do not help the tree conduct fluids from one part to another. The other main type of cell in a hardwood is the *vessel cell*. Vessel cells perform the fluid-transfer function necessary for the tree to maintain itself. These cells are large, thin-walled, and hollow.

1–6. Trees with broad leaves are classified as hardwoods. Hardwoods have a trunk that may branch off in several directions as the tree grows.

When boards are cut from a tree, some of the vessel cells are sliced through. These openings in the surface of the board are known as *pores*. Some species, such as oak, have very prominent pores. These species are called *open-grained woods*. Species such as maple that have small, less noticeable pores are called *closed-grain woods*.

Hardwoods are also classified as either ring-porous or diffuse-porous. In *ring-porous woods,* such as oak, ash, and elm, most of the vessel cells are concentrated in the earlywood. This gives these woods a distinctive grain pattern, but it also tends to make them uneven-grained and therefore more difficult to work. *Diffuse-porous woods,* such as birch, alder, and basswood, have their vessel cells distributed evenly throughout the annual ring. They are very even grained and easy to work. Some woods—black walnut, for example—fall between these two classifications. They are called *semi-ring-porous*. In these woods, the earlywood has large pores that gradually diminish in size as they reach the latewood (**1–7**).

Density

The actual measure of a wood's hardness is its density. Wood density is measured by specific gravity, which is the ratio of the weight of a substance to the weight of an equal volume of another substance, that of water. Specific gravity numbers of less than one indicate that a material will float in water. The harder the wood, the higher is its specific gravity.

1–7. Hardwoods are divided into three smaller classifications according to the arrangement of their vessel cells. The maple, on the left, is an example of a diffuse-porous wood. The vessel cells are distributed evenly throughout the wood and are not very discernible. The walnut, in the middle, is an example of semi-ring-porous wood. The vessel cells are more prominent in the earlywood, and diminish in size throughout the latewood. The oak, on the right, is an example of a ring-porous wood. The very prominent vessel cells are concentrated in the earlywood part of the ring.

You can see by looking at **1–7** that the terms *hardwood* and *softwood* are misleading. The least-dense wood in the table is balsa, and balsa is a hardwood. Southern yellow pine, which is a softwood, is almost as dense as black walnut, which is a hardwood, and considerably denser than several other hardwoods, such as basswood, cottonwood, and alder.

Most of the popular cabinet woods have a specific gravity of between 0.4 and 0.7. Wood in this density range is hard enough to withstand physical abuse, yet soft enough to be worked with ordinary tools.

Wood with a specific gravity of 0.5 to 0.6 is ideal for cabinetmaking. Black walnut, black cherry, and mahogany fall into this range. Although softer woods, such as pine, dent too easily to be used for desks or tabletops, they are frequently used for cabinets where denting isn't a problem. Harder woods, such as oak and maple, are used for cabinets that will receive a lot of abuse.

Moisture Content

Green wood freshly cut from a tree is almost 30 percent water. As this water evaporates, the wood shrinks. Because of variations in cell structure, some parts of the wood shrink more than others. This sets up internal stresses that cause boards to twist, warp, and split. Before using a board, you want it to be dimensionally stable. A dimensionally stable board has a moisture content of approximately six to nine percent.

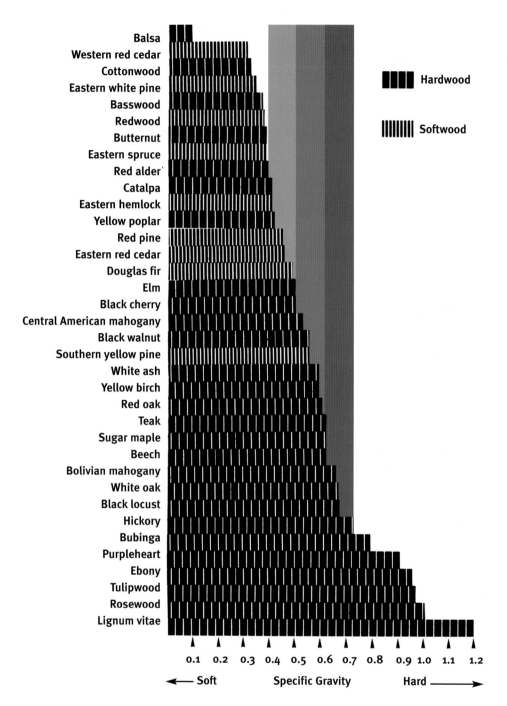

Balsa
Western red cedar
Cottonwood
Eastern white pine
Basswood
Redwood
Butternut
Eastern spruce
Red alder
Catalpa
Eastern hemlock
Yellow poplar
Red pine
Eastern red cedar
Douglas fir
Elm
Black cherry
Central American mahogany
Black walnut
Southern yellow pine
White ash
Yellow birch
Red oak
Teak
Sugar maple
Beech
Bolivian mahogany
White oak
Black locust
Hickory
Bubinga
Purpleheart
Ebony
Tulipwood
Rosewood
Lignum vitae

▮▮▮▮ Hardwood

|||||| Softwood

0.1 0.2 0.3 0.4 0.5 0.6 0.7 0.8 0.9 1.0 1.1 1.2

◀── Soft   Specific Gravity   Hard ──▶

1–8. Specific gravity is a measure of wood density. Density affects the working properties and wearing qualities of the wood. In this chart, any wood represented by a band that touches a brown area is considered a cabinet wood. Medium-gray areas represent those woods that combine good-working properties with good-wearing properties. The light-gray band represents woods that are very easy to work, but may not be hard enough to withstand heavy use. The darkest gray band represents woods that are a little more difficult to work, but will withstand heavy wear. Woods outside of the gray area can be used in cabinetmaking; however, they are not considered primarily cabinet woods.

Moisture is removed from lumber in two ways: by *air drying* or *kiln drying*. Air drying relies solely on natural evaporation. The wood is stacked so that air can circulate freely around it. This process can take up to several years and usually won't lower the moisture content below 12 percent. Most cabinet-grade lumber is kiln-dried. With kiln-drying, large ovens bake out the moisture. Kiln-dried lumber has a moisture content of five to nine percent.

Even kiln-dried lumber shrinks or swells slightly with changes in humidity. Usually, woods with higher specific gravity shrink and swell more than the less-dense woods. If you don't account for this shrinking and swelling when you build a cabinet from solid lumber, cracks and loose joints will result.

The problem of wood movement is exaggerated by modern central heating. An antique that has survived for hundreds of years in a drafty old house may crack and loosen when moved to a centrally heated, modern setting. For this reason, it may be necessary to modify the design of an antique reproduction to allow for wood movement. For example, some Shaker furniture isn't designed to allow for much wood movement since the humidity was fairly constant in the old Shaker buildings. If you follow an old Shaker design exactly, you may have problems with the piece in a modern building. Solutions to this problem are covered in chapters 4 and 6.

Knots

A knot is actually the joint between the main trunk of a tree and its limb. A tight knot forms at the base of the limb, where its fluid channels connect to the fluid network of the tree. A tight knot in a board will not fall out since it is firmly attached to the surrounding wood. This type of knot presents some problems in working with the wood, because the growth pattern changes abruptly around the knot, making operations such as planing and surfacing more difficult.

As long as the branch is alive, new connections will be made to the fluid channels and the knot will remain tight. However, if the limb dies due to damage or lack of light, a loose knot will form as the tree increases in diameter past the point where the limb is attached. The trunk will grow around the limb, but the wood of the limb will be separated from the wood of the trunk by the limb's bark. Wood with tight knots can be used to good effect to create a rustic-looking cabinet (1–9). Wood with loose knots should be avoided, because the knots will eventually fall out of a cut board, leaving a hole.

1–9. Wood with tight knots can be used to good effect to create a rustic-looking cabinet. Wood with loose knots should be avoided, because the knots will eventually fall out of a cut board, leaving a hole.

How Wood Is Cut

THE WAY WOOD IS CUT into boards can affect the grain pattern and the dimensional stability of the board. The basic grain pattern of a log is a set of concentric rings. Cutting through these rings at various angles produces a variety of grain patterns. Solid lumber is cut in basically two ways: *plain-sawn* and *quarter-sawn* (**1–10**).

Cabinetmakers use two words, *grain* and *figure*, to describe what most people simply refer to as grain. To a cabinetmaker, *grain* refers to the direction of the tracheid, or fiber cells, in the wood. The way the board is cut creates a grain direction in the board. The fibers may intersect the surface at an angle, as shown in **1–11**. *Figure* is the design created by cutting through the concentric rings at an angle. In practice, the terms grain and figure are frequently interchanged, and, in casual conversation, many cabinetmakers refer to both properties as *grain*. However, when clarity is essential, cabinetmakers will distinguish between the two words.

Plain-sawn boards are cut from the log with the saw blade tangent to the annual rings. With this method, the blade cuts through relatively few rings and the board contains a larger segment of each ring than quarter-sawn lumber. The plain-sawn method produces a figure pattern on the surface of the board that consists of parabolas (U- or V-shapes) and ellipses (ovals). When softwoods are cut in this manner, they are usually called *flat-sawn boards* or *flat-grained* boards (**1–12**).

Quarter-sawn lumber is cut so that the saw blade passes at a right angle to the rings. This means that many rings are cut through, but the board contains only a small segment of each ring. The face of the board shows only the edge of the rings, so the figure is a series of closely spaced parallel lines. Softwoods cut this way are frequently referred to as *edge-grained* or *vertical-grained*.

Woods such as oak that have large ray cells produce an interesting effect when they are quarter-sawn (**1–13**). Since the ray cells run at right angles to the rings, the saw blade may slice through them lengthwise. This produces interesting, irregularly shaped marks on the surface of the board.

In practice, many boards are cut at angles ranging between tangent to the rings and 90 degrees to the rings. For the purpose of classification then, an arbitrary division has been set at 45 degrees. A board that has been cut so that its rings form an angle that is between 45 degrees and 90 degrees with its surface is called *quarter-sawn,* whereas a board with rings that form an angle of less than 45 degrees is called *plain-sawn.* A board that falls in the midrange at approximately 45 degrees exhibits characteristics of both types of cutting. Oak boards cut in this midrange are sometimes called *rift-cut* if they don't exhibit much ray figure (**1–14**).

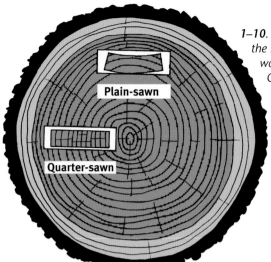

1–10. Plain-sawn lumber is cut so that the faces of the board are tangent to the rings. This produces a pleasing figure on the face, but boards cut this way are more apt to cup and change dimension across their width. Quarter-sawn lumber is cut so that the face forms a 90-degree angle with the rings. Quarter-sawn wood is more dimensionally stable than plain-sawn wood; its width does not vary as much with moisture change, and it has less of a tendency to cup.

1–11. Grain direction is important when using tools such as chisels or planes. The chisel on the left is cutting with the grain. Notice how the chip tends to break off above the cutting line, leaving a smooth, even cut. The chisel on the right is cutting against the grain. The wood tends to tear ahead of the chisel, causing chipping, gouges, tear-out, and a rough cut.

1–12. Plain-sawn boards have a figure pattern that consists of parabolas (U- or V-shapes) and ellipses (ovals).

1–13. The figure of some quarter-sawn wood like oak is embellished by wild ray marks.

1–14. The oak on this chest is rift-cut. It has the characteristics of quarter-sawn oak without prominent ray marks.

When wood is tangent to the rings, it shrinks and swells about twice as much as it does when it is perpendicular to the rings. This means that in a plain-sawn board most of the shrinkage and swelling takes place across its width, whereas in a quarter-sawn board most of the dimensional change takes place across its thickness. Since the width of a board is greater than its thickness, any change in width will be more critical than a change in thickness. For this reason, quarter-sawn boards are considered more dimensionally stable than plain-sawed boards. Plain-sawn lumber has a tendency to cup in the direction shown in **1–10**, whereas quarter-sawn lumber usually remains flat as it dries.

When uneven-grained wood, such as fir, is plain-sawn, it is difficult to get a truly flat surface, because the softer sections of the grain tend to wear down faster during sanding operations. It is easier to get a flat surface on quarter-sawn lumber, because the soft sections of the wood are less exposed.

Because of its greater stability, quarter-sawn lumber has been the cabinetmaker's choice for hundreds of years; however, the figure of plain-sawn lumber makes it more popular in some applications. The choice then boils down to a trade-off between figure and dimensional stability. Each project is different, so you should make your choice based on the function of the cabinet and the way you want it to look.

Lumber Grades

WHEN YOU BUY LUMBER, the grade you choose will determine the finished look of the cabinet. Usually you will want to use the highest grade that you can afford to avoid defects and discoloration; however, if you want a distinctive look, you may choose a lower grade that has more variation in color and minor defects that will add interest (**1–15**). There are two grading systems for lumber: one for hardwoods and one for softwoods.

1–15. These cabinets are made from common-grade maple. The variation in color and minor defects give them a distinctive rustic look.

Hardwood Grades

There are five grades of hardwood in the system used by the National Hardwood Lumber Association. The grading system is based on a principle called *clear-face cuttings*. **Illustration 1–16** demonstrates this. There is also a minimum size for each grade (**1–17**).

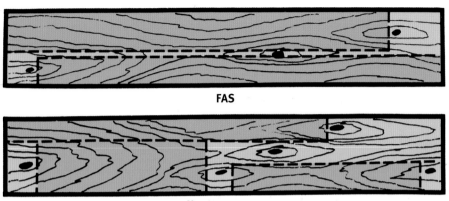

FAS

No. 1 common

1–16. The placement of knots or other defects in a board determines the largest board that can be cut that would miss all the defects. When the defects are placed in a manner that allows a few large clear boards to be cut from the original board, the board receives a higher grade than a board that would have to be cut into several smaller boards to avoid all the defects. Clear-face cuttings are purely imaginary; it is the principle of clear-face cuttings that gives the cabinetmaker an idea of the size of usable boards that can be cut from a board of a particular grade. You can cut the first and seconds (FAS) board, on the top, into two large pieces with almost no waste. You would have to cut the No. 1 common board, on the bottom, into three smaller boards with a considerable amount of waste to obtain clear-face cuttings.

Minimum Sizes for Hardwood Grades

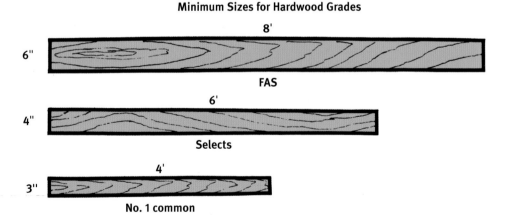

1–17. In addition to the placement of defects, hardwoods are graded according to size. This illustration shows the smallest board for each grade.

FIRST AND SECONDS (FAS)—This is the highest grade. These boards are almost completely free from knots or defects. They are six inches or wider and eight inches or longer. The boards yield 83⅓ percent clear-face cuttings that are 4 inches or wider by 5 feet or longer, or 3 inches or wider by 7 inches or longer.

SELECTS—This grade has one side that is equal to FAS and one side that is No. 1 common. This grade is useful when you only need one good side. The boards are 4 inches or wider by 6 feet and longer. They yield 83⅓ percent clear-face cuttings.

NO. 1 COMMON—This grade is more economical for small projects when long, wide boards are not necessary and you can cut parts from clear sections between defects. The boards are 3 inches or wider by 4 feet or longer. They yield 66⅔ percent clear-face cuttings that are 4 inches or wider by 2 feet or longer, or 3 inches or wider by 3 feet or longer.

Two additional grades are also available, but they are usually not used in cabinetmaking; they are **NO. 2 COMMON** and **NO. 3 COMMON**.

Softwood Grades

The Western Wood Products Association has designated many grades of softwood, but the ones most useful in cabinetmaking are listed here.

C SELECT AND BETTER—This is the best grade; it has only minor imperfections. It can be very expensive.

D SELECT—This is still a very high quality grade. It will contain a few sound defects.

NO. 1 COMMON—This grade has more knots and defects than D select, but it is still useful for making the smaller cabinets since you can cut around the defects.

NO. 2 COMMON—This is also called shelving grade. It has quite a few knots and it is only useful for cabinets when you want a knotty effect. This is the grade most commonly sold at lumberyards. If you want a higher grade, you will usually need to go to a lumber dealer that sells to professionals.

NO. 3, 4, AND 5 COMMON—These lower softwood grades are usually unsuitable for cabinet work.

Surfacing

WHEN A BOARD IS FIRST sawed from a log, it has a rough surface and may vary in thickness and width, and the edges are not square with the face of the board. You can buy this rough-cut lumber just as it left the saw, but you need a jointer and a surface planer to work with it. That is what most commercial cabinet shops do, and now that inexpensive surface planers are available many do-it-yourselfers also surface their lumber (**1–18**). However, when you are first starting out and you don't have the equipment for dealing with rough-cut lumber, you can pay a little more to get lumber that has been surfaced at the mill.

There are several different types of surfacing available. For most beginners, the best is S4S, which means surfaced four sides. An S4S board has smooth and parallel faces as well as smooth edges that are square with the face.

If you own a jointer, you may want to buy S2S (surfaced two sides). This type of board has smooth and parallel faces, but the edges are still rough and uneven. To use this type, first surface one edge with a jointer (1–19). Then saw the board to width on the table saw with the jointed edge against the fence.

There are two other types of surfacing, but they are not frequently stocked by most dealers. They are S1S1E (surfaced one side one edge) and S1S2E (surfaced one side two edges).

1–18. This type of portable surface planer is inexpensive enough to consider using in a home shop.

Lumber Sizes

YOU CAN PURCHASE lumber in random widths and lengths or by standard dimensional lumber sizes. Rough-cut lumber and most S2S boards are only sold in random widths and lengths. Large cabinet shops buy lumber in large units. These large units of random widths and lengths provide a variety of sizes that will meet most shop needs with little waste.

Do-it-yourselfers usually want to buy only enough lumber for one project at a time, and they need specific sizes. You have two choices: You can buy standard-size dimensional lumber, or you can go to a lumber dealer that lets you sort through various random sizes to find what you want.

1–19. You can use a jointer to produce a smooth, straight, and square edge on a board that has rough edges.

Standard Sizes

The nomenclature used for designating standard sizes can be a little confusing to the beginner. The actual size of a board is always smaller than the nominal size used for designating the board. The sizes refer to the rough-cut size of the board. Planing and smoothing operations reduce the thickness. This means that a board with a nominal thickness of 1 inch is actually about ¾ inch thick when surfaced. For thicknesses greater than

1 inch, there is a difference in the actual thickness between hardwoods and softwoods.

The thickness of a rough-cut board can also be designated by a system called the *quarter designation*. In this system, the nominal thickness is designated in quarters of an inch. Therefore, 1-inch-thick rough-cut boards are called *4/4's*. A 4/4's rough-cut board will usually be approximately ¾ inch when it is surfaced. If you wanted a surfaced board that is closer to a full inch when surfaced, you would use ⁵⁄₄'s rough lumber to begin with.

Pricing

Since dimensional lumber is commonly priced by the piece, it is easy to tell how much it will cost. If it is not priced by the piece, it will usually be priced by the linear foot, so you simply multiply the cost per foot by the length. Rough-cut lumber is sold by the board foot. One board foot is 144 cubic inches. A board that is 1 inch thick and 12 inches x 12 inches is 1 board foot; so is a 1-inch-thick board that is 6 inches x 24 inches. Any combination of width, length, and thickness that equals 144 cubic inches is 1 board foot. Anything less than 1 inch thick is still calculated as 1 inch thick. Therefore, up to 1 inch, you can figure board feet the same way as square feet: Simply multiply the length times the width. If the measurements are in feet, then you have board feet. When the measurements are in inches, you need to divide the total by 144. Anything thicker than 1 inch is figured in increments of ¼ inch. Thus, a board that measures 1¹⁄₁₆ inches thick would be figured at its nominal size of 1¼ inches. For calculations, this translates into 1.25 inches. To get board feet in this instance, figure the square feet and then multiply your answer by 1.25.

Most lumberyards have a chart that gives board feet equivalents for most sizes of boards, so calculations are usually unnecessary. Simply find the section of the chart for the correct thickness; then find the point where the length and width line up on the chart. Once you have the board feet, you can figure the total price by multiplying the board feet by the price per board foot.

Veneers

SOLID WOOD THAT IS less than ¼ inch thick is referred to as *veneer*. Usually made from expensive wood, veneer is used for covering the face of a less expensive wood. The log or piece of log from which veneers are cut is called a *flitch*. Veneers are usually sliced from the flitch with a large mechanical knife, but they can also be sawed.

Veneers are sliced in four ways. *Flat-sliced* veneers are the equivalent of plain-sawn lumber. *Quarter-sliced* veneers are the equivalent of quarter-sawn

1–20. The variations in the figure of these oak veneer samples are caused by the way they have been sliced. From left to right, they are: plain-sliced, quarter-sliced, and rift-sliced.

1–21. The figure produced by rotary cutting is quite different from that produced by the other methods. The narrow annual ring is exaggerated in width because the cut is so close to parallel with the ring. This example of rotary-cut oak exhibits a wilder figure but is still suitable for use on fine cabinetry.

lumber. *Rift slicing* is a method used to reduce the fleck pattern in oak or other woods with prominent medullary rays; otherwise, the figure looks like quarter-sliced (**1–20**). The fourth method is *rotary slicing* and it has no equivalent in solid lumber.

With rotary slicing, the log is mounted in a large lathe and rotated. A knife slices a thin sheet of veneer from the log as it rotates. The cut is made almost parallel to the rings. This method produces a large sheet of veneer without any seams. The figure produced by rotary cutting is quite different from that produced by the other methods. The narrow annual ring is exaggerated in width because the cut is so close to parallel with the ring. Some species, such as fir, produce a wild figure when rotary-cut. Other species, such as oak and birch, produce a pleasant figure that is very suitable for use on fine cabinetry (**1–21**).

You can purchase quarter-sliced and flat-sliced veneers by the flitch. Each sheet is stacked in the order it was sliced. The figure on adjacent pieces will almost be identical. You can put these pieces together in patterns.

Plywood

PLYWOOD IS A MANUFACTURED product produced by laminating veneers together (1–22). Wood has been laminated for hundreds of years, but early laminates had all of the grain running in the same direction. Plywood, on the other hand, has every other sheet of veneer running with the grain direction at a 90-degree angle to the previous sheet. Plywood always has an odd number of laminations so that both face veneers will have their grain running in the same direction.

A major advantage of plywood is its dimensional stability. Because the grain is running in two different directions, the effect of changes in moisture content is minimized. Plywood simplifies construction practices, because special precautions to account for dimensional change are not needed. Another advantage of plywood is that it is available in large sheets, so you can make large cabinet parts from a single piece instead of from several boards glued together. In the United States, the standard size for plywood is 4 feet x 8 feet. Metric plywood is available is several sizes, but the most common sizes are 2400 mm x 1200 mm and 2700 mm x 1200 mm.

Plywood is available with a softwood-face veneer, usually fir, or with a variety of hardwood-face veneers. There are various grading systems for softwood and hardwood plywoods.

Softwood Plywood Grades

Softwood plywood is graded according to the type of wood used, the type of glue used for laminating the plies together, and according to the quality of the face veneers.

Although fir is the most commonly used wood for softwood plywood, there are approximately 30 species of softwood used in plywood manufacturing. These species are classified into four groups, according to their structural stiffness.

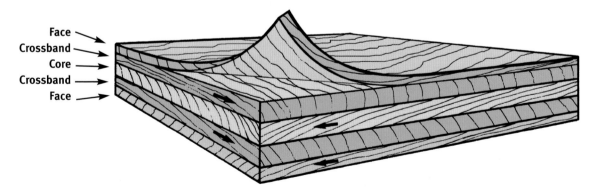

Face
Crossband
Core
Crossband
Face

1–22. Plywood is composed of veneers called plies that are laminated together. The outside plies are called faces. The middle ply is called the core. Plies that have a grain direction opposite the grain direction of the face plies are called crossbands.

GROUP 1 includes Douglas fir that originates in the American Northwest, western larch, tanoak, and several varieties of pine.

GROUP 2 includes Douglas fir that originates in the southwestern United States, several other varieties of fir, Port Orford cedar, western hemlock, lauan, western white pine, and Sitka spruce.

GROUP 3 includes lodge pole pine, ponderosa pine, redwood, Alaska yellow cedar, and red alder.

GROUP 4 includes sugar pine, aspen, cottonwood, incense cedar, and western red cedar.

GROUP 5 includes basswood and poplar.

You may have noticed that a couple of hardwoods, such as lauan and alder, are included here. Even though they are technically hardwoods, they are included in the list of softwood species used by the American Plywood Association.

Two types of glue are used: *interior*, which is moisture-resistant but not waterproof, and *exterior*, which is fully waterproof.

The quality of the face veneer is designated by a letter. The highest quality is N, which means natural or that the face veneer is suitable for a natural finish. However, this veneer is not commonly stocked by most dealers. The highest grade commonly available is A. This grade is smooth with only slight repairs. Grade B is a solid-surface veneer that permits plug repairs and tight knots. With a grade-C face veneer, knot holes to 1 inch in diameter are permitted and small splits are also allowed. The lowest grade available is D, which permits knot holes to 2½ inches along with some splits.

Different combinations of face veneers are available, with one side that is a higher grade than the other.

As previously mentioned, N-grade face veneers are the highest quality available. They are usually only available as a special-order item and are very expensive. N-N has N veneers on both sides, N-A has an A veneer on the back, and N-B has a B veneer on the back. N-N, N-A, and N-B are only available in a ¾ inch thickness. N-D has a D-back veneer and it is only available in a ¼ inch thickness.

A-A is the highest quality that is commonly available. It is used when both sides of the sheet will be visible.

A-B is the type that is usually used for cabinet work. It has one good face with a back that is almost as good.

A-C is only available with exterior glue. This is a good choice for cabinets that will be subjected to a great deal of moisture.

A-D is frequently used for the bottom or back of a cabinet, where the back of the plywood will not be visible.

B-C is only available with exterior glue. It is not commonly used for cabinetmaking.

C-D (commonly called *CDX*) is available with exterior glue and has two rough faces. Intended for building construction, it is not generally used for cabinetmaking. This type of plywood is supposed to be used in large sheets. When it is cut into smaller pieces, it frequently has separated plies.

Softwood plywood is often available in the following thicknesses: 5/16, 3/8, 1/2, 5/8, 3/4, and 7/8. Thicker plywood is available for structural applications, but it is not commonly used for cabinetmaking.

Hardwood Plywood Grades

THE GRADING SYSTEM FOR PLYWOOD with a hardwood-face veneer is different from the grading system for softwood plywood. There is a separate grading system for face veneer and back veneer used on hardwood plywood.

The system used for face veneer is similar to the softwood plywood grading system.

AA is the highest grade. The veneers used are almost totally free from defects. When more than one piece is used for covering the sheet, the figure and color are carefully matched.

A is the second grade. The veneers are almost the same quality as AA, but they are not as carefully figure-matched. However, they are color-matched.

B uses veneers that are very high quality, but they are not matched for color or figure.

C allows for some small defects in the veneer and unlimited color and figure variation.

D allows for large defects such as 3-inch-diameter knot holes. The defects are plugged, but will be noticeable.

E is the lowest grade and is only useful when a very rustic appearance is acceptable.

The first three grades, AA through B, are acceptable as face veneers for cabinetmaking. They are equally smooth and free from defects. The major difference is in the amount of care taken in figure and color matching.

The system for grading the back veneer uses numbers. **GRADES 1** and **2** may have small repaired defects. **GRADES 3** and **4** may have open defects like splits and knot holes.

The grade of a sheet of hardwood plywood is designated by listing the face grade first and then the back grade. For example, a sheet with a high-quality face and a back with no open defects would be A1, while a sheet with a high-quality face and a back with open defects would be A4. In both cases, the face veneer is the same quality, so you can save money by using the A4 in cases where the back will not be visible.

The best way of buying hardwood plywood is selecting the individual sheets yourself. You may find that you prefer the pattern of the unmatched veneers on a particular sheet of a lower grade over the matched veneers of a higher grade. A-grade veneers are uniform, and this is appropriate for many uses. But some of the lower grades that allow for more color variation have more individual character, so select your plywood on the basis of what you want your finished project to look like.

There is one additional grade called *SP*, or *specialty*. Veneers in this grade may have certain defects such as knots or worm holes that, under the normal grading system, would allow them only to be used as backings. However, since their specific defects give beauty or character to the wood, these veneers are used as face veneers and are graded SP. In some instances, SP veneers may be more expensive than A veneers, and they are only available in limited quantities.

As with softwood plywood, different combinations of face and back veneers are available in hardwood plywood. One of the most popular combinations for cabinetmaking is A-2. This combination actually gives you two good sides. Some of the more expensive varieties—walnut, for example—are available with birch backs. It's best to use them when only one side of the plywood will show. Most of the ¾-inch hardwood plywood readily available does not have a back any lower than grade 2; however, ¼-inch plywood is often available with a grade-4 back.

There are more than 150 species of wood available as face veneers for hardwood plywood, but most of them are only available as special-order items. The most common species that you will find at most dealers are birch, lauan, oak, walnut, mahogany, basswood, and cherry. These are roughly listed according to their availability. Almost every lumberyard carries birch, lauan and oak plywood, because they are widely used in the building trades. The other varieties listed are usually only available at the largest outlets, or by special-order from local lumberyards or mail-order lumber outlets. The mail-order outlets sell hardwood plywood in small parts of a sheet, which is an advantage with the more expensive species. If you special-order them locally, you will probably have to purchase a full sheet.

The veneers used for hardwood plywood can be cut in one of four ways: *plain-sliced*, *rift*, *quarter-sliced*, or *rotary-cut*. Oak and birch produce a pleasing figure when they are rotary-cut, so rotary-cut veneers from these species are frequently used for plywood. Most other species are only readily available plain-sliced. Quarter-sliced veneers are used only on special-order plywood. If you special-order hardwood plywood, you may be able to specify the way you want the face veneer to be matched. For example, you could specify a book-matched pattern, or you could specify that the face be made from one whole piece of veneer.

Almost all of the hardwood plywood readily available is interior plywood, which uses a water-resistant glue. The exterior type of hardwood plywood uses a waterproof glue. Hardwood plywood is also available with a lumber core (**1–23**). This type is frequently used in cabinetmaking. It has a face veneer, a thin crossband on each side, and a thick core of solid lumber.

Plywood edges that are visible from the exterior of the cabinet usually must be covered in some way to make them visually acceptable. Several types of edge treatment that can be used with plywood cabinetry are discussed in detail toward the end of this chapter.

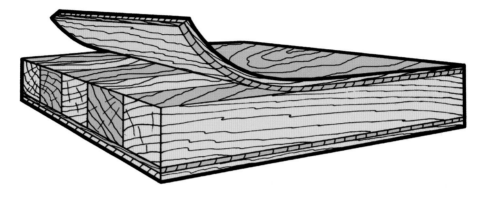

1–23. Lumber core plywood is a good substitute for solid lumber. Strips that are glued together into a panel form the core ply of a plywood sheet. The core is much thicker than the core of standard plywood and the crossbands are thinner.

Reconstituted Wood Products

PROJECTS LIKE THE CLOSET ORGANIZER shown in **1–24** can be made of the less expensive reconstituted wood product and still look good when the product is covered with a decorative overlay material.

Reconstituted wood products can produce durable cabinets when used correctly, but some deviations in standard design practices are necessary. The span of reconstituted wood products is not as great as the span of plywood or solid lumber, so additional supports for shelves and tops may be necessary. Because ordinary screws don't hold very well in reconstituted wood products, you should use special fasteners, as described in chapter 5. You should not attach hinges and other hardware to an edge; you need to use special hardware that attaches to a face. Reconstituted wood products are usually not very water-resistant and lose strength quickly when exposed to water. (Plastic laminate on the face can help to alleviate this problem.) Some joints are not suitable for use with reconstituted wood products (see chapter 4).

Because of the high percentage of glue in reconstituted wood products, cutting tools dull rapidly. If you will be using reconstituted wood products extensively, you should use carbide-tipped cutting tools.

As with plywood, the exposed edges of reconstituted wood products need to be covered in some manner. Various types of edge treatment are discussed later.

There are a number of wood products that are made of wood chips, particles, or fibers. These products are all made by combining the small pieces of wood with glue and then bonding them with heat and pressure **(1–25)**.

Particleboard

Particleboard is probably the most widely used reconstituted wood product for cabinetmaking. It is made from very small particles of wood bonded with a large percentage of glue. The high glue-to-wood density makes particleboard very hard and heavy. A sheet of particleboard weighs more than a sheet of plywood. Two types of particleboard are available: *underlayment* and *industrial grade*. Underlayment is meant to be used as a flooring material under carpet or vinyl. It doesn't have the density or surface finish needed for most cabinet work. Cabinetmakers use industrial-grade particleboard. It has a very smooth, dense surface. Industrial particleboard is further classified into three grades. The lightest grade is *M1*. It is a 43-pound density panel that is a good choice for applications where screw-holding is not a priority.

When rigidity and screw holding are important, M2 and M3 grades are better. They are 45-pound and 48-pound density panels, respectively. Industrial-grade particleboard is usually sanded to a 100-grit finish and comes in 49-inch-x-97-inch-size panels. The extra inch over the 4-feet-x-8-feet size is handy when you are cutting out parts, because it allows you to use dimensions in full one-foot increments. For example, you can't cut four 12-inch pieces from a 48-inch-wide sheet, because the

1–24. This closet organizer is made of an inexpensive reconstituted wood product that is covered with a decorative overlay material.

1–25. Reconstituted wood products, from top to bottom: particleboard, MDF (medium density fiberboard), hardboard, and oriented strand board.

blade thickness (kerf) will remove approximately $\frac{1}{16}$ inch with each cut, leaving the last piece $11^{13}\!/_{16}$ inches wide, but with a 49-inch-wide sheet all four pieces can be a full 12 inches.

Particleboard is generally available in $\frac{1}{2}$-inch, $\frac{5}{8}$-inch, and $\frac{3}{4}$-inch thicknesses. It is dimensional stable, so it makes a good lamination substrate.

MDF (Medium Density Fiberboard)

MDF is made from wood fibers that have been "cooked" in a moderate-pressure steam vessel (digester). This makes the fibers less susceptible to moisture and less brittle. During the manufacturing process, the fibers are formed into bundles, which form a strong random mat. A resin binder glues the fibers together and the sheet is hot-pressed. MDF accepts paint better than particleboard, so it is a good choice when you will be using paint as a final finish.

Hardboard

Hardboard is a compressed, composite board. Saturated wood fibers are compressed in a wet process, and an overlay of fine fibers is applied to create a smooth face that is typically a light brown color. It is most often used in $\frac{1}{8}$- or $\frac{1}{4}$-inch thicknesses for cabinet backs and drawer bottoms.

Hardboard is made from wood fibers that are combined into a mat and compressed by rollers into sheets. It is available with either one smooth side or two smooth sides.

Three grades of hardboard are available: *service*, *standard*, and *tempered*.

SERVICE GRADE is a low-density panel that you should only use when high strength is not required.

STANDARD GRADE is the type most frequently used in cabinets. It has high strength and a dense surface that finishes well.

TEMPERED HARDBOARD has resins added to the fibers, and it is heated during manufacturing to improve its stiffness and water resistance.

Oriented Strand Board

Oriented strand board (OSB) is made from larger chips of wood, instead of from the fine particles used in particleboard. Because its strands are oriented in layers, as with plywood, OSB has much more strength than particleboard. However, because of its rough surface, it is not often used in cabinetmaking.

Decorative Overlays

Since reconstituted wood products have no figure on the surface, they are not usually used on the exterior of cabinets without some form of decorative overlay except in utility cabinets. To make reconstituted wood products more useful as a cabinet-making material, manufacturers have developed products that have decorative surfaces on their faces. One type is similar to hardwood plywood. It is called *composite plywood*. It has face veneers of hardwood, thin crossbands, and a thick particleboard or MDF core.

The other types use a thin overlay that has imitation wood grain, solid color, or some other decoration imprinted on it. This overlay can be made from melamine, vinyl, or paper (1–26). Melamine overlay is popular among commercial cabinet-makers, because it eliminates all finishing steps and the plastic laminate surface is durable and easy to clean. A similar product is vinyl overlay. As the name indicates, the surface is covered with a thin sheet of vinyl. This product is frequently used for drawer construction or for cabinet backs. It is water-resistant and easy to clean, but not as abrasion-resistant as melamine.

1–26. Reconstituted wood products are available with a variety of decorative surfaces.

When durability is not an issue, you can use the less expensive paper overlay products. They are covered with a thin sheet of paper that is printed with a wood grain or other design. The paper is not water- or abrasion-resistant, so it is easily damaged.

Edge Treatments for Plywood and Reconstituted Wood Products

WHEN RAW EDGES OF PLYWOOD or reconstituted wood products are visible from the outside of a cabinet, you will usually want to cover them.

Edge Banding

One of the most popular types of edge treatment for plywood and reconstituted wood products is edge banding. This is a thin tape that is applied to the edge with glue (1–27). For plywood, an unfinished veneer tape made of the same wood species as the face veneer of the plywood is usually used. It is applied before the wood is stained. Once the project is finished, the edge banding will match the face veneer in color and appearance.

1–27. Edge banding is a type of tape made from wood veneer or plastic. It is available in various widths and with or without hot-melt adhesive on the backing.

Veneer tape is a very thin piece of wood bonded to a paper backing. The paper reinforces the veneer so that it is more flexible and can be made thinner than unreinforced veneer. It is available in most of the popular wood species. It comes in rolls eight feet long or longer. It is usually available in two widths: $13/16$ and 2 inches. The $13/16$-inch width is the most widely used; it will fit standard ¾-inch plywood. This size is also used for thinner plywood with the overhang trimmed off.

For reconstituted wood products with an overlay, matching edge banding made of melamine, polyester, or PVC is usually used. This type and the wood veneer type are available with a hot-melt adhesive back or without adhesive.

Edge banding can be applied before or after the cabinet is assembled. Commercial shops use a special edge-banding machine to apply the edge-banding tape. In this case, the edge banding is applied after the parts are cut to size but before they are assembled. Do-it-yourselfers usually apply the edge banding tape by hand. When you apply the tape by hand, you can apply it after the cabinet is assembled.

Applying Edge Banding by Hand

To apply edge banding by hand after the cabinet has been assembled, the hot-melt adhesive type is attached by passing a hot iron over the tape, whereas the plain type is applied with contact cement. Simple butt and miter joints are used where pieces of tape meet, so even though a bookcase may have dado joints for the shelves, the tape is applied in a continuous strip along the side; the tape on the shelves butts into the side tape. The corners are usually mitered. The same bookcase may have a rabbet at the top corner, but the tape will be mitered (**1–28**). You should carefully think through the order in which you will apply the tape to make the application easier. Joints are made during application. Cut the pieces of tape slightly long; at first. Don't attempt to apply all of the tape at once; each edge should be applied and trimmed separately.

If you are using the heat-activated tape, use a hot iron to press the tape in place and melt the glue, in one operation. When making joints, don't pass the iron over the piece of tape that overlaps the first one applied; stop just before you get to the joint. After you've trimmed the joint, iron it down. If you are using the type without hot-melt adhesive, apply contact cement to both the back of the tape and the edge of the cabinet and let it dry.

1–28. Usually you can use simple butt or miter joints when applying edge banding, even if the underlying joint is a dado or rabbet, as shown here.

Place the tape on the edge so that it overhangs the end and on both sides. Press the hot-melt adhesive tape down with a hot iron (1–29). If you are using contact cement, lightly rub the tape down with your fingers. Now use a pair of scissors to trim the overhang at the ends close to the wood. If you look at a pair of scissors, you will see that if you cut in one direction, the flat inside of one blade will rest against the end of the board; try to cut this way because it will trim closer than it would if you held the scissors in the other direction (1–30).

Pressing the hot-melt tape down with the iron will firmly attach it to the wood; however, if you are using contact cement, you will next need to use a small wallpaper seam roller to roll down the tape to get a firm bond. Be sure to trim the ends of the tape before using the roller. If you roll down the tape before trimming the ends and the roller slips off the end with some tape overhanging, the tape will break and tear out fibers from the good part of the tape.

Now use a razor knife or a special edge banding trimmer to trim the excess from the sides. Press the side of the knife against the plywood so that it will follow the edge (1–31). If the grain direction of the wood veneer type of tape starts to pull the knife into the good portion of the tape, stop cutting and cut from the opposite direction.

If you are using plastic edge banding, no further trimming is necessary. If you are using wood veneer, you should sand the edges. After the edges have been trimmed with a knife, wrap a piece of 150-grit sandpaper over a small block of wood and sand off the last of the overhang. Sand with the folded edge of the sandpaper facing forward (1–32). If you hold the block so that a cut edge of the sandpaper is forward, the edge may catch on the grain of the tape and tear the tape. Hold the block on a slight angle so that it touches only the edge until the tape is even with the edge; then flatten out the block a little. The edge of the tape

1–29. Use a hot iron to press down the edge banding. This will activate the hot-melt adhesive.

1–30. You can use scissors to trim edge banding. Notice how the scissors are positioned so that the flat-inside edge of the lower blade is resting against the wood.

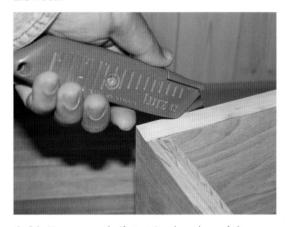

1–31. Use a razor knife to trim the edges of the edge banding flush with the sides of the board.

MATERIALS   33

1–32. Bevel the edges of the tape with sandpaper. Notice how the sandpaper is held on the block; the fold is facing forward to prevent the edge from catching on the tape and tearing out a sliver.

1–33. Use a combination square and a razor knife to cut a miter at the corner where two pieces of edge banding meet.

1–34. Cutting through both pieces of edge banding at the same time ensures a perfect-fitting miter joint. After cutting the joint, peel back the lower piece and remove the triangular scrap.

should be slightly beveled to prevent it from catching and being torn off later. At this point, the joint between the tape and the face veneer of the plywood will be almost invisible. Next, sand the ends. Use only a downward stroke to sand the ends; any upward movement of the sandpaper will tend to tear up the tape.

Now cut the joints. Use a combination square for guiding a razor knife. Butt joints need to be trimmed back so that the extra width of the tape is removed and the edge of the butt is even with the edge of the wood. To do this, place the square against the side of the cabinet and line up the edge of the blade with the edge of the plywood; now use the edge of the square as a guide for the knife to trim the tape.

To make a miter joint, apply both pieces of edge banding before cutting the joint. At this point, don't worry about the joints; simply let the edge banding overhang the ends. If you are using glue, be careful not to get any glue on the lower piece of edge banding. If you are using the hot-melt type, don't iron down the overlapping section.

When the edges have been trimmed and sanded, cut the joints. Place the 45-degree face of the square against a side of the cabinet and line up the edge of the blade with the corner of the joint. Use the knife to make a 45-degree cut through both pieces of edge banding (**1–33**). Use the point of the knife to lift the corner of the scrap piece and then remove it; the joint should match perfectly (**1–34**). Use the iron to press the joint area down (if you are using contact cement, use the roller to press the joint down), and then continue on to the next piece of tape.

Making Your Own Edge Banding

You can make your own veneer edge banding, but since it won't have the paper backing, it won't be as flexible and it will need to be a little thicker. To make your own edge banding, use a piece of solid lumber of the same species as the face veneer of the plywood. The board should be slightly thicker than the plywood if possible.

Joint an edge of the board. Set the table-saw fence so that the distance between the far side of the blade and the fence is 1/16 inch less than the width of the board. Run the board through the saw with the freshly jointed edge on the outside of the blade. This should produce a 1/16-inch-thick strip. Joint the edge of the board again to remove the saw marks, and then move the fence 1/16 inch closer to the blade and make another cut.

Continue in this manner until you have enough strips. As the fence gets closer to the blade, be sure to use a push stick. Don't try to use every last piece of the board; discard it when it becomes too small to be handled safely.

If you would like the strips to be a little thinner, you can sand the back side with a belt sander. Clamp one end of the strip to the bench, and hold the sander so that the motion of the belt pulls the strip away from the clamp. If you try to sand in the other direction, the strip will simply curl up and break.

This type of edging is applied in much the same manner as the commercial type, but the joints must be cut differently. Cut the joints with a backsaw and a miter box before applying the tape.

Plastic T Molding

Plastic T molding is a type of edge treatment that doesn't require glue. It is a plastic molding that has a cross section shaped like a T. The tail of the T is barbed with small ridges (1–35). This molding is available in solid colors, such as brown or black, or with a wood-grain pattern.

1–35. You insert plastic T molding in a kerf cut in the edge of the board. Barbs on the tail of the molding hold it in place.

Applying Plastic T Molding

You apply molding by cutting a narrow kerf in the middle of the board edge. The barbed tail of the molding fits into the kerf and the barbs keep it in place. You can cut the kerf with a table saw, but the blade must be thinner than usual or the molding will not fit tightly. A special router bit is available to make the kerf; it has a ball-bearing pilot to keep the bit in position even around curves.

Place the molding in the kerf, and then drive it home with a rubber mallet or a hammer and a block of wood to protect the molding. If the molding is a little too wide, you can trim it with a razor knife after it is in place.

You can bend molding around corners, but you must trim the tail away from the bend. Cut a V-shaped notch at the point of the bend. Make the cuts at 45-degree angles. Commercial shops use a special nipper to make the cut in a single operation. Slightly round the corners of the board where the T molding must be bent. When trimming parts such as doors or drawer fronts that will have molding on all four edges, apply the molding in one piece. Notch the molding to bend at the corners. Plan the position of the notches so that the two ends of the molding will join in the middle of the least-visible edge.

Other Methods

There are several other methods for hiding the raw edges of plywood or reconstituted wood products. One popular method is to cover the edge with a strip of solid wood. You can use a wide strip of wood of a matching or contrasting color wood and make it part of the design (1–36). Use biscuit joints to attach the wide strip to the edge.

1–36. You can make the edge covering a decorative part of the design by using a wide strip of contrasting wood.

If you want to make the edging less noticeable, use a narrow strip of wood that blends with the face. Apply the narrow strip with glue and small brads, or with glue alone. You can use contact cement, in which case no clamping is needed. If you use glue that requires clamping, pieces of masking tape placed at close intervals will be sufficient. For cabinets that will be painted, pine screen mold is often used. Screen mold was originally designed to hide the edges of the screen in screen doors and windows; however, because it is ¾ inch wide and ¼ inch thick, it makes a perfect edge covering. The corners are slightly rounded, but the face is flat.

If only one face of the plywood will show, you can cut the edge at a 45-degree angle, as if you were making a miter joint. Take the piece that was cut off the edge, reverse it, and glue it back onto the edge so that the face veneer is on the front edge. You can also use a wedge of solid wood that has been cut to a 45-degree angle.

A similar method employs a V-shaped groove. This method is a little more difficult, but it looks good from both sides. Set the table-saw blade to a 45-degree angle, and then cut the groove in two passes. Make a wedge of solid wood to fit into the groove, and then glue it in place. After the glue has dried, sand the corners until they are flush with the faces.

Another method for edging plywood involves cutting a ⅛-inch-deep groove in the edge with a dado blade. Set up the saw so that only the face veneer is left on either side of the groove, and then cut a solid-wood strip to fit into the groove.

Plastic Laminates

PLASTIC LAMINATES ARE OFTEN used for covering countertops or entire cabinets (1–37). They are available in a wide range of colors and patterns (1–38). This product is made from layers of Kraft paper that are impregnated with phenolic plastic resin. The top surface of the laminate is made of rayon paper impregnated with melamine plastic resin. It can be imprinted with an imitation wood grain, a solid color, or another pattern. High heat and pressure bond the paper and resin into a tough, durable material. Plastic laminate can be used to cover the edges as well as the face of the substrate. When the same plastic laminate is used to cover the edge, it is called a self edge (1–39).

Plastic laminate is available in two thicknesses: $\frac{1}{16}$ inch for countertops and $\frac{1}{32}$ inch for other parts of the cabinet. It is commonly available in sheets up to 5 feet x 12 feet. When you buy plastic laminate, always get a piece larger than you need to allow for fitting and trimming. If you will be using a self edge, be sure to add the width of the edge to the size when you buy the material.

Plastic laminate is quite flexible, but it is also brittle. Handle it carefully to avoid cracking it, and don't try to bend it around too sharp of a corner.

1–37. Plastic laminates are often used for covering countertops or entire cabinets. This cabinet has been covered with plastic laminate on all exposed surfaces, including the drawer fronts and edges.

1–38. Plastic laminate comes in a wide range of colors and patterns. These samples represent just a small portion of the colors and patterns available.

1–39. You can use a strip of plastic laminate to cover the edges a project; this is called a self edge.

Plastic laminate can be cut with ordinary woodworking tools, but this will dull them quickly. If you will be cutting a lot of plastic laminate, you should use carbide-tipped tools that will last longer.

You can cut plastic laminate on the table saw. The sharp chips that fly off the laminate as it is being cut can be dangerous, so wear eye protection, preferably a full-face shield. If there is a gap between the bottom of the fence and the saw table, the plastic laminate will slip under the fence and the cut will be off. To avoid this, clamp an auxiliary wooden fence to the rip fence and make sure that it is tight against the table.

The flexibility of the laminate makes it difficult to handle by yourself on the saw. Large pieces may require three people: one to guide and support the front, another person to support the side, and someone else to support the rear. It is easier to handle a large piece if you bend it across the width. Keep it flat against the table near the blade and fence, but lift the far side off of the table. This will make the piece more rigid and give you more control.

Instead of cutting the laminate with a saw, you can cut it the same way as you cut glass. For this, you will need a special carbide-tipped knife. Use a straightedge to guide the knife and scratch a line on the face side of the laminate (1–40). Go over the line several times to make sure it is deep enough. Place the piece on a bench with the line barely overhanging the corner. Apply downward pressure to the overhang, and the plastic laminate will break along the line.

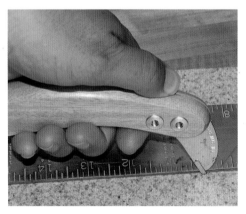

1–40. Instead of cutting the laminate with a saw, you can cut it the same way as you cut glass. For this, you will need a special carbide-tipped knife. Use a straightedge to guide the knife, and scratch a line on the face side of the laminate. Go over the line several times to make sure it is deep enough. Place the piece on a bench with the line barely overhanging the corner. Apply downward pressure to the overhang, and the plastic laminate will break along the line.

Working with Plastic Laminates

To apply plastic laminates, you need to follow special procedures. The first step is cutting off the self-edge strip, if you will be using one. For countertops, the edge is usually 1½ inches, but the strip should be cut two inches wide to allow for trimming.

Next, cut the main piece, allowing for about a ½-inch overlap on all edges.

The self edge is a narrow band of plastic laminate used for covering the edges of a countertop. If the counter has rounded corners, you can bend the self edge around the corners. Test a scrap to see how sharp of a bend the laminate can make before it breaks. If you need to make a sharper bend, try heating the laminate with a hot-air gun or use a belt sander on the back surface of the laminate to decrease its thickness in the area that must bend.

Glue the self edge in place with contact cement. Apply the cement to both surfaces with a brush or roller, and let them dry for the amount of time specified on the cement

1–41. Using a router equipped with a laminate-trimming bit is one of the most efficient ways of trimming the overhanging edges of the plastic laminate. The bit has a pilot that rides against the side of the board to guide it. The pilot will follow curved surfaces as well as flat ones. It will also follow irregularities in the surface of the board, so you should fill them in or sand them out before you apply the laminate. Notice that the pilot tends to accumulate small bits of glue. Clean the bit after each cut to avoid irregularities in the next cut.

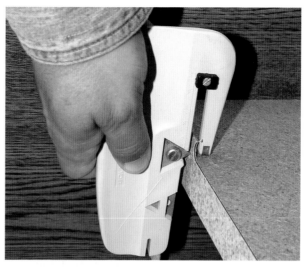

1–42. This hand scoring tool has a guide to keep the cut aligned with the edge.

1–43. You can use tin snips to trim areas that can't be reached with a router. They will leave a rough edge, so don't trim right to the edge; leave some overhang and remove it with a file.

container. The contact cement will grab as soon as the two surfaces touch, so position the edging carefully. Bend the laminate away from the edge, except at one end. Line up that end, and then slowly bring the rest of the strip into contact with the edge. Use a roller to press the laminate firmly in place.

Now trim off the overhang. You can use a router or a special carbide-tipped hand-cutting tool. A special router bit is required for trimming plastic laminate. It has a pilot that rides against the surface of the work (1–41). Always clean off any glue that accumulates on the pilot before making another cut or the bit won't cut accurately. There are two types of trimming bit. One makes a square cut; the other makes a bevel cut. To trim the self edge, you need to use the square-cutting bit.

When a counter butts against a wall, it is difficult to trim all the way to the wall, because the router base hits the wall before the cut is complete. In this case, trim as close as you can with the router; and then use a hand scoring tool or a pair of tin snips to cut off the remaining part. You can buy a hand scoring tool that has a guide to keep the cut aligned with the edge (1–42).

After you score the line, press backward on the overhang to snap off the excess. The tin snips will leave a rough edge, so don't cut right next to the edge. Leave a little overhang and file it off; finally, smooth the edge with a file (1–43).

After trimming the laminate with the router or hand cutter, use a file to make the top edge of the laminate exactly flush with the wood. Hold the file flat against the wood to guide it. Don't rock the file, or the edge will be rounded and a gap will show when you apply the next piece.

Before applying glue to the main piece, make sure it fits correctly. If any of its edges must butt against a wall or another part of the cabinet, it may be necessary to fit the edges by scribing. (See chapter 10.) You can use a block plane or a file for trimming to the line. *The edge can became very sharp while you are planing, so use care when you are trimming with a block plane. Try to position your fingers so that they won't hit the edge of the laminate should the plane slip off the edge.*

When the edge is trimmed completely, apply contact cement with a brush or roller to the back of the plastic laminate and the surface where you are applying it.

If the piece of plastic laminate is large, it will be difficult to position accurately. If you can get help, have someone else hold one end high above the work, while you position the other end, and gradually lower the laminate and press it in place as you go.

Another method that is very useful when the pieces are difficult to handle involves covering the wood with strips of scrap wood or plastic laminate. Then put the piece of plastic laminate on top of the strips and slide it into position. Pull one of the strips out at one end, and press that end down. Work from that end to the other, pulling out one strip at a time and pressing the laminate in place. If you use scraps of plastic laminate, use only pieces that have never had contact cement applied to them or else they will stick to the surface.

Some say that paper should be used for this purpose, but it seldom works very well. Even when completely dry, contact cement is somewhat tacky. The paper often sticks to the cement and rips, making a mess that is very difficult to remedy.

Use a roller to firmly press the laminate to the wood (**1–44**). You can also use a block of wood and a hammer to press it down, but the bond won't be as good. Hammering on the wood block only creates a small bond area directly below the block, whereas rolling bonds the entire surface.

Now trim the excess laminate from the edges. You can use the bevel type of router bit for this operation. When covering an entire cabinet with plastic laminate, very simple joints are usually used in the cabinet construction since the plastic laminate will cover them completely. You can drive nails and screws in the face of the board if you set them and putty them over before applying the laminate. The laminate is usually applied in this order: first the sides, then the front, and finally the top.

There are two ways to apply the laminate to a face frame. The first method is easy, but wastes some of the laminate. Apply a single piece of laminate to the entire front. Drill an entrance hole into each opening and use the router to trim the laminate out of the openings. Finally, use a file to square up the corners (**1–45**). The second method conserves material, but is more difficult. Cut the laminate into strips and apply them individually to each stile or rail. When a stile meets a rail, cut the laminate to make a miter or a butt joint (**1–46**). A miter is easier in this case because it allows you to let the strips overhang. If you make a butt joint, you have to line up the edge of the strip with the edge of the board as you apply it.

1–44. Use a roller to firmly press the laminate firmly to the wood.

1–45. The front of this cabinet has been covered with a continuous piece of plastic laminate. After the laminate was applied, entrance holes were drilled in the opening and a router with a laminate trimming bit was used to cut out the waste inside the opening. Finally, a file was used to square up the inside corners.

1–46. This face frame has been covered with individual strips of plastic laminate.

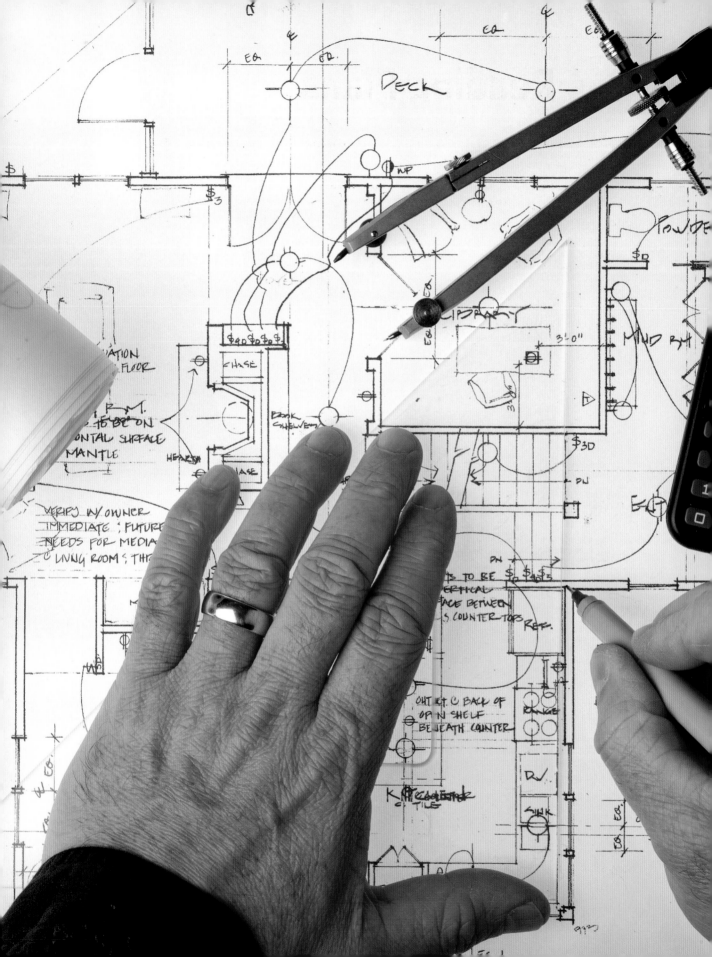

② Reading Plans

Y OUR FIRST PROJECTS WILL PROBABLY BE EASIER and turn out better if you use a prepared set of plans. In the final chapters of this book, I have included plans for both freestanding and built-in cabinets. Several magazines specialize in woodworking plans, and most of the popular do-it-yourself magazines contain one or two woodworking projects per issue. There are also many books of plans in print. In addition, you can purchase plans from many of the mail-order woodworking-supply houses, and there are many plans available for downloading on the Internet. Once you have selected a set of plans to work from, you need to know how to read the plans before they will do you any good (**2–1**).

2–1. The ability to read plans is the first skill you will need to develop before you can build cabinets successfully.

Types of Lines

ALL DRAWINGS ARE MADE OF LINES. Just as different letters of the alphabet are put together into words, different types of lines are put together to make a drawing. Different types of lines have different meanings (2–2).

Visible Lines

A thick, solid line is called a *visible line*. It is used to represent the visible outline of an object. This type of line is used only to represent what you could actually see if you viewed the object from the exact angle that the drawing shows.

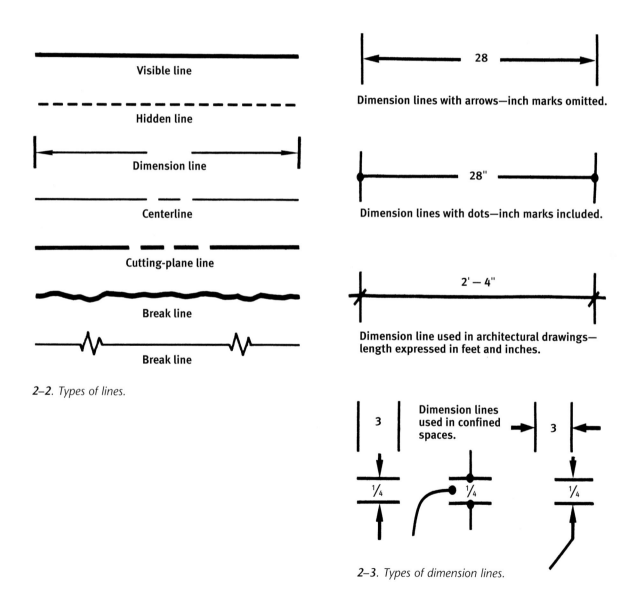

2–2. Types of lines.

2–3. Types of dimension lines.

Hidden Lines

Any part of the object that is hidden from view is represented by a dashed line of medium thickness. The dashes are equal in length and equally spaced. In woodworking, one of the most important functions of hidden lines is to show how a joint is constructed. Parts of an object may show up as hidden lines when drawn from one viewpoint and as solid lines when drawn from another.

Dimension Lines

To actually build the object portrayed in a plan, you need to know the size of each part. Two thin lines, called *extension lines*, project from the part to be measured. Another thin line, called a *dimension line*, connects the extension lines. Where the dimension line touches the extension line, there is frequently an arrowhead or a dot. Somewhere along the dimension line, there is a space where the actual measurement of the part is written in.

For cabinet work, dimensions are usually given in inches, and the symbol for inches (") is omitted. However, when both feet and inches are used on the same drawing, feet are indicated by a single mark (') and inches are indicated by two marks ("). When there isn't enough room on the drawing to write in the measurement between the extension lines, the measurement is written close by and an arrow called a leader line connects the measurement to the correct part. The leader line may be straight or S-curved (2–3).

Centerlines

A centerline is a type of extension line. It is used for indicating the middle of a hole (2–4). A centerline is the same thickness as an extension line, but there is a small dash where the line crosses the middle of the hole. It takes two centerlines crossing at right angles to indicate the middle of a hole. Dimension lines are drawn from a good reference point, such as the edge of a board, to the centerline.

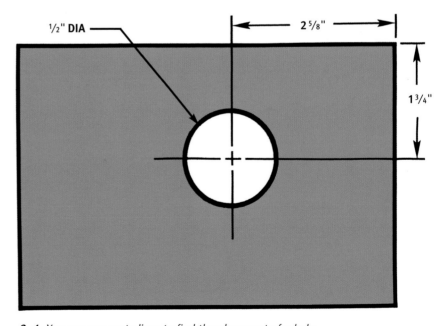

2–4. You can use centerlines to find the placement of a hole.

Centerlines make it easy to position a hole. When you are building a project, you simply measure from the reference point shown in the drawing and make a cross that indicates the point where you will place the middle of the drill bit. The diameter of the hole is given either by a dimension line running diagonally across the hole or by a leader line. The measurement given will be followed by DIA, indicating diameter, which is the distance from edge to edge, or by R, indicating radius, which is the distance from the middle to the edge.

Most simple drawings will contain only the lines mentioned here. Complex drawings, on the other hand, may also include some of the other lines shown in 2–2.

Types of Drawing

THERE ARE SEVERAL TYPES of drawing used in woodworking plans; some are more difficult for the drafter to draw than others, and some are better suited than others for a particular project. You will find all of the following types of drawing used in plans, so you need to be familiar with them all. Generally, the drawings that are the most difficult for the drafter to draw are the easiest to understand. Plans in magazines and books that are intended for the beginning woodworker generally use some of the most sophisticated types of drawing so that all the aspects of construction are clearly shown (2–5). On the other hand, plans intended for professional use generally use simple drawings, because it is assumed that the reader is familiar with the construction techniques and skilled at reading plans.

Many plans available on the Internet are in a CAD format. CAD stands for Computer Aided Drafting (or Drawing or Design). CAD drawings follow the same conventions as other drawings.

2–5. Plans in magazines and books generally use some of the most sophisticated types of drawing so that all the aspects of construction are shown clearly. This is an example from a magazine article that I wrote.

Multiview Drawings

The multiview drawing is the most fundamental type of drawing used in cabinet plans, but for the beginner, it has a couple of drawbacks. It is difficult to visualize an object from a multiview drawing unless you are experienced at reading plans, and many details appear as hidden lines, making the drawing confusing. The advantage of a multiview drawing, however, is that all parts of the plan are the same scale and appear in their true shape. Other types of drawing distort scale and shape in order to show perspective. Because of this, a multiview drawing is ideal for dimensioning. Usually a set of plans includes a multiview drawing to show the dimensions and other drawings to clarify the details.

A multiview drawing is based on the fact that a cube has six sides. This means that there are six possible ways of viewing any three-dimensional object. A multiview drawing of a child's block with a different letter on each side appears in 2–6. You can see that each side is drawn independently of the others. Only what you can see by looking directly at one face of the block appears in each view.

In most cases, only three views of an object are needed to define its shape: the top, the front, and the right side. For this reason, multiview drawings are frequently called *three-view drawings*. The views are usually placed in the same relationship on the page, so they are not normally labeled.

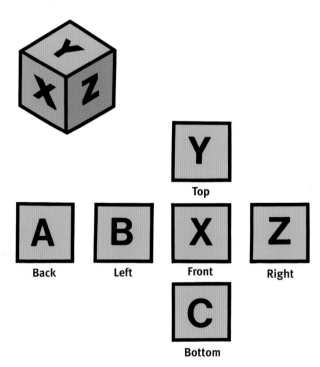

2–6. A child's block illustrates how the six views of a multiview drawing are placed on the page.

Illustration 2–7 shows the conventional placement of the standard three views. In some cases, a nonstandard view gives more information than the standard three views. Sometimes the bottom is shown instead of the top, or the left side is substituted for the right side. If the views are not labeled, you can tell what view is used by its placement on the page, as shown in 2–6. If nonstandard placement is used, the views will be labeled.

In some cases, when one view is not important, only two views are shown. For example, the top view in 2–7 doesn't add much information other than the shape of the glue blocks. If a set of plans covered the base construction with other detail drawings, the top view of this drawing would probably be omitted. Notice that the top view is omitted in 2–8.

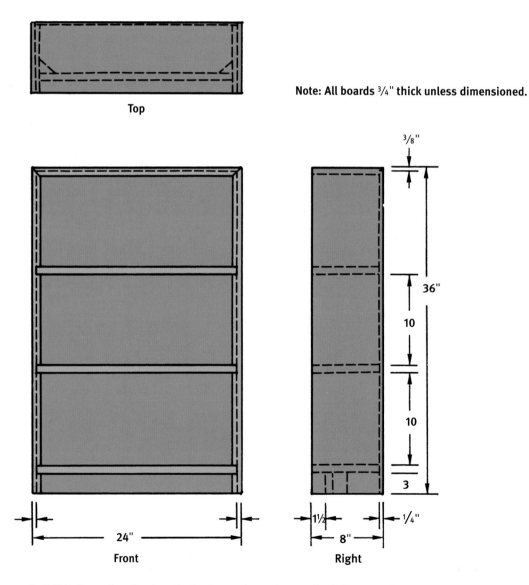

Top

Note: All boards ³⁄₄" thick unless dimensioned.

Front

Right

2–7. This three-view drawing of a bookcase shows the standard placement for top, front, and right-side views.

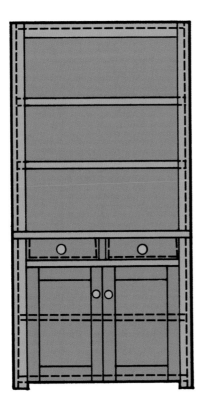
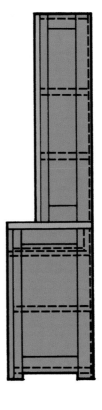

2–8. This drawing of a breakfront illustrates how different planes are distinguished in a multiview drawing. There is no apparent difference between the top section and bottom section in the front view. The side view shows that the top section is not as wide as the bottom section.

To determine all of the dimensions of any one piece of a project, you need to refer to more than one view. For example, in **2–7**, you can get the width of the back from the front view, but the side view shows the height and thickness.

One aspect of three-view drawings that often confuses people is the way parts on different planes are depicted. For example, in the multiview drawing of a breakfront in **2–8**, the top section is recessed back from the lower section; however, in the front view, the top and bottom appear to be on the same plane. The offset only appears in the side view. Anything you can see from the front is drawn in the front view whether or not it is on the same plane. In multiview drawings, you always need to look at more than one view to determine the shape of the object.

Visible lines take precedence over hidden lines; so, in some views, the visible lines hide details that would otherwise be shown by hidden lines. Usually you need to look at two views to understand what a particular hidden line means. In the top view in **2–7**, there are diagonal hidden lines in the corners. The part that these lines represent may be positioned anywhere from the top to the bottom of the cabinet. To find out where they are, look at the side view. The only line that matches the diagonal lines in the top view is a short hidden line in the base of the cabinet. Together, these lines describe two triangular glue blocks in the corners of the base. Another example is the hidden lines in the middle of the front edges of the top and sides on the front view in **2–7**. By looking at the side view, you can see that this indicates the ¼-inch-plywood back and the rabbet into which it fits.

To keep multiview drawings from looking cluttered, only essential dimensions are shown. When parts are the same size, dimensions may be given for just one part. And some dimensions must be calculated from other dimensions that are given. For example, the length of the shelves in the bookcase is not given, but an overall width is given, and the distance from the outside to the end of the shelf is given. To get the shelf length, you have to subtract the distance from both sides from the overall length.

Pictorial Drawings

It is difficult to visualize an object from multiview drawings because they lack a three-dimensional quality; therefore, pictorial drawings are used to give a clearer idea of the shape of an object. Pictorials are usually supplementary drawings used in conjunction with a multiview drawing. Most of the dimensions are usually shown on the multiview drawing. Hidden lines are omitted from pictorial drawings unless they are needed for clarity. Pictorials may use wood-grain patterns or shading to add to the illusion of depth and to distinguish solid areas from open areas.

Oblique Projections

In an oblique projection, all three of the standard views in a multiview drawing are combined into a single view. The front view appears just as it would in a three-view drawing. The top and the right-side views are attached to the front view with their receding lines drawn at an angle. Any angle may be used, but a 45-degree angle is the most common. This type of drawing presents all three views in a single image. While not exactly the same as photographic realism, an oblique projection does give a three-dimensional effect, making it much easier to interpret than a multiview drawing.

When its receding lines are drawn the same length, as they would be in a three-view drawing, the drawing is called a *cavalier projection* (**2–9**). However, normally receding lines are foreshortened by the eye. The *cabinet projection* (**2–10**) has a more true-to-life appearance, since its receding lines are drawn one-half the length that they would be in a three-view drawing.

All dimensions that can be placed on a three-view drawing can also be placed on an oblique drawing. Dimensions on the front view appear the same as they would on a three-view drawing. Dimension lines for the side and top views follow the angle of the receding lines, but otherwise they appear the same as they would on a three-view drawing.

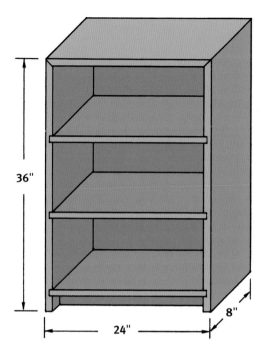

2–9. This oblique cavalier drawing shows how dimensions can be placed on an oblique drawing. Notice that the shelves appear deceptively deep. Cavalier drawings tend to distort depth perception.

2–10. This cabinet drawing gives a more accurate idea of the depth of the shelves. All the receding lines are drawn one-half scale. The wood grain and shading add to the realism of the drawing, but the wood grain isn't just decorative—it shows you how to orient the grain direction on each part.

Isometric Drawings

An isometric drawing is similar to an oblique drawing, but the object appears to have been rotated so that you are looking directly at one corner (**2–11**). As with an oblique drawing, all three views are presented in a single image; the difference is that all of the lines appear to be receding lines. This type of drawing is slightly more realistic-looking than the oblique projection, but both are about as easy to read. If dimension lines are used, they are placed parallel to the lines to which they refer, but frequently, isometric drawings are used for clarifying the shape of the object, and dimensions are given on another drawing.

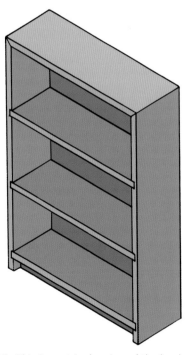

2–11. This isometric drawing of the bookcase in 2–10 has more realism. Dimension lines can be included on isometric drawings in the way that is shown in 2–9.

Perspective Drawings

Perspective drawings are complex to draw, yet objects drawn this way are some of the easiest to visualize, because the drawing clearly shows what the completed project should look like (**2–12**).

Dimensions can be placed directly on a perspective drawing, but frequently a perspective drawing is used to give you an overall idea of a project, with a multiview drawing giving you the actual dimensions.

Exploded Views

An exploded view is a good way to show how all of the parts of a project fit together. In an exploded view, each part of the project is drawn separately but in proper relationship to the rest of the parts in the project. When it is unclear where a particular part goes, dashed lines are used to indicate where the part is attached. Exploded views do not usually have dimensions, but the parts may be keyed to other drawings with letters (**2–13**).

Details

ANYTHING THAT NEEDS TO BE enlarged or otherwise clarified in the main drawing is circled and labeled "Detail," followed by a letter. The cutaway in **2–14** is a detail of the bookcase in **2–12**. There are several types of detail. Some details are simply enlargements of small areas on the main drawing; others may be cutaways or cross sections.

Cutaways

In a cutaway drawing, part of the exterior surface of the project is removed to make hidden details more clear. A thick, irregular line, called a *break line*, indicates the section that has been removed. Solid areas under the broken-out section are indicated with *section lines*, which may appear as a wood-grain pattern or simply as equally spaced diagonal lines (**2–15**). The detail shown in **2–14** is a cutaway. When thin materials, such as ¼-inch plywood, are drawn in a cutaway, a gentle curving line is frequently used as a break line (**2–16**).

Cross Sections

Another type of detail is the cross section. In a cross section, you can see what a part would look like from the end if you were to saw through the part at the point indicated by a cutting-plane line. A cutting-plane line is a thick dashed line. Its ends extend past the end of the object and are bent at a right angle to the main part of the line. Each end has an arrowhead drawn on it. The arrows point in the direction of view. Therefore, if the

Detail A

2–12. Of the various types of drawing, perspective drawings look the most natural. The area labeled "Detail A" is enlarged and cut away in 2–14.

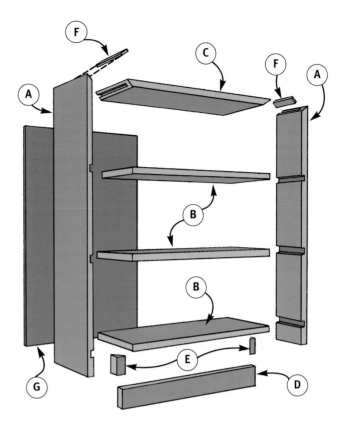

2–13. Exploded views show how the various parts are assembled. The letters refer to the parts in the instructions and on the Bill of Materials. The dashed line connecting part A to part F clarifies where part F fits.

Universal

End grain

2–15. Types of section lines.

Edge grain

Face grain

Plywood

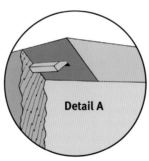

Detail A

2–14. This detail is an enlarged corner of the bookcase shown in 2–12. Part of the side is cut away to reveal the spline that joins the two parts.

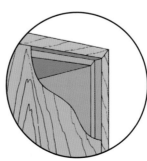

2–16. This detail shows how the back of the bookcase fits into the sides and top. This gentle, curving type of break line is used when the material being represented is thin—that is, ¼ inch thick or less.

arrows point to the right of an object, the cross section is drawn as if you were standing to the left of the object looking at the right half after having cut away the left (**2–17**).

When the cutting plane passes through a solid part of the object, the area on the cross-sectional view is covered with section lines (**2–18**).

Revolved Sections

Sometimes a cross section is simply drawn on top of the place where a cutting plane would be drawn. This is called a *revolved section*, because it is as if you cut a small slice out of the part and revolved it 90 degrees. The table leg in **2–19** shows how revolved sections can clarify the shape of a part.

Long Breaks

Another form of break line is used for shortening long details in a drawing. A table leg is an example (**2–20** and **2–21**). This type of break line indicates that a section of the line is missing to make the drawing fit on the paper. When long breaks appear, you can assume that the broken-out section is identical to the rest of the part shown in the drawing.

Centerlines

Centerlines can be used as break lines on symmetrical objects (**2–22** and **2–23**).

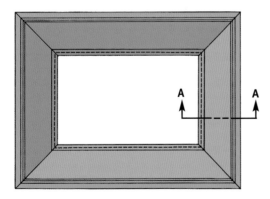

2–17. This plan for a mirror frame shows how the cutting-plane line is placed on a drawing.

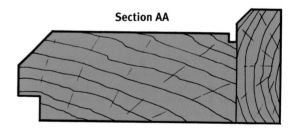

Section AA

2–18. This sectional view shows the cross section of the mirror frame at the point indicated by the cutting-plane line in 2–17.

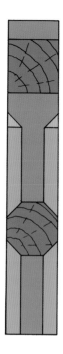

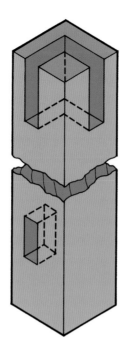

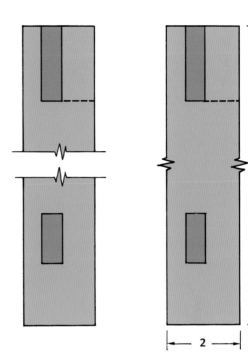

2–19. Revolved sections show the cross section of a part without separate details drawn in. The cross section is drawn in the position where the cutting-plane line would appear.

2–20. Break lines shorten a long object so that you can use a larger scale for the drawing. You can assume that the broken-out section is similar to the areas that are drawn in.

2–21. Here is another form of break line that is used for shortening long objects on the drawing.

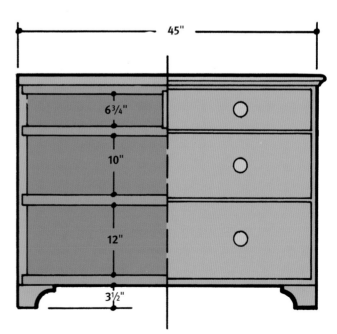

2–22. When an object is symmetrical, as is this lathe-turned leg, it is common practice to draw only half of the outline, stopping at a centerline.

2–23. You can also use a centerline as a cutaway point to show interior details of the object.

Full-Size Patterns

SOME SETS OF PLANS that you can purchase include full-size patterns. A full-size pattern is one view from a three-view drawing that is drawn the exact size of the completed part. It is especially useful for irregularly shaped parts, such as gingerbread trim or carved legs. Since you can transfer a full-size pattern directly to the wood, chances for error in measurement are minimized.

Architectural Drawings

ARCHITECTURAL DRAWINGS, such as house plans, include drawings for the cabinet work that will be included in the project. However, the architect assumes the cabinetmaker knows all about standard construction practices, so the cabinet plans included in architectural drawings usually only indicate the outside dimensions and placement of the cabinets (2–24).

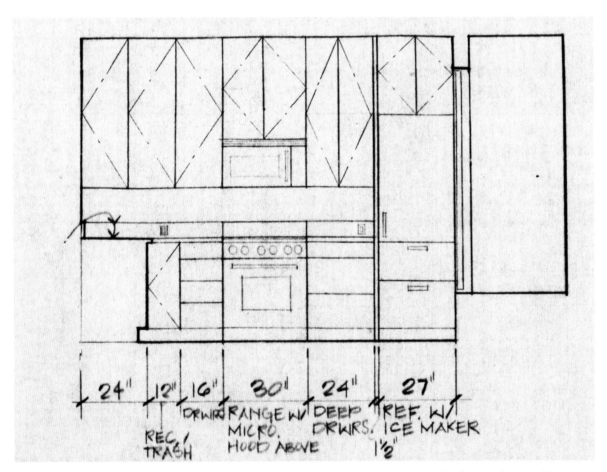

2–24. Architectural drawings are not as detailed as drawings intended for less experienced cabinetmakers. In this drawing, the diagonal lines with dashes in the middle point to the hinge side of each door.

The cabinetmaker is expected to furnish a set of shop drawings, showing the construction details of the cabinets. Cabinets in architectural drawings are shown in elevations that are equivalent to the front view of a three-view drawing. Shop drawings are usually three-view drawings. Generally, shop drawings don't show every joint; several details of typical joints are shown, and it is left up to the cabinetmaker to use these typical joints in their proper applications.

Choosing a Set of Plans

WHEN CHOOSING A SET OF PLANS, there are several things to look for. First, the drawings should be clear and appropriate for the project. A simple project may only require a single three-view drawing, whereas a complex project may require several types of drawing with details, exploded views, and cutaways. Make sure that there is a detail for anything that isn't clear on the main plan.

Generally, for your first projects, it's a good idea to choose simple projects that have very detailed plans. The plans found in magazines are some of the best. They often include step-by-step instructions and detailed photos that help to clarify the construction process. They also usually include a Bill of Materials that lists all the lumber and hardware that is required so that you can purchase the right amount of materials.

Plans that can be purchased by mail vary in quality. Some mail-order full-size plans are little more than giant three-view drawings with no instructions or details, whereas others include detailed directions and all of the necessary drawings.

Scaling

WHEN YOU LAY OUT THE PARTS of a project on the wood, you need to know every dimension of each part. If the dimension is not given on the drawing, it is still possible to get the dimension if the drawing is drawn to scale.

On a scale drawing, each measurement is a fraction of the actual measurement. The scale of the drawing is noted somewhere on the drawing, usually in the right-hand lower corner. On cabinet drawings, the scale is usually given in relationship to 1 foot, such as 1" = 1', or as half size, eighth size, etc. However, not all drawings are to scale. If no scale is given or if the words "not to scale" appear, you can't get measurements directly from the drawing unless they appear in dimension lines.

By measuring the length of a line on a scaled drawing and multiplying the measurement as indicated by the scale, you can find any measurement.

For example, if a drawing is half-scale and you measure a line as ⅜ inch, the actual measurement is ¾ inch. With some scales, such as half-scale, it's easy to convert the measurements, and you can use an ordinary tape measure or ruler to scale from the drawings. However, because most standard measuring devices are divided into 16 divisions per inch, some scales are difficult to convert.

A measuring tool that eliminates having to calculate the scale is the *architect's scale*. This is a special ruler that has a standard scale plus 10 reduced-size scales (**2–25**). Using an architect's scale, it is possible to read the measurement directly without any calculation. To conserve space on the scale, each line contains two different scales, except for the full-size scale, which has only one. Each scale is designated by a number at the end of the scale. The full-size scale is designated by 16, which means the scale is divided

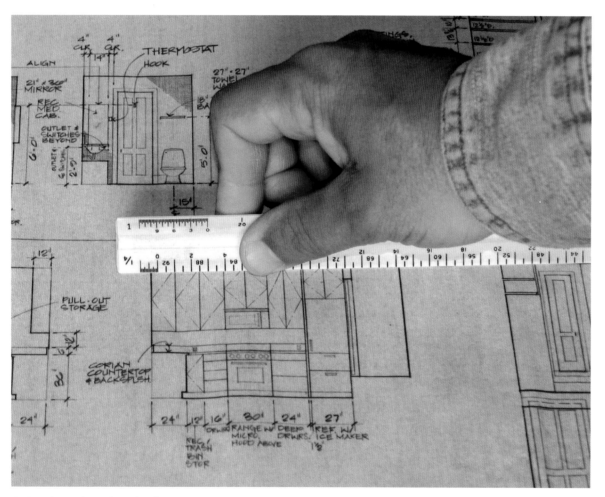

2–25. The architect's scale allows you to take direct measurements from a scaled drawing. In this case, a scale of ¼ inch = 1 inch is being used. Since two scales overlap on each side of the scale, every other number refers to a different scale. The "92" refers to the scale that starts at the other end; it is also one-half foot on the ¼-inch scale. The "2" is the 2-foot mark on the ¼-inch scale. Inches are read in the section between 0 and the end of the scale.

into sixteenths of an inch. The reduced-size scales are designated by the number of inches equal to 1 foot; therefore, the scale marked ½ means that ½" = 1'. This is not the same as half-scale, which means 6" = 1'. There are two scales per line; so ¼ and ⅛ share the same line, but they start at opposite ends of the scale. Thus, reading left to right produces ⅛, whereas reading right to left produces ¼. The divisions on the scale equal one foot, except for a one-foot section between zero and the end of the scale that is divided into smaller increments. To measure distances less than one foot, use this section of the scale. To measure distances more than one foot, place the scale so that one end of the line to be measured falls on an even foot mark and the other end falls in the section past zero that is divided into smaller increments. The total length of the line is the number of feet shown on the scale plus the inches and fractions of an inch shown in the section past zero.

Remember, when scaling from oblique cabinet drawings, that the receding lines are drawn at one-half the scale of the rest of the drawing. Generally, perspective drawings cannot be scaled.

Transferring Full-Size Patterns

THERE ARE TWO METHODS for transferring full-size patterns to the wood. With one method you use *carbon paper*, and with the other you use a tool called a *pounce wheel*.

With the first method, you thumb-tack the plan to the wood so that it can't move and then you slide a piece of carbon paper under the plan. The type of carbon paper specifically made to be used with a pencil works better than the type made for a typewriter.

Now trace over the lines on the plan to transfer them onto the wood. You can use a pencil or you can make a stylus by sharpening a dowel in a pencil sharpener. The stylus won't leave pencil marks on the plan, making the plan easier to use again. When you have finished tracing over one section, slide the carbon paper to a new section and trace it. When all the tracing is done, remove two of the thumb tacks, but leave the other two in place and lift the plan to see if all the lines transferred onto the wood. By leaving two thumb tacks in place, you can lay the plan back down in the proper position if it is necessary to retrace a line that didn't show up.

With the second method, you thumb-tack the plan in place and roll the pounce wheel over the lines. The pounce wheel has many small points around its edge that make small dents in the wood. If the dents are not visible enough, you can rub a little bit of powdered chalk from a chalk line over them to make them stand out. Although some woodworking dealers sell pounce wheels, you can also find them at fabric stores because they are used for transferring sewing patterns onto fabric as well.

The pounce wheel can also be used with a special type of carbon paper sold at fabric stores. This carbon paper is available in several colors, which is an advantage on dark-colored wood, where the standard blue carbon paper is sometimes hard to see.

Transferring Grid Patterns

PLANS THAT COME FROM MAGAZINES and books don't usually include full-size patterns. To get a full-size pattern for a complex shape, you must enlarge a grid pattern, which they usually provide. The grid pattern is covered with grid lines that are similar to those on graph paper (2–26). Somewhere on the drawing, the scale of the grid, such as 1 square = 1 inch, is noted. To enlarge the pattern to the correct size, draw a grid on a large sheet of paper, spacing the lines the distance specified in the note—in this case, 1 inch. Now draw in the lines that appear in the small grid into the large grid freehand. This is fairly easy to do because the grid lines give you a point of reference.

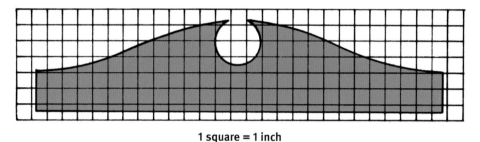

1 square = 1 inch

2–26. When a complex shape is drawn less than full-scale, it is common to draw grid lines over the area. The grid lines are used to enlarge the pattern to full size.

Don't worry about the overall shape; just concentrate on the square where you are working. For example, if the line in one of the small squares goes from the lower right corner of the square to the upper left corner of the square, draw a line in the corresponding large square from the lower right corner to the upper left corner. If the squares in the small grid are spaced closely enough, you won't have to worry too much about curves. Most details can be broken down into fairly straight lines within the square, but the overall effect of many squares will create the correct curve.

The *pantograph* is a machine that can enlarge or reduce drawings. It has levers with variable pivot points that control the amount of reduction or enlargement. A stylus on one lever is traced over the plan, and a pencil attached to another lever redraws the plan at the desired size. You can purchase a pantograph from one of the many mail-order woodworking-supply companies.

There are other ways of enlarging a pattern, thanks to modern technology. One of the best is by using a photocopy machine that is capable of enlargement or a computer with a scanner. Photocopy machines usually can't enlarge more than 200 percent at one time, so you may have to place the first enlargement back in the machine and enlarge again to get the size you need. Keep enlarging in this manner until the grid lines are the correct size. A computer gives you better control over the size. Using photo-editing software, you can easily adjust the size to the desired enlargement. Print out the enlarged drawing and trace it onto the wood. You will need to enlarge very large patterns in sections using this method.

For very large patterns, you can use a projector that connects to a computer. With this method, you scan the pattern into the computer and project the image on a wall. Adjust the projector's distance from the wall until the grid lines are the proper size, and then tape a piece of paper on the wall and trace the pattern onto it. When you are using this method, be sure that the projector is square with the wall and is not tilted up or down; otherwise, you will get distortions.

You can achieve a similar result by taking a photograph of the plan using slide film and then projecting the slide in a projector. When you take the photograph, be sure that the camera is perfectly square with the plan so that there won't be any distortion.

Computer-Aided Drafting (CAD)

MANY PLANS ARE DISTRIBUTED in electronic CAD file format on disk or over the Internet. To open a CAD file, you will need to install a CAD program on your computer. You can download free CAD viewing software that will let you look at CAD files, but you won't be able to modify them. CAD files are usually formatted in Drawing Exchange Format (DXF). This is a format that can be read by any CAD program. You will also see files formatted for specific CAD programs; DWG is the format used by many professional CAD programs.

Reading a CAD drawing is basically the same as reading other drawings, but there are added advantages. One advantage is that you can enlarge an area on the drawing to get a better view of a detail. To do this, you select the "zoom in" command (2–27). Another useful feature is that you can get accurate measurements on any part even if it is not dimensioned by using the measuring tool in the CAD software. From the "tools" menu, select "inquiry" and "distance" and then use the mouse to trace across the part you want to measure (2–28). The "inquiry" tool also lets you measure area. This can be useful in estimating the amount of material you will need.

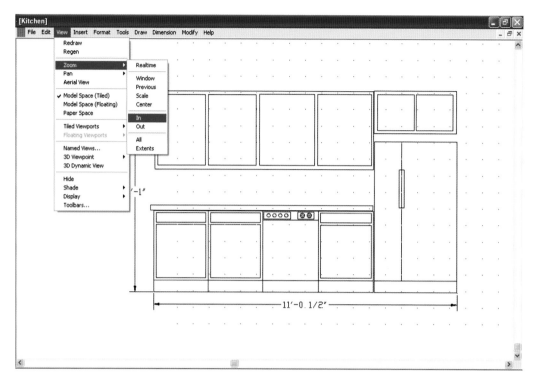

2–27. You can enlarge an area on a CAD drawing by selecting the "zoom in" command.

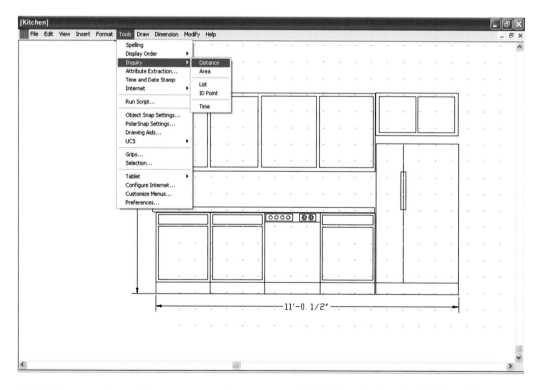

2–28. You can get accurate measurements for any part of a CAD drawing by selecting from the "tools" menu "inquiry" and "distance" and then using the mouse to trace across the part you want to measure.

Bill of Materials

MANY BETTER-QUALITY PLANS include a Bill of Materials (also called a Cutting List). This is a list of all the parts in the project, including the sizes and materials that are used. The parts are usually keyed to one of the drawings with letters. If the Bill of Materials includes a note saying "All Dimensions Actual," then board widths are given exactly as they will measure when cut. If this note is not included, the width and thickness may be nominal sizes that will vary from the actual size. Here is an example of a Bill of Materials for the bookcase in **2–13** (*page 53*).

Bookcase Bill of Materials
(All Dimensions Actual)

Part	Description	Thickness	Size	Number Req'd
A	sides	¾" plywood	36 x 8	2
B	shelves	¾" plywood	23¼ x 7¾	3
C	top	¾" plywood	24 x 8	1
D	toe-kick	¾" plywood	22½ x 3	1
E	glue blocks	pine	1¼ x 1¼ x 3	2
F	spline	¼" hardboard	7½ x ¾	2
G	back	¼" hardboard	33 x 23¼	1

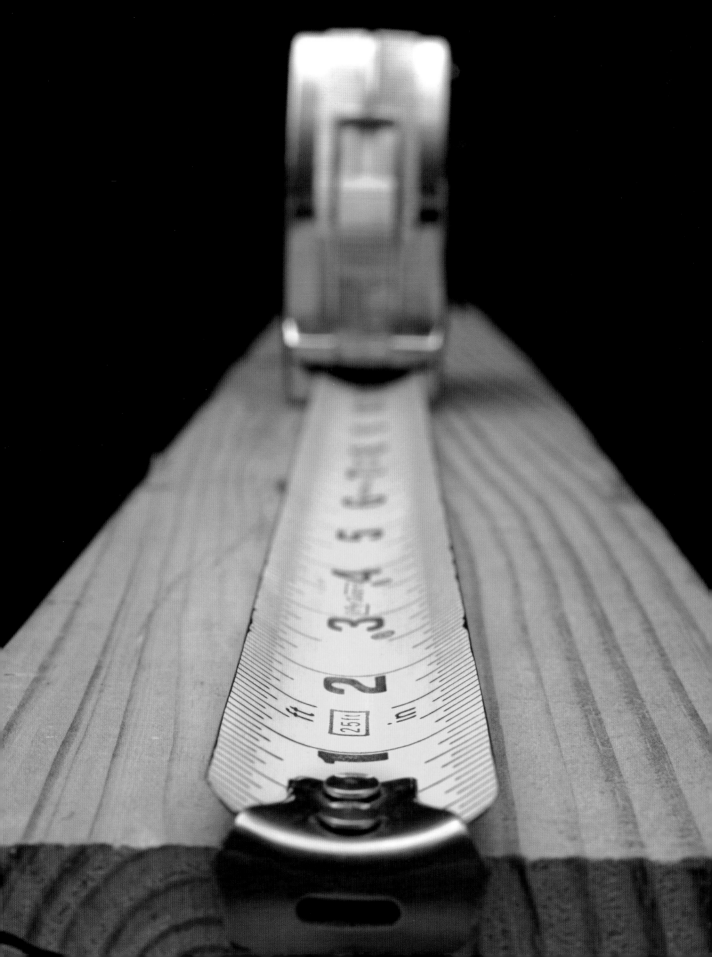

③ Laying Out, Squaring, and Cutting the Parts

....

WHEN YOU BEGIN A PROJECT, you first need to lay out the sizes of the pieces onto the wood. The parts of the project must be square and flat. If the boards you are using are not square, then you need to square them up. Next, the parts should be cut to size. These first three steps are critical to the entire cabinetmaking process. Inaccuracy in any one of them will affect all of the operations that follow.

Laying Out the Parts

IT IS OFTEN SAID THAT WOODWORKING only needs to be accurate to $\frac{1}{16}$ inch, but a $\frac{1}{16}$-inch gap in a joint looks pretty bad on a piece of cabinetry. Obviously, cabinetmakers need to measure much more accurately than plus or minus $\frac{1}{16}$ inch. Accurate layout, therefore, is essential to quality work.

It is not necessary or even desirable to lay out all the parts at once. It is very difficult to account for losses in size that result from saw kerfs (the widths of the cuts made by the saw) or from jointing boards between cuts. It is much better to lay out the parts individually when you are ready to cut each part, but you need to plan ahead and have a firm idea of how you will cut out the parts if you want to make the best use of your material.

Some plans include a cutting plan that shows you how to fit the parts onto the stock. This is especially important when you are using material such as plywood or particleboard that comes in large sheets. If your plans don't include a cutting plan, sketch one for yourself before cutting out the parts (**3–1**).

In making a cutting plan, you have to keep two things in mind: ease of cutting and making the most efficient use of your materials. Where grain direction is important, you need to keep that in mind as well. It is difficult to

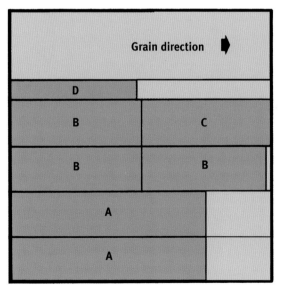

3–1. A cutting plan helps to minimize waste and make cutting easier. The light-colored areas are unused.

stop a cut partway through a large sheet. Lay out the parts so that pieces of the same width line up; that way, you can cut all the way through a sheet without stopping. This may involve some waste, but it makes cutting much easier. Also, keep in mind that you will lose approximately $\frac{1}{16}$ inch for each saw kerf, so you can't get four 12-inch-wide shelves from a 4-foot sheet of plywood. You either have to split the difference between each shelf or settle for three shelves from that sheet.

The Story Stick

ONE OF THE CABINETMAKER'S secret ways of measuring more accurately than plus or minus $\frac{1}{16}$ inch is by using the story stick. A story stick is simply a scrap of wood that is 1 or 2 inches wide and a little longer than the length of the board being measured. You should use the story stick when you need to make multiple joints in several boards (3–2). Lay out the position of the joints on a story stick, and then transfer the marks to the boards from the stick; this way, you minimize the chance for error by only measuring once. Another advantage of the story stick is that you can use it for setting up machines to make joints or holes. You can make a test cut on the story stick to make sure that the setup is right, and if the setup is wrong, you haven't ruined the actual board.

Another way cabinetmakers measure very accurately is by taking measurements directly from the work whenever possible. Once you have one part cut, use it as a reference for parts that have to match it. If you are using a table saw for cutting out the parts, make all the cuts that are the same size before moving the fence or stop.

You shouldn't lay out or cut certain parts, however, until you have begun the actual assembly of the cabinet. For example, a flush door needs to be custom-fit to the opening after the cabinet has been assembled. Some parts, such as face-frame stiles and rails, can be marked for length directly from the boards where they are attached. To do this, hold the part in place and mark its length directly from the side of the adjoining board.

3–2. A story stick is useful when you are making multiple joints in several boards. Lay out the position of the joints on a story stick, and then transfer the marks to the boards from the stick.

This method totally eliminates the need for using a tape measure and the tendency to round off to the nearest $\frac{1}{16}$ inch. One caution when using this method: Don't tilt the board by putting one end inside the opening and letting the long end hang over the end, or you will end up with an error. The board must be held square with the front. On larger projects, it is difficult to hold the actual board in place, so you should use a story stick to transfer the measurement. With the story stick, you also have the added advantage of being able to cut it to length and test-fit it before you cut the actual part.

Of course, you can't use these methods in every case, so you also need to learn how to accurately read a tape measure.

Using a Tape Measure

The tape measure is one of the fundamental tools of the cabinetmaker. Most cabinetmakers use a 12-foot tape with a ¾-inch-wide blade. The accuracy of the tape depends on the end hook on the blade. Good-quality tapes have a hook that is either loosely attached to the blade or swings out of the way for inside measurements. The loosely attached type is the most convenient, because it automatically compensates for inside measurement. There is exactly the right amount of play in the attachment holes so that the hook pulls out slightly when it is hooked over the end of a board and it pushes in when it is pressed against something for an inside measure (**3–3**). This way, the end of the tape is in the same position in both cases. Most

3–3. To compensate for the thickness of the hook, the end of this tape measure has exactly the right amount of play in the attachment holes, so that the hook pulls out slightly when it is hooked over the end of a board and it pushes in when it is pressed against something for an inside measure.

tape measures are divided into sixteenths of an inch, but some are divided into thirty-seconds for the first foot and sixteenths thereafter.

When you use a tape measure, you must keep it flat and straight. Line up the tape with an edge of the board. If you place it at a slight diagonal, you will get an incorrect measurement. Also, keep the tape flat against the board all along its surface. If the board has a slight bow in it, and you let the tape span the bow, the measurement will be incorrect. When measuring a board with a bow, put the tape on the crown side (the side that is high in the middle); this makes it easier to keep the tape flat against the surface.

To read the tape, look squarely at the edge you want to measure. Viewing the tape from an angle leads to inaccuracies.

Since most tapes are marked in sixteenths of an inch, there is a tendency to subconsciously round off the reading to the nearest sixteenth. To avoid this, cabinetmakers think in terms of fat sixteenths and thin sixteenths. If the measurement is exactly at a sixteenth mark, they call it *dead on* or *on the money*. If a board measures a little longer than 11⁷⁄₁₆ inches, but it is closer to ⁷⁄₁₆ inch than ½ inch, you would call it *11 and a fat ⁷⁄₁₆ inches*. If the board is really closer to ½ inch but not dead on, call it *11 and a thin ½ inches*. When measuring this way, try to immediately transfer the measurement to the work, so that you can keep the visual image in your mind of exactly where the mark should fall between the sixteenth marks on the tape. When you are laying out a project from the plans, always make your measurements dead on. Only use fat and thin measurements when you are fitting a part to another part that has already been cut.

There are two ways of making inside measurements. Most tapes have a note on the case, such as "add 2½ inches for inside measure." This means that if you butt the hook against one side and the back of the tape case against the other and then take a reading at the point where the tape exits the case, you can get the actual inside measurement by adding 2½ inches. Although this method tends to be awkward, it is probably the best way for a beginner to take inside measurements. However, many experienced cabinetmakers prefer bending the tape up the opposite side and reading the dimension directly, but this takes experience because the tape is bent right at the point where you need to read. To learn this method, take readings both ways and notice where the actual measurement falls on the curve. Although this method may seem inaccurate, someone who is experienced with it can usually get an accurate reading.

Making Marks

A sharp pencil is the usual marking tool for most cabinetmakers; however, when very accurate marks are required, a sharp knife or an awl will make a finer line. When you make a mark, draw a small arrowhead with its point at the exact measurement. It's difficult to line up exactly on a single line, because the line is seldom perfectly square and you are often left wondering whether it was the low side or the high side of the mark you meant to use. An arrowhead, on the other hand, leaves no room for doubt. Make an X on waste areas to avoid confusion later on.

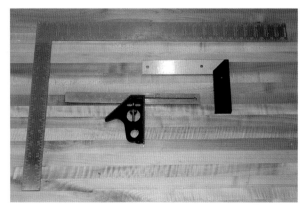

3–4. *Top to bottom: framing square, try square, and combination square.*

Using a Square

Once you have a measurement marked on the board, use a square to draw a cutting line. A try square or a combination square works well on boards up to approximately 10 inches. For larger boards, it's best to use a framing square (**3–4**). Place the square against the best edge; a factory edge or a jointed edge is preferable.

Occasionally check your square for accuracy by performing this test: Choose a scrap board with a good straight edge, and then place the square against the edge and draw a line. Next, flip the square over so that it is still against the same edge, but on the opposite side of the line, and then align the square with the line you just drew. It should line up perfectly; if it doesn't, your square has lost its accuracy. Dropping the square or other rough treatment can account for the inaccuracy.

Truing and Squaring

THE BOARDS YOU USE FOR BUILDING a cabinet must be flat and square. Both faces should be parallel to each other, and the edges should be square (exactly 90 degrees) with the face and parallel to each other. For your initial projects, it's a good idea to use plywood, particleboard, or high-grade S4S lumber. Plywood and other manufactured sheet material are very dimensionally stable and resist warping; they are surfaced at the mill to be smooth and flat. Sheet material also comes with four factory edges that are square and true, so you have a good square reference point for all other cuts. High-grade S4S lumber is also surfaced at the mill to be flat and have true, square edges.

If you choose your lumber carefully, you won't need to do any initial surfacing or squaring; however, a time will come when you will need to know how to true and square a board. Sometimes a board may warp after you buy it. Some boards have internal stresses; when you cut into the board, you upset the balance of stresses, and the two pieces will curve off in different directions. If you want to work with rough lumber, you definitely need to know how to true and square a board.

The plane is the traditional hand tool that is used for truing and squaring lumber. However, today most cabinetmakers will usually use power equipment for this job. In terms of power equipment, the jointer and the surface planer are the most useful.

Using a Plane

Using hand methods can be an enjoyable for small projects, but if you are building many cabinets you will probably want to use power equipment for surfacing. If you are interested in learning how to use hand planes, refer to my book *Plane Basics* for a complete discussion. I will give a brief introduction to planes here, but the main focus of this book is on modern power tool techniques.

If you want to use hand planes, you should start with a block plane and a jack plane in your basic set of tools. The block plane is used mostly for fitting and trimming. For truing and squaring, the longer jack plane is especially useful. An even larger plane, called a jointer plane, can also be used for truing and squaring.

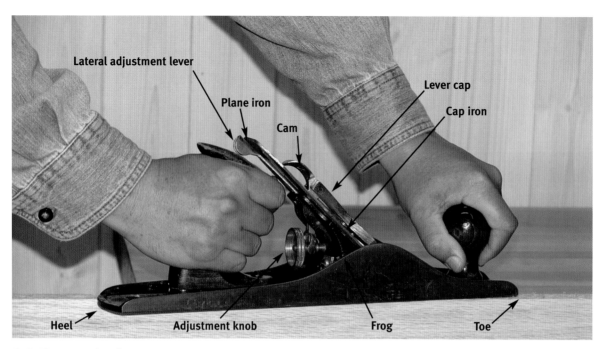

Lateral adjustment lever

Plane iron

Cam

Lever cap

Cap iron

Heel

Adjustment knob

Frog

Toe

3–5. The parts of a plane.

Illustration 3–5 shows the parts of a plane. For rough cuts, turn the adjustment knob to expose more of the blade; then pull the blade in some for fine-finishing cuts. The cap iron should be set at approximately ³⁄₃₂ inch away from the cutting edge for rough cutting; for finish work, move the cap iron closer. For most work, ¹⁄₁₆ inch is a good distance; but for very hard wood, move the cap iron even closer to the cutting edge. The lateral adjustment lever keeps the blade straight in the throat. Grasp the plane, as shown in **3–5.** Apply forward pressure on the rear handle and downward pressure on the front handle. At the end of the cut, release the pressure on the toe of the plane.

When you set a plane down, put it on its side. This protects the blade and the surface you are setting it on. When you put a plane away, retract the blade. This will protect the blade from getting nicked by some other tool.

Correcting Defects

The four most common problems you will run into are *cupping, bowing, twisting,* and *edges that aren't true.*

Cupping

This usually occurs in plain-sawn boards. The board curves, or cups, in the direction that is opposite to the annual rings. To test for cupping, place the blade of a square on the board, as shown in **3–6.** If you can see light between the blade and the board at the edges on one side of the board and in the middle on the other side, the board is cupped.

To correct cupping with a plane, clamp the board to a workbench so that the high edges are up. Plane down the high edges. Take a medium cut with the plane, and hold the plane at about a 10-degree angle to the grain direction. Push the plane parallel to the grain direction. If the blade catches or tears out chips of wood, plane in the opposite direction. Periodically check the surface with a square, and stop planing when the blade of the square rests flat all across the surface. Now turn the board over and repeat the process, only plane down the high point in the middle of the board. When both sides are flat, set the plane for a shallow cut and dress up both sides to get a smooth surface.

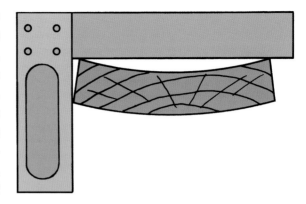

3–6. *Using a square to test for cupping.*

To correct a cupped board with power equipment, you need a jointer and a surface planer. First run the side with the high edges over the jointer until the blade is cutting all the way across the face (**3–7**). Next, place the board with the jointed side against the table of a surface planer and run the board through the planer until the high middle of the board has been cut off (**3–8**). Simply running a cupped board through the surface planer without jointing it first won't correct most cupped boards. This is because the feed rollers will press the board flat against the table during the cutting, but the board will spring back to a cupped shape after it leaves the outfeed rollers.

3–7. *Using a jointer to correct cupping.*

Correcting a cupped board decreases the thickness of the board. Extremely cupped boards may become so thin that they are useless for their intended applications. If a board is too cupped to salvage by planing, save it for a time when you need some thin strips. If you rip a cupped board into several smaller boards, the cupping in each of the smaller boards will be minimal. You can then use these smaller boards the way they are, or you can correct them with some minor planing.

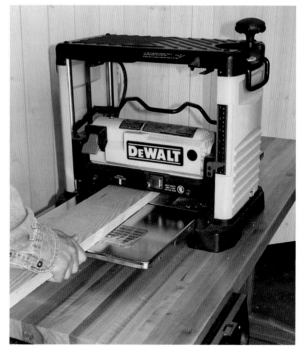

3–8. *Using the surface planer.*

Bowing

This is a curvature along the length of a board. Although you can usually see bowing by sighting along the board, you can also test for it by placing a straightedge along the board. You can usually use slightly bowed boards without correcting them. This is because clamping the bowed board during assembly will frequently take the bow out and other parts of the cabinet where the board is attached will hold it straight once the glue sets or fasteners are installed.

If a board is badly bowed, use it for shorter parts. Cutting it into smaller lengths will usually bring the bowing into acceptable limits.

If you have no other alternatives, you can use a plane to remove the bow. Place the board on a bench with the crown (the side that is high in the middle) up. Clamp or nail a small board to the bench at one end of the board that will act as a bench stop. This prevents the board from moving as you plane. Plane down the crown, pushing the plane in the direction of the bench stop. Check your progress by placing a long straightedge on the face of the board; when it lies flat on the face of the board, stop planing and turn the board over. Repeat the process, but remove wood from the high ends of the board instead of from the middle. This process will make the board thinner than its original thickness; if that is unacceptable on the cabinet you are building, your only alternative is using another board.

It is difficult to remove a bow using power equipment because both the jointer and the surface planer tend to follow the bow. One method that works, however, is using the jointer to remove wood from the high ends by placing the board over the blade past its middle and pushing it through, and then turning the board end-for-end and repeating the process. When the ends are cut down to the level of the middle, put the jointed side down on the surface-planer table and take a cut off the top. Set the cutting depth very shallow because the board gets thicker toward the middle.

Twisting

Boards tend to twist along their length due to internal stresses set up as the cells dry out. A board that is cut from a part of the tree that has an uneven cell structure will likely twist as it dries. Slightly twisted boards can be clamped flat during assembly, but a badly twisted board may pull the rest of the cabinet out of square.

The best solution for a twisted board is cutting the board into smaller parts. You can plane diagonally from one high corner to the other on both sides of short boards to remove the twist.

Truing an Edge

The edges of a board must be straight (without high spots or dips) and square with the face of the board. This is especially important when two boards will be edge-joined together to form a larger part. To see if the edge is straight, place a straightedge on the edge or sight along the edge (3–9). Use a square to see if the edge is square with the face (3–10).

Truing an edge—or *jointing*, as it is commonly called—is the primary job of the jointer. The jointer will remove irregularities in the edge and make it square with the face. The main thing to remember is to keep the face of the board against the fence at all times to ensure that the edge will be square (3–11). The two edges of a board must be parallel. You can't achieve this with the jointer alone. If you use the jointer on both edges, they will not be parallel. To ensure that the edges are parallel, joint one edge, and then use a table saw to rip the board to width with the jointed edge against the saw fence.

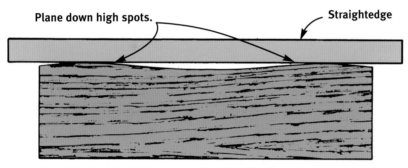

Plane down high spots.   **Straightedge**

3–9. Checking for high spots with a straightedge.

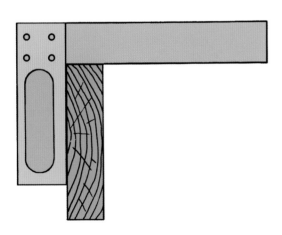

3–10. Checking the edge-to-face angle with a square.

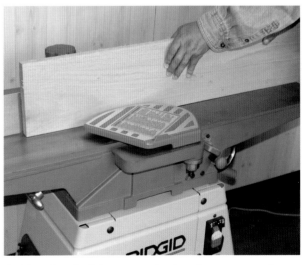

3–11. Using the jointer to make the edge square and true.

If you don't have a jointer and a table saw, you can still true the edges using a portable circular saw and a saw guide. I will explain this process in detail in the section about cutting.

For those who want to use traditional hand methods, you can joint the edges with hand planes. When you find the high spots on the edge, make a mark on the face of the board where they begin and end. Marking on the face is better than marking on the edge, because marks on the edge are liable to get planed off. Clamp the board in a vise with the edge up, and plane down the high spots, checking your progress with a straightedge. When the edge is straight, set the plane for fine cut and take one long continuous pass along the entire edge of the board.

If the edges are not square with the face, clamp the board edge up in a vise, hold the plane square with the face, and plane along the entire edge. If you have difficulty holding the plane square with the face, try using a shooting board (3–12). The shooting board guides the plane and keeps it square. Rub some paraffin on the part that the side of the plane rides on to lubricate it. Place the board to be planed on the shooting board with the edge projecting approximately ⅛ inch past the lip of the shooting board. Place the plane on its side and rest it against the shooting board. Now plane along the entire edge of the board, making sure that the side of the plane is always resting on the shooting board.

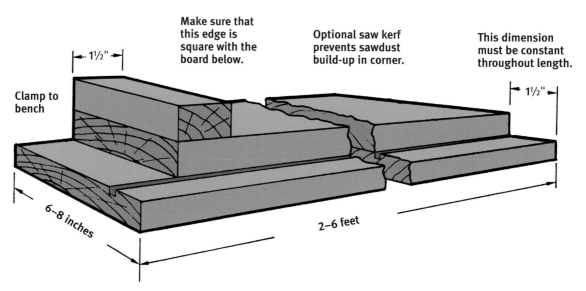

3–12. A shooting board helps to guide the plane when truing an edge. You should place the board with its end against the stop on the shooting board and the edge to be trued slightly overhanging the lipped section of the shooting board. The plane needs to be placed on its side on the lipped part of the shooting board. Keeping the side of the plane against the shooting board ensures a square edge on the board being planed.

Surfacing and Squaring Rough Lumber

When you are working with lumber that has been surfaced at the mill, you have at least one flat surface to use as a reference point for squaring the other edges. With rough lumber, on the other hand, you don't have any flat surfaces to begin with. Thus, your first task is getting one flat surface.

Examine both faces and choose the one that appears to be the flattest. If the face isn't cupped and contains only minor irregularities, you can place that face on the table of the surface planer and surface the other side until it is flat, and then you can turn the board over and surface the first side. If neither side is flat enough to be placed directly on the planer table, you will have to run one side over the jointer first. You will need a large jointer if you plan on surfacing wide boards. Run one face over the jointer until it is flat, and then place that face against the table of the surface planer and surface the other face.

When you have both faces flat, choose the best edge and run it over the jointer. When that edge is square, you need to cut the other edge so that it is parallel to the jointed edge. The easiest way of doing this is setting the rip fence of a table saw to the width of the narrowest part of the board (or to a specific width if you are cutting the board to width at this time). Place the jointed edge against the fence and run the board through the saw.

Finally, square the ends by placing a square against the jointed edge and marking a square cut across the face.

You can also square and surface rough lumber by hand. If you plan on doing very much hand planing of rough lumber, it would be a good idea to invest in a jointer plane. This plane is approximately 23 inches long. The long sole spans low spots and allows the blade to cut down high spots, making it easier to get a flat surface (3–13).

Begin by planing one face flat. Set the plane for a deep cut and plane diagonally across the surface. When the surface is fairly flat, reduce the thickness of the cut and plane with the grain. When you have finished one face, turn the board over and plane the other side. The trick is keeping the two faces parallel. Measure the thickness of the board at several points along both edges. Take more wood off the thick areas so that the board is uniformly thick throughout.

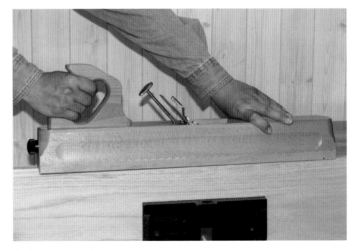

3–13. Jointer plane.

When you have finished the faces, use a shooting board to joint one edge. Now, measuring from the jointed edge, mark a line parallel to the jointed edge on the other edge of the board. If there isn't a large variation from parallel on the rough edge, simply plane to the line to bring the edges parallel. When a lot of wood needs to be removed to make the edges parallel, saw along the line with a ripsaw and then dress up the cut with a plane set for taking a thin shaving.

Cutting Techniques

WHEN YOU HAVE A FLAT AND TRUE board and you have laid out the cuts, the next step is cutting the parts to size. To begin with, you need to learn the terminology I will be using to describe the cutting process. Crosscutting refers to making cuts across (perpendicular to) the grain of a piece of solid lumber. A crosscut saw has specially sharpened teeth that cut the longitudinal fibers in a board (3–14). Ripping is the process of cutting with (parallel to) the grain of a solid piece of lumber. The ripsaw has teeth shaped like small chisels that shave away the wood parallel to the grain (3–15). The kerf is the area removed by the saw. You must take the width of the kerf into consideration when you are cutting out parts. A saw kerf is typically about ⅟₁₆ inch to ⅛ inch wide. Always place the saw so that the kerf will be on the waste side of the line; otherwise, the parts will be too small.

You cut plywood and reconstituted wood products the same way as solid lumber, but grain is less of a consideration. You should use a special combination blade or plywood blade that combines the features of a crosscut saw and a ripsaw. If the sheet has a face veneer, the grain of the veneer should be taken into consideration.

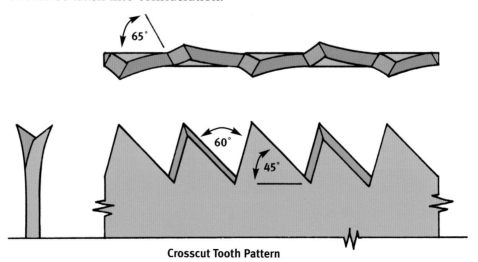

Crosscut Tooth Pattern

3–14. The teeth of a crosscut saw resemble a knife blade. This type of saw cleanly shears off the wood fibers.

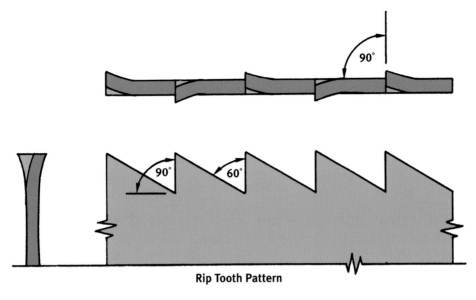

Rip Tooth Pattern

3–15. Rather than shearing off the fibers, the ripsaw actually planes away small shavings from the saw kerf.

When crosscutting the face veneer, it will tend to chip and splinter along the cut. Using a fine-tooth blade will minimize this, but in extreme cases you may need to take further measures. One way of minimizing this is by placing masking tape on both faces of the plywood so that it covers the area of the cut. Make your cutting line on top of the tape so that you can see it. Press the tape down firmly so that it adheres to the wood. After you make the cut, remove the tape. The tape should prevent most of the chipping, but some types of plywood will chip even when you use the tape. If this happens, place a straightedge along the cut line and cut through the face veneer with a sharp knife before making the cut with the saw. This should eliminate all chipping, as long as the saw doesn't stray past the knife cut. Usually it is only necessary to make the knife cut on the face of the board most susceptible to chipping; however, in severe cases, you may need to make a knife cut on both faces.

Using Power Saws

Four types of power saw are usually used for cutting parts to size: the *portable circular saw*, the *table saw*, the *power miter saw*, and the *radial arm saw*. The portable circular saw is the least expensive of the four and the one most frequently used by do-it-yourselfers. Large cabinet shops usually have table saws and radial arm saws, which are especially suited for specific jobs even though they are both multipurpose machines. The radial arm saw works well for crosscutting and, in a large shop, is usually set up for that job alone. The table saw is especially good for ripping, but it can handle crosscutting as well. The power miter saw is a fairly inexpensive piece of equipment that can be used for crosscutting boards to length as well as cutting miter joints. I will cover this saw in more depth in chapter 4.

Whenever you use power equipment, follow all of the manufacturer's directions and safety precautions, keep all parts of your body away from the blade, and use the guards that are provided.

Basic Safety Instructions for Portable Circular Saw Use

1. Place the work on a good support like a cutting table. This is because if the work sags during the cut, the kerf will close and cause the blade to bind. This can lead to kickback.

2. Kept the saw cord out of the path of the saw.

3. Before starting the saw, place it on the work, but make sure that the saw teeth are not touching the work.

4. Don't overreach or get into an awkward position as you cut.

5. Let the saw stop before removing it from the work and placing it down.

3–16. This aluminum saw guide incorporates clamps that slide in a channel to firmly attach the guide to the sheet being cut.

Portable Circular Saw

Most of the time, modern cabinets are made from materials that come in 4-foot x 8-foot sheets. Short of a professional panel saw, the portable circular saw is really the best tool for cutting large sheets. However, to make the cuts accurately, you should use a saw guide that clamps to the sheet. A saw guide can be as simple as a long piece of wood clamped to the sheet that the saw base rides against, but for really accurate cuts, I recommend that you buy a commercial cutting guide. They are usually made of aluminum and have a built-in clamping system to hold them firmly in place on the sheet (**3–16**).

There are two types of commercial cutting guide. The first type is really just a straight edge that guides the saw base. To use this type, you must measure the distance from the edge of the saw base to the blade, and offset the guide from the cutting line by this measurement. As you cut, you must make sure that the saw base always stays in contact with the guide. If it wanders away from the guide, the cut will not be straight.

The second type of commercial cutting guide includes an auxiliary base that attaches to the base of the saw. It has grooves that fit over a track on the guide. I recommend this second type because the saw cannot wander from the straight line. Also, since the saw sits on top of the guide, there is no need to offset the guide from the cutting line. You can simply line up the edge of the guide with the cutting line and be assured the cut will fall exactly on the line. This type of guide can also be used as a router guide when making joints. I'll tell you more about this in chapter 4.

When you make the cuts, you will need some way to support the work. Sawhorses can do the job, but a cutting table is better (**3–17**).

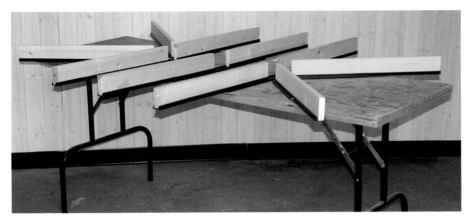

3–17. A cutting table supports a full sheet of plywood for cutting. This is a commercial model that has adjustable tracks for the spacer blocks, but you can make one without the tracks by attaching 1-x-3 lumber to a tabletop.

A cutting table is a sturdy folding table with spacers made of 1-x-3 lumber attached to the top. When you make a crosscut, the saw blade usually goes between the spacer blocks. When you make rip cuts, the saw will cut into some of the blocks. The blocks are replaceable if they get really chewed up, but as long as they can support the sheet, cuts in them won't hurt anything.

The blade that usually comes with a portable circular saw is designed for house framing. It is great for cutting 2 x 4s, but the cut is too rough for cabinet work. Buy a blade designed for making fine cuts in plywood. This type of blade will have more teeth than a framing blade and will produce a thinner kerf.

Before cutting with a portable circular saw, set the depth adjustment so that only about ¼ inch of the blade will protrude from below the board. Place the board with the good side down. Because of the direction the saw blade rotates, there will be more chipping on the side facing up. When you lay out the cut, mark the waste side with an X and position the guide so that the cutting line is left on the good side of the cut. Then clamp the guide in place.

Place the saw on the guide. Make sure that the blade is not touching the wood, and then start the saw. *Keep your fingers away from the cutting path, both in front of and behind the saw.* Advance the saw into the board at a speed that doesn't lug down the motor (**3–18**). When you have finished the cut, release the trigger and let the blade stop before lifting the saw.

3–18. Cutting a large sheet with a portable circular saw and a saw guide.

If you don't have a jointer, you can use a portable circular saw and a saw guide to make a true edge on a board. Clamp the guide to the board approximately ¼ inch in from the narrowest part of the board, and cut off the irregular edge with the saw. Remove the guide and mark the desired width from the true edge near both ends of the board. Line up the guide with these two marks and clamp it in place. Because you measured from the new true edge in two locations, this next cut will be parallel to the first.

Basic Safety Instructions for Radial Arm Saw Use

1. Don't try to cut short pieces on the radial arm saw; it is only intended for cutting pieces off long boards.

2. Keep your hands at least 6 inches from the blade while cutting.

3. Make sure that the blade guard operates correctly.

4. Keep the work firmly against the table fence; otherwise the work can kick back violently.

Radial Arm Saw

Because of the popularity of the power miter saw, the radial arm saw has fallen out of favor with most do-it-yourselfers. Most manufacturers no longer make an inexpensive do-it-yourself model of a radial arm saw. However, production shops still use this saw, because it is one of the most efficient ways to cut multiple parts to length.

To crosscut with a radial arm saw, place the board on the table with the good side up. Put the best edge against the fence. To lay out a board for cutting on the radial arm saw, it is only necessary to make a small mark on the edge of the board at the correct length. The saw will make a square cut automatically. With the saw off, line up the mark with the blade, making sure that the entire kerf will be in the waste. Turn on the saw and pull it through the board. *Always keep your arms and hands out of the blade path and return the saw to the rear of the track after each cut.*

You can make multiple cuts of the same length by placing a stop on the fence at the proper position and then by positioning each board against the stop. Try not to hit the stop too hard with the board to keep from moving the stop. You can use a commercial stop or simply clamp a small scrap to the fence.

You can also make rip cuts with the radial arm saw up to the length of its arm. Lock the saw head in position on the arm and rotate it 90 degrees. Place the board against the fence and feed it into the saw.

Table Saw

The table saw is a versatile piece of equipment that is used by do-it-yourselfers and professionals alike. There are many models available ranging in price from a few hundred dollars to several thousand dollars.

*3–19. Set the table saw blade to protrude approximately ⅜
inch above the board being cut. (The guard is removed for
clarity in the photo. You should use the guard provided
with your saw.)*

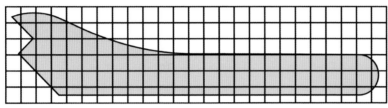

1 square = ¹/₂ inch

*3–20. A push stick is a necessity when using a table saw. This shape is
comfortable to use, but you can make a simple push stick by cutting a notch
in a scrap of wood.*

The blade on a table saw should be set so that only approximately ⅜ inch protrudes above the board being cut; this is not
only safer, but it also helps to minimize chipping (**3–19**). Don't
make any adjustments to the saw while it is running. When cutting on the table saw, the good side of the board should be up.
*Stand off to the side of the blade line to avoid being hit if the board
kicks back.* When the saw is running, keep your hands at least six
inches away from the blade in all directions. If you need to cut
something smaller than six inches, use a push stick that will
keep your hands six inches away from the blade (**3–20**).

Don't reach over the blade to catch a board; let the board fall
on the floor or use a *take-off table*. This is a long thin table that is exactly
the same height as the table of the table saw. The take-off table should be
placed behind the saw so that it will support the board as it leaves the saw.
Instead of a take-off table, you can buy adjustable roller stands that will
support long boards as they exit the saw (**3–21**).

*3–21. These roller stands can be
adjusted to the exact height of
your table saw. They will support
long boards as they come off the
back of the saw table.*

3–22. To set the rip fence to the correct width, measure from the face of the fence to the fence side of a saw tooth that is set in the direction of the fence. In this photo, I'm setting the width to 2 inches.

To rip on the table saw, set the rip fence at the correct width. Measure from the face of the fence to the fence side of a saw tooth that is set in the direction of the fence (**3–22**). This will put the entire saw kerf in the waste. Turn on the saw and put a jointed edge against the fence. Feed the board into the saw, making sure that you keep the edge of the board against the fence.

Ripping long boards is usually a two-person operation. Have someone else support the boards as they leave the back of the table. That person should only support the wood; you should do all of the feeding and guiding. If you have a take-off table, you can rip long boards by yourself.

When ripping anything smaller than approximately 6 inches wide, you should use a push stick when the end of the board needs to be pushed past the blade. A push stick doesn't have to be fancy; a scrap of wood with a notch cut in the end will do.

To crosscut with the table saw, you need to use the miter gauge. The miter gauge has markings indicating degrees for angle cuts; it should be placed at 90 degrees for square cuts. It's a good idea to check the gauge's accuracy by placing a square against the blade and the miter gauge. Place a jointed edge against the gauge. Mark the length of the cut on the edge of the board closest to the blade, and line up the mark with the blade. Turn on the saw. Hold the board firmly against the miter gauge, and push the miter gauge forward to feed the board into the saw.

There are two ways of making multiple cuts of the same length using the table saw. The first method uses the fence. However, the fence should not be used in conjunction with the miter gauge unless you take certain precautions; otherwise, there is a strong possibility of kickback. To use the fence as a stop and also avoid kickback, clamp a short piece of scrap to the front part of the fence. This clearance block should stop before it reaches the blade. Set the fence so that the distance between the clearance block and the blade is the length of the piece. With the miter gauge pulled back even with the clearance block, position the board to be cut against the clearance block. Hold the board firmly against the miter gauge and feed it into the saw. The board should not be in contact with the clearance block when the cut is complete.

The other way of making multiple cuts of the same length with the table saw is by attaching a wood extension to the face of the miter gauge. The extension should be a little longer than the board being cut. Clamp or nail a stop block to the extension at the correct length. Then simply position the board so that it rests against the stop block and proceed as you normally would with the miter gauge.

Using Handsaws

Nowadays, most cabinetmakers will only use a handsaw on rare occasions. However, for cutting moldings and narrow boards like face frame parts, a backsaw and a miter box can be almost as efficient as a power saw. I will tell you more about this in chapter 4. For those of you who are interested in using traditional hand tools, here is some information about handsaws.

Using a Crosscut Saw

You should use the crosscut saw for making cuts across the grain. The easiest way of cutting small boards is by firmly clamping them to a workbench. It's easy to cut larger boards if you hold them down with your knee on a sawhorse. Place the board with the good side up, because the crosscut saw tends to tear small splinters from the bottom side of the board.

Position the saw blade so that the entire cut will be made on the waste side of the line. Hold the saw at about a 30-degree angle to the edge and square with the surface. Hold the saw in your dominant hand (right or left) and place your other hand on the board with your thumb resting against the smooth steel of the blade, just behind the teeth. Your thumb acts as a stop, preventing the blade from wandering past the line until it gets started.

To start the cut, pull up on the saw without exerting much pressure to get a small kerf started; then push downward, exerting a little pressure and using a short stroke. As the blade enters the wood, lengthen your stroke and exert more pressure. The saw cuts on the downward stroke, so don't exert any pressure on the return stroke. When the blade is approximately 1 inch into the wood, begin taking long strokes that travel almost the full length of the blade and continue sawing in a steady, moderate rhythm. Short, fast strokes only wear you out and are not as productive as long, rhythmic strokes. When you get near the end of the cut, support the waste end of the board with your free hand and revert back to short, gentle strokes to avoid breaking the waste off before finishing the cut. If the waste is not supported, it will break off prematurely, tearing a splinter out of the face of the board.

Using a Ripsaw

You should use the ripsaw for making cuts parallel to the grain. When you cut with the ripsaw, you follow the same basic procedures you used with the crosscut saw, except you hold the saw at a steeper angle—at approximately 45 degrees. And since rip cuts are usually longer, you need to use a different method for supporting the board.

For short boards, simply hang one end of the board a few inches off the bench and begin cutting. When the saw gets near the edge of the bench, stop cutting and move the board farther out past the edge. Continue in this manner until there is too much of the board hanging off the bench for you to handle. At this point, it will be easier if someone else supports the end of the board for you. If you can't get help, turn the board around so that the cut portion is on the bench and finish the cut working away from the bench. Keep the saw as close to the bench as you can to minimize up-and-down movement of the board.

For longer boards, support the board with two sawhorses. A handy accessory for making rip cuts is the *ripping horse* (**3–23**). This is a sawhorse that has an extra-wide top and a slot running down the middle. Simply place the board to be ripped on the horse, leaving enough room between the end of the board and the end of the slot for the saw, and then begin ripping.

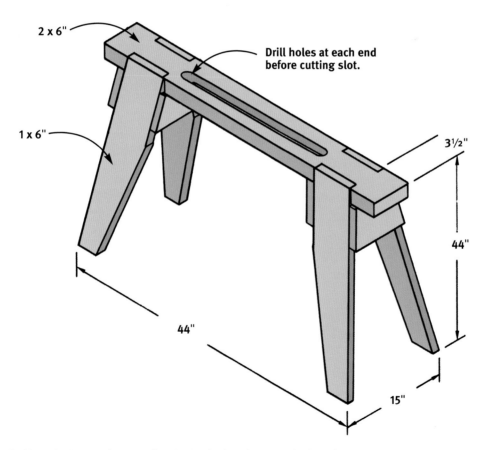

2 x 6"

Drill holes at each end before cutting slot.

1 x 6"

3½"

44"

44"

15"

3–23. A ripping sawhorse makes ripping by hand easier. The board is positioned over the slot so that the saw is in the slot. For long cuts, the board is moved forward each time the saw reaches the end of the slot.

Making Curved Cuts

So far, all of the saws described make only straight cuts. Curved cuts can be used to add decorative effects to cabinets (**3–24**). They are also necessary when fitting a cabinet to an irregular wall. When you need to make a curved cut, you need to use a different type of saw. The handsaw most commonly used for making curved cuts is the *coping saw*. Three power saws often used for making curved cuts are the *jigsaw,* the *scroll saw,* and the *band saw.*

Using a Coping Saw

The coping saw has a very thin blade stretched across a springy metal frame. The distance between the blade and the frame determines how deep you can cut into a board. The coping saw is one of the few Western saws that cuts on the back stroke. When inserting a new blade, position it so that the teeth point toward the handle. By rotating the handle and the blade attachment at the other end of the frame, you can rotate the blade to any position relative to the frame. This feature is very useful because it lets you move the frame out of the way when you make long cuts.

3–24. Not all cuts need to be straight. This cabinet uses a curved cut on the doors to add a decorative detail.

Clamp the board to be cut to the bench with the cutting line overhanging the edge. Try to keep the overhang to a minimum to prevent the board from springing back and forth. For long cuts, you may need to reposition the board several times.

Hold the saw only by the handle; applying any pressure to the other end of the frame may cause the blade to come unhooked. When cutting a board that is laying flat on the bench, hold the handle of the saw under the board and follow the line on the top of the board. If the board is clamped vertically in a vise, hold the handle on the side facing you and follow the line on that side (**3–25**).

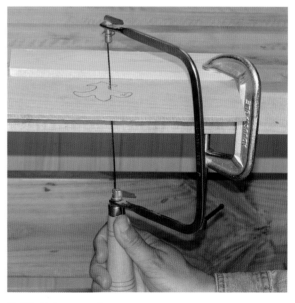

3–25. Using a coping saw.

You can use the coping saw for making inside cuts by drilling an entrance hole inside the waste area of the cutout. Remove the blade from the saw and place it through the hole, and then reinstall it in the handle.

To make a square corner on an inside cut, cut all the way to the line from one direction and then back the saw up a little and make a smooth curve around the corner through the waste. When you have completely cut around the cutout, remove the waste and go back to each corner and cut from the other direction to square the cut.

3–26. A jigsaw.

Using a Jigsaw

The jigsaw, or saber saw, is an inexpensive piece of portable power equipment that many beginners buy soon after they start cabinetmaking. It performs basically the same function as the coping saw. The jigsaw has a short, stiff blade that is moved rapidly back and forth by an electric motor (3–26).

You can make inside cuts with the saber saw by drilling an entrance hole or by plunge cutting. To make a plunge cut, hold the saw so that the front of the shoe is resting on the face of the board and the blade is almost touching the wood. Turn on the saw and then slowly lower it so that the blade begins to cut into the face of the board. Continue slowly lowering the saw until the shoe is flat against the face and the blade has cut all the way through the board. Now proceed with normal cutting.

Don't force the saber saw, or the blade may break. Since a saber saw blade is wider than a coping saw blade, it won't cut as sharp a corner. To make very intricate cuts, you may need to first remove most of the waste with a rough cut as close to the actual shape as you can make it and then go back and cut the details. To cut inside corners, use the same procedure described for the coping saw. You can make bevel cuts by adjusting the angle of the shoe.

As with all power saws, keep your fingers away from the blade while it is in motion.

Using a Scroll Saw

The scroll saw is like a motorized coping saw. The blades are very similar, but the scroll saw blade doesn't have the cross pin attachment; instead, it is clamped into a screw-tightened jaw.

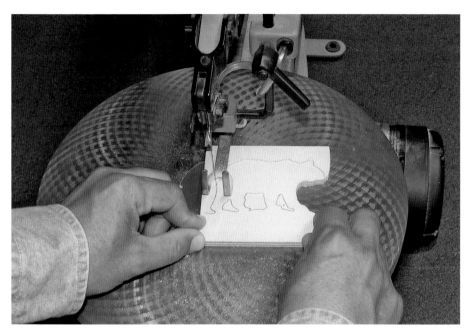

3–27. A scroll saw.

The blade on the scroll saw is positioned for cutting on the downward stroke. The motor is below the table, and the upper end of the blade is supported by an overarm. As with the frame of the coping saw, the distance between the blade and the overarm limits the depth of cut. The blade can be rotated 90 degrees in the chuck to permit long cuts (**3–27**).

The scroll saw has a hold-down attachment that keeps the board flat against the table. You need to adjust this attachment so that there will be enough force to keep the board from clattering up and down with the blade.

Cutting with a scroll saw is similar to cutting with a coping saw, except that the board is moved and the saw remains stationary. You can make inside cuts in the same manner described for the coping saw. And you can make bevel cuts by tilting the table. The scroll saw is capable of making very intricate cuts. This can be useful in cabinetmaking for cutting designs used to decorate a cabinet. The wildlife scene shown in **3–28** decorates the area under the sink on a set of kitchen cabinets.

Using a Band Saw

In production work, where speed is important, you should use a band saw for making curved cuts. The band saw has a long, flexible blade joined into a continuous loop. The blade travels over two wheels, one above the table and one below the table. The blade cuts in a downward motion toward the table. Because the blade travels in only one direction, the board doesn't need to be held down with a special attachment, as with the scroll saw. The band saw has a sliding bar that resembles the hold-down

3–28. A scroll saw can make intricate designs that can be used to decorate cabinets.

attachment on the jigsaw, but its function is guiding the blade. You should position the blade guide near the surface of the board, but not touching it (3–29).

There are two sets of blade guides: the one just described and another set below the table. These guides must be properly adjusted for the saw to cut correctly. There are guide blocks or wheels on either side of the blade and a rear guide that controls the blade's front-to-back position.

To initially adjust the guides, back off the adjustments until none of the guides are touching the blade. The blade tension should be set so that it takes a moderate amount of finger pressure to deflect the blade. Manually rotate the lower wheel and adjust the upper-wheel tilt control until the blade is riding in the middle of both wheels. Stand clear of the saw and turn it on for a few seconds until the blade position stabilizes on the wheels. If the blade moves too far from the middle of the wheel, readjust the tracking adjustment. Turn off the saw and adjust both rear guides so that they almost touch the rear of the blade.

Now adjust the side guides so that the teeth of the blade are outside of the guide. Finally, move the side guides in so that they barely touch the blade on each side without deflecting it. If the guides are adjusted properly and you have a sharp blade, you can make very accurate cuts with the band saw.

Blades in a variety of styles and widths are available for the band saw. You should use blades with fine teeth for thin stock and blades with coarser teeth for thicker stock. Wide blades make straighter cuts, but they can't turn tight curves. Narrow blades are best for tight curves. Generally, most cabinet work can be done with a ¼-inch-wide blade. Don't force the board into the blade, and don't force a wide blade around a sharp bend.

For intricate work, it may be necessary to make relief cuts. A relief cut is a straight cut from the waste edge to the cutting line. You make the cut and then back the saw out. When backing out long distances, it's a good idea to turn off the saw so that the blade won't be drawn off the wheels. The relief cut allows you to remove a section of the waste at the point where a difficult turn must be made, permitting the blade to turn without binding. You can make bevel cuts with the band saw by tilting the table. In most cases, the band saw is not suitable for making inside cuts. To make an inside cut, you either need to make an entrance cut through a good section of the board and later glue it back together or you need to cut the blade and weld it back together inside of an entrance hole.

As always, keep all parts of your body away from the moving blade and keep the guards in place.

3–29. You should position the band-saw blade guide near the surface of the board, but not touching it.

④ Joinery

THE SEPARATE PARTS OF A CABINET are held together with joints. The process of cutting the joints is called joinery. Over the centuries, cabinetmakers have developed hundreds of specialized joints. Before the development of modern glues, joinery had to be quite complex; many types of self-locking joints were developed that would stay together even if the glue failed. Modern glues have simplified joinery. The main objective now is providing the greatest surface area for gluing (**4–1**).

4–1. There are literally hundreds of different types of wood joints, but you can make practically anything with the joints shown here.

IT IS MORE DIFFICULT to separate a glue joint by spreading the joint apart than it is by applying a shear force, so many joints are designed to minimize forces on the joint. Solid lumber expands and shrinks with changes in humidity, so joints used with solid lumber need to allow for dimensional changes. Manufactured materials, such as plywood and particleboard, are dimensionally stable, but they require specialized joints that account for their unique properties. The type of jointused with particleboard is particularly important, because, while very strong in compression, particleboard has low shear strength.

Sometimes joints are used for purely decorative reasons. They may or may not contribute to the strength of the cabinet. Decorative joints can range from simple, exposed dowels to hand-cut dovetail joints. In this book, I will focus on the most useful basic joints. If you are interested in more advanced joints, consult my book *Wood Joiner's Handbook*.

Joinery Tools

VARIOUS TOOLS ARE USED in the process of making joints, but there are several tools that are used extensively for joinery. They are the *chisel*, the *backsaw*, the *router*, the *plate (biscuit) joiner*, the *dowelling jig*, and the *pocket-hole guide*.

Chisel

A chisel is simply a heavy blade set into a handle, but it can perform a number of different operations (4–2). The blade is similar to a plane iron, only it is stouter. It can therefore withstand pressure without the support the plane iron receives from the other parts of the plane. The chisel is used mainly for chopping and paring.

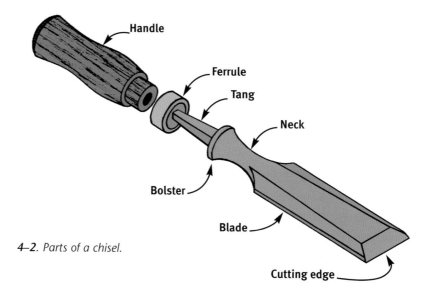

4–2. Parts of a chisel.

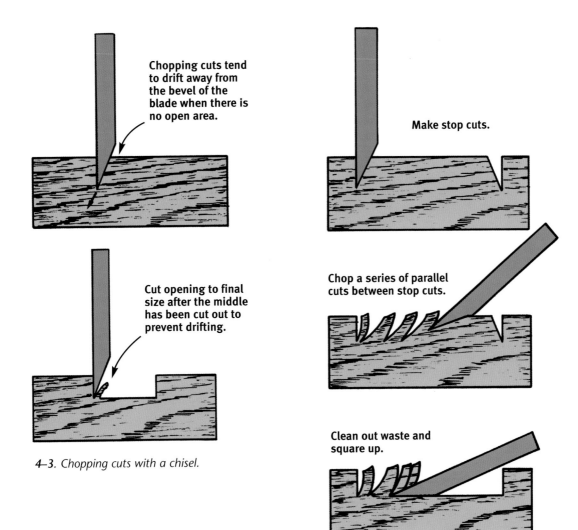

Chopping cuts tend to drift away from the bevel of the blade when there is no open area.

Cut opening to final size after the middle has been cut out to prevent drifting.

4–3. Chopping cuts with a chisel.

Make stop cuts.

Chop a series of parallel cuts between stop cuts.

Clean out waste and square up.

4–4. Using a chisel for removing wood between stop cuts.

Chopping is the process of cutting at approximately a 90-degree angle to the face of the board. It is usually done with the aid of a hammer or mallet. Chopping is usually used for defining the edges of a section to be cut out with the chisel. Chopping around the edges of a cutout cuts the wood fibers so that they won't tear past the line (**4–3**).

Chopping is also used for removing large amounts of wood and bringing a cut to its approximate depth. Hold the chisel so that the bevel is facing the wood and the blade is at about a 60-degree angle. Use a hammer or mallet to drive the chisel, and chop into the wood, as shown in **4–4**. Notice that the cut is made across the grain. Use a chisel that is approximately the same width as the cut you are making. Stop the cut a little short of the correct depth. Make a series of parallel cuts in this manner—from one end of the cutout to the other. Break out the loose chips, and then begin using the chisel for paring.

When paring, the chisel blade resembles a plane iron in the way it shaves off a slice of wood. Paring is used for removing wood inside of a cutout and for smoothing the surface of the wood at the bottom of the cutout area. You can pare with the grain or across the grain. You can tap the handle with a hammer or mallet, or you can use body force to move the chisel. *Whatever method you use, remember to keep both hands behind the cutting edge of the chisel to prevent accidents if the blade should slip. When paring, the board should be firmly clamped down.*

There are two ways you can hold the chisel for paring. For roughing out a cutout, hold the chisel so that the bevel of the blade is facing the wood. This places the handle on an angle away from the wood, making the chisel easy to hold and control. To make a very smooth finishing cut, you can pare with the flat back of the blade resting against the wood. This places the handle down low against the wood, making the chisel awkward to use in some situations (**4–5**).

Paring all the way across a board can lead to tear-outs at the edge. To prevent this, pare from both sides toward the middle (**4–6**). Giving a slight twisting motion to the chisel will help to cleanly shear off the fibers when paring end grain or across the grain.

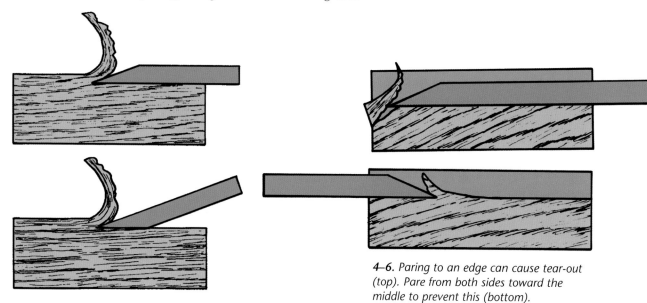

4–5. *You can make paring cuts with the chisel in one of two positions. With the bevel up and the back of the blade flat against the surface, you can make fine cuts although you are limited by the length of the chisel blade (top). With the bevel down and flat against the surface, you can make cuts of any length (bottom).*

4–6. *Paring to an edge can cause tear-out (top). Pare from both sides toward the middle to prevent this (bottom).*

Backsaw

The backsaw and its cousins, the tenon saw and dovetail saw, are very useful for making joints (**4–7**). The backsaw has a stiffener along its back that keeps it straight and eliminates whipping. You hold a backsaw with its teeth flat against the wood, instead of at an angle, as you would hold a panel saw. You make the cut across the entire surface at once; this means that the cut will be very straight and you can stop the cut partway through the board and get a flat-bottomed cut. This is very

4–7. Backsaws come in several sizes; the smaller ones are often called tenon saws or dovetail saws.

important for making certain joints, such as the rabbet and dado. The teeth on a backsaw are finer than those on most panel saws, so there is less tearing and chipping. A backsaw is often used with guide blocks or a miter box to hold the saw in exact alignment.

Router

The router is basically an electric motor that turns at a high speed of 11,000 to 23,000 rpm. The motor is mounted in an adjustable base that controls the depth of cut. A chuck or collet is connected to the motor shaft and different bits or cutters can be mounted in the chuck (**4–8**). Routers are available with a ¼-inch collet or a ½-inch collet. For joinery, the ½-inch collet type is best because there is less possibility of bit chatter.

Many types of bits are available for the router. Specially shaped bits are used for making decorative edges; however, for joinery, the most useful bit is simply the straight bit. Straight bits come in several sizes. You can get a bit that will cut the exact size of the groove you need, or you can use a smaller bit and make more than one cut.

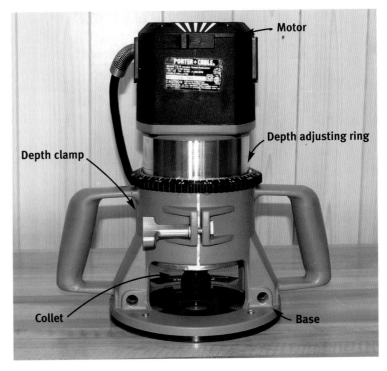

4–8. Parts of a router.

Another useful joinery bit is the *rabbeting bit*. This bit has a guide called a *pilot* that rubs against the edge of the board. The pilot keeps the cut parallel to the edge. If the edge is straight, the cut will be straight. The pilot bit will also follow a curved edge, so it is very useful for making joints in curved parts. More expensive pilot bits have small ball bearings mounted on the pilot; this makes the bit less likely to burn the edge.

You can guide a router freehand to make rough cutouts or to do decorative carving; however, for most joinery tasks, you need to use some type of guide to keep the router straight. Using an auxiliary fence is one way to guide the router. The fence attaches to the router base and will guide the router parallel to an edge of the board.

Another way of guiding the router is by clamping a board that has a straight edge to the work and letting the base rub against the board. If it is important for the router not to stray from the line in either direction, as when making a dado, then you can use two boards, one on either side of the cut. By using clamped boards as a guide, you can make cuts that are not parallel with an edge of the board. This can be useful if you need to make joints at odd angles.

One of the best ways to guide a router is with an aluminum cutting guide. Usually you can use the same guide that you would use for guiding a portable circular saw. You will need to measure the offset from the bit to the edge of the router base and use this measurement to position the guide. If you are using the straight edge type of guide, hold the router base against the guide as you make the cut. The track type of guide has an accessory router guide that attaches to the router base (**4–9**). The advantage of the track type of guide is that it prevents the router from wandering away from the guide as you make the cut.

A third way of guiding the router uses a special template-following collar that is mounted around the bit on the base of the router (**4–10**). The collar is used with a template usually made of ¼-inch hardboard, plastic, or aluminum. The collar will follow the shape of the template exactly. The template size is slightly larger than the actual cutout to allow for the thickness of the collar. This type of guide is useful for making mortises or for cutting gains for hinges. It is also used with a dovetail tail template to make dovetail joints.

4–9. A track-type of router guide.

4–10. Template-following collar.

You can mount the router in an accessory table, which makes it operate in the same way as a small shaper. The router table incorporates an adjustable fence that can be used for guiding the work. A router table is a useful accessory for working with small parts because the wood is moved instead of the router.

The router can throw wood chips at high velocity, so always wear eye protection. Keep a firm grip on the router so that it won't get out of control if the bit grabs.

Plate Joiner

The plate joiner is a machine that cuts a slot for plate splines; it is basically a plunge-cutting circular saw with a 4-inch-diameter blade (**4–11**). It will cut a slot anywhere in the face or edge of a board and align it easily and accurately.

A plate, or biscuit, spline is a type of manufactured spline of compressed wood. The splines are made of beech wood with the grain running diagonally to the length; this gives the joint increased shear strength because the grain runs across the joint line. The shape and embossed pattern of plate splines make them resemble a biscuit or cracker, so they are often simply called biscuits (**4–12**). Since the wood is compressed while being manufactured, the splines expand as they absorb moisture from the glue, creating an extremely tight-fitting joint.

The plates are available in three sizes, but they are all ⁵⁄₃₂ inch thick. No. 0 is ⅝ inch x 1¹³⁄₁₆ inches, No. 10 is ¾ inch x 2³⁄₁₆ inches, and No. 20 is 1 inch x 2⅜ inches. An adjustment on the machine sets the depth of cut for each size of plate (**4–13**). For long joints, several plates should be used,

4–11. Biscuit or plate joiner.

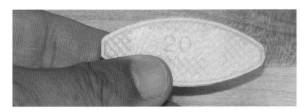

4–12. A plate spline, or biscuit, is made from compressed beech wood with the grain running diagonally.

4–13. This adjustment on the plate joiner sets the depth of cut for each size of plate.

spaced every four to six inches. For maximum strength, the plates can be spaced as closely as 2½ inches from the middle of one to the middle of the next. Two rows of plates will give added strength for boards ¾ inch thick or thicker (**4–14**). Since the slots are slightly longer than the plates, you can slide the parts into alignment during assembly. There is approximately ½ inch of lengthwise adjustment in the joint.

To lay out the joint, place the parts side-by-side, and make a pencil line across both parts at the middle of the slot location (**4–15**). The exact procedure for aligning the machine differs from one manufacturer to another, but the joiners usually can be guided either by a fence or by resting the base on the bench top. For joints such as frame butts and face miters, place the part on a flat working surface, and rest the base of the plate-joining machine on the same surface. Align the locating mark on the machine with the mark on the joint, and make the cut (**4–16**). Make sure that you have the same face against the bench for each part of the joint. Case butts, however, require a slot in the end of one board and in the face of the other. When the joint is far from an edge, to guide the cut you can clamp a board to the face of the part.

A 45-degree fence attaches to the base of the machine to make the slots in an edge-miter joint (**4–17**). In this joint, the parts are placed on the workbench with the inside face up. The fence on the plate joiner rests on the bench or the face of the board and will guide the cut perpendicular to the joint face.

Apply glue to the slots and insert the plate splines. Assemble the joint and clamp. Manufacturers typically recommend clamping until the glue is set, but you can sometimes remove the clamps after the biscuits have swollen enough to hold the joint tight.

Dowelling Jig

Dowels are wooden pegs used to reinforce many types of joint. Dowels used in joints should be chamfered at the ends to allow easy insertion into the holes, and they should have small grooves in their side to allow glue to escape from the holes. You can buy ready-made dowels that are cut to length and chamfered and have spiral or straight grooves (**4–18**). If you prefer to buy dowelling in 3-foot lengths and cut your own dowels, chamfer the ends on a sander and scratch a groove in the side of the dowel with an awl.

A dowelling jig (also called a *dowel jig*) is a tool that guides a drill bit to make a hole for a dowel. It helps to position the hole and keeps the bit straight as you drill. There are many types of dowelling jig on the market. They don't all function the same way or make the same type of joints, so you should decide what types of dowel joint you will be making before you buy a jig.

4–14. Two side-by-side biscuits can be used to give added strength when joining thick boards.

4–15. To lay out the biscuit locations, place the parts side-by-side, and make a pencil line across both parts at the middle of the slot location.

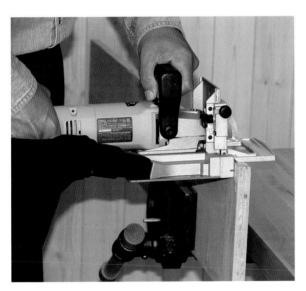

4–16. Cutting a slot with the plate joiner.

4–17. A fence on the plate joiner base can be adjusted to make miter joints.

4–18. These ready-made dowel pins have chamfered ends and many grooves in the side. The grooves allow the excess glue to escape and ensure a tight fit.

4–19. This jig can be used to make frame and panel joints.

4–20. The two jigs shown here can make case, edge, frame, and panel joints. The jig on the left clamps both boards, speeding up the process. The front jig operates in a similar way, but you must clamp it with a separate C-clamp to each board individually.

4–21. The notches in this jig allow you to line up the second hole by inserting dowels into the first hole and placing the notch over the dowel.

Two types of jig are depicted in the illustrations in this chapter. The first one is representative of a number of jigs that can be used to make frame-and-panel joints (4–19). This jig clamps to the edge or end of a board. Several sizes of interchangeable bushings are used to guide the drill bit. To center the hole position, you loosen a wing nut and align a mark with a graduated scale.

Other similar jigs operate about the same way, but a rotating turret may be used instead of the loose bushings. Some jigs are self-centering, which means that the holes will be drilled close to the center of the board no matter what the thickness of the board. Since the holes will not be drilled exactly in the center of the board, to ensure a perfect fit position the jig so that the fence is against the same face on both boards. This will compensate for any error.

To make case and edge joints, you will need a different type of jig (4–20). This type of jig can be used to make case, edge, frame, and panel joints.

Both jigs pictured have three built-in bushings for ¼-, ⁵⁄₁₆-, and ⅜-inch bits. There is no provision for centering the holes. The bushings are positioned so that the ¼-inch hole is approximately centered on a ½-inch-thick board, the ⁵⁄₁₆-inch hole will be close to the center of a ¾-inch-thick board, and the ⅜-inch hole is near the center of a one-inch-thick board. This lack of adjustment is the one limitation of this type of jig, but it is not usually a problem if you are careful to always place the jig fence against the same face on both boards.

This type of jig has notches that allow you to align the jig for the second set of holes by placing the notch over a dowel placed in the previously drilled holes in the mating board (4–21). This simplifies the joint layout.

There are several other types of dowelling jig on the market. Most of them operate about the same way as the two described here. Before buying one, make sure that it is capable of making the type of joints needed.

The dowel holes should always be a little deeper than the length of the dowel to allow for expansion and shrinkage and to allow a space for excess glue. You can use a piece of masking tape wrapped around the drill bit to indicate the depth, or you can use a commercial drill stop to keep all of the holes the same depth. Most dowelling jigs come with a set of depth stops.

When you apply glue to the mating surfaces of the joint, drip a little glue into the dowel holes, and then use a splinter to spread the glue around inside the holes. Don't use too much glue or the joint won't pull together.

Pocket-Hole Guide

One of the simplest ways to reinforce a joint is to drive screws through the joint; however, most of the time you don't want the screw heads to be visible. The pocket-hole guide allows you to hide the screws on the back of the joint where they will be less noticeable. The guide clamps to the face of a board and guides a special drill bit at a very low angle (4–22). This creates a pilot hole for the screw and an angled pocket for the screw head (4–23). This type of reinforcement works well for cabinet face frames, because the holes can all be made in the back of the frame where they won't be visible. If you must drill the holes in a visible area, you can plug the holes with specially made wooden plugs (4–24). After the plugs are glued in place, you can sand them flush with the surface of the board.

4–22. The pocket-hole guide clamps to the rear face of the boards you are joining.

4–23. The angled pocket hides the screw head.

4–24. These wooden plugs can be used to hide the pocket hole after the screw is installed.

The Five Basic Joints

OUT OF THE HUNDREDS OF JOINTS developed, five have become so popular that they can be called the basic joints of cabinetmaking. They are *butt, rabbet, dado, miter,* and *half-lap joints.* You can cut all of these joints with simple hand tools or with power equipment. Using these five basic joints, you can build almost any type of cabinet.

As you advance, you will want to use some of the more advanced joints, but you will probably still find that the five basic joints will fulfill most of your needs.

These five basic joints are recommended for all materials—solid lumber, plywood, and particleboard. Some of the more advanced joints, on the other hand, are designed specifically for solid wood and won't perform well when used with manufactured materials.

Butt Joint

The butt joint is the simplest joint to cut. However, the butt joint requires some type of reinforcement to give it strength and it is not self-aligning during assembly, so the butt joint is not always the simplest one to use.

You can use the butt joint to make a corner or to edge-join two boards into a larger panel. When a butt joint is put together so that the end grain of one part attaches to the long grain of another part, the joint must always be reinforced. Otherwise, the difference in expansion and shrinkage between end grain and long grain will eventually cause the joint to fall apart. When boards are joined long grain to long grain and a fairly large gluing surface is present, as is the case when two boards are joined to form a larger panel, no reinforcement is necessary when using modern glues.

Frame and Case Butt Joints

You can use the butt joint to make two types of corner. One type of corner is used when you are making face frames. The end of one board is joined to the edge of another; this is called a *frame butt* (**4–25**). The other type of corner is used for a situation such as joining the side to the top of a cabinet. In this case, the square end of one board is attached to the flat face of the other board; this is called a *case butt* (**4–26**). You can also use butt joints to join parts, such as shelves, to the sides of a cabinet; this is called a *T butt* (**4–27**).

The ends must be cut perfectly square and the face must be truly flat or the contact point will be too small for a good glue bond. Small projects that won't be subjected to very much stress can use butt joints that are simply glued and firmly clamped; however, in most cases, the butt joint must be reinforced in some manner. The simplest type of reinforcement is nailing

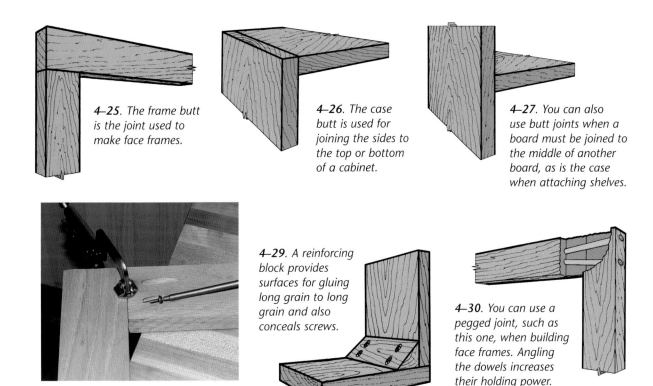

4-25. The frame butt is the joint used to make face frames.

4-26. The case butt is used for joining the sides to the top or bottom of a cabinet.

4-27. You can also use butt joints when a board must be joined to the middle of another board, as is the case when attaching shelves.

4-29. A reinforcing block provides surfaces for gluing long grain to long grain and also conceals screws.

4-30. You can use a pegged joint, such as this one, when building face frames. Angling the dowels increases their holding power.

4-28. Pocket holes and screws can be used to reinforce frame butts.

through the joint. Screws are another form of simple reinforcement. Yet both of these methods leave visible holes in the exterior of the joint that must be filled when appearance is important. For frame joints, pocket holes are a good way to hide the screws (**4–28**).

A reinforcing block strengthens a case butt joint and allows screws to be put in from the back (**4–29**). A smaller reinforcing block without screws is called a *glue block*. You need to spread glue on the sides of the glue block and press it in place, and then rapidly rub it back and forth in place until the glue grabs. The reinforcing block is clearly visible from the inside of the joint; if this is not desirable, dowels or biscuits are a good alternative.

Dowel joints are fairly easy to make, and they adapt well to production-line work. They have therefore become very popular in inexpensive, mass-produced cabinetry. However, dowel joints that join end grain to long grain tend to loosen over time.

The simplest type of dowel joint uses the dowel in much the same way as you would use a nail or screw. When used in this manner, the joint is frequently called a *pegged joint* (**4–30**). Pegs can be used to reinforce any type of butt joint. **Illustration 4–30** shows a pegged frame butt, and **4–31** shows how pegs can be used in a case butt. The hole for the dowel is drilled after the joint has been assembled, and the dowel is driven into the hole and cut off flush. This type of dowel joint will be much stronger if the dowels are angled slightly. Dowels can shrink and become loose in their holes; angling them makes it more difficult for the parts to separate than if you used straight dowels.

When you do not want the end of the dowel to show, you should use a blind dowel joint (4–32), although this joint is not as strong as the pegged joint. With the blind dowel joint, neither end of the hole comes to the surface of the board and the holes must be drilled before the joint is assembled. You can lay out the position of the holes manually or use one of the jigs described earlier to align the holes.

To lay out the position of the holes, clamp the two boards together, as shown in 4–33. Use a square to mark the position of the holes across both boards at once. Use a marking gauge or set the blade of a combination square to act as a marking gauge, and mark the middle line of the holes. Make sure that you hold the marking gauge against the same face on both parts to compensate for any error.

Dowel centers are an easy way of locating blind dowel holes. Drill the holes in one of the parts, and then insert the dowel centers into the holes. The dowel centers come in several popular sizes that fit most standard-dowel sizes. In the middle of the dowel center, there is a small point. This point makes a mark indicating the middle of the hole on the corresponding part. Simply clamp the two parts together temporarily in their correct alignment to make the marks. Dowel centers have the advantage of automatically compensating for errors in layout (4–34).

Another way of reinforcing a butt joint is by screwing on steel reinforcing angles. The flat kind frequently used works well. However, the type called a *chair brace* is more rigid; its shape helps to hold the joint square and it has less of a tendency to bend (4–35).

Another reinforcement similar to the angle brace is the *knock-down fitting*. This is a brace that comes in two parts; one part fits on each board. The two parts can be locked together or taken apart at any time. This type of fitting is sometimes used in commercial cabinets so that they can be shipped flat to save shipping costs. The cabinets can easily be assembled on the job. There are more details on knock-down fittings in chapter 5.

Splines are thin strips of wood that are sometimes used to reinforce a butt joint (4–36). The splines are usually approximately ⅛ or ¼ inch thick for use with ¾-inch-thick lumber. Thicker lumber requires a thicker spline. Splines may be made of solid wood, plywood, or hardboard. Hardboard is easy to work with, and it makes a very strong spline. This is especially true of the tempered hardboard. You can also use plywood, especially when you need a thicker spline.

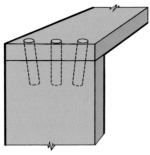

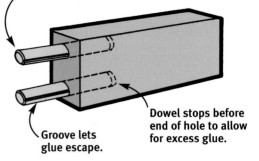

Chamfered end makes it easier to insert dowel.

Dowel stops before end of hole to allow for excess glue.

Groove lets glue escape.

4–31. You can also use pegged joints when joining the top to the sides of a cabinet. Note that the middle dowel is straight and the two outside ones are angled.

4–32. Blind dowels are concealed completely. Care must be taken to allow clearance for excess glue, or else hydraulic pressure may split the wood or hold the joint open when clamped.

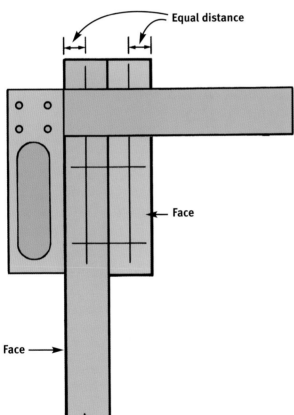

Equal distance

Face

Face

4–34. Dowel centers provide an easy and accurate way of transferring hole positions from one board to the other.

4–33. To mark dowel positions, place the parts together with the faces to the outside. Measure from the face of each board.

4–35. Steel reinforcing angles can be used to reinforce butt joints. The flat kind frequently used works well. However, the type called a chair brace is more rigid; its shape helps to hold the joint square and it has less of a tendency to bend.

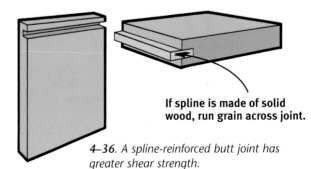

If spline is made of solid wood, run grain across joint.

4–36. A spline-reinforced butt joint has greater shear strength.

If you use solid wood for a spline, the grain should run across the width. This is 90 degrees from the direction you normally orient the grain of a board. If the grain of a spline runs lengthwise, there is a tendency for the spline to split along the grain at the joint line.

You can cut the slots for the splines with a handsaw. Mark the middle of the joint and draw a line on either side of the middle, indicating the width of the spline. Make a saw kerf on each of those lines, keeping the saw inside the line. You can usually break out the thin strip of wood left in the middle by giving the saw blade a little twist. For larger splines, you may need to make several kerfs between the two outer ones.

You can easily make the kerfs with a table saw. If you use a wide blade, you may only need to make one kerf for a ⅛-inch spline. Set the rip fence to center the blade in the joint, and raise the blade so that the depth of cut is a little greater than one-half the width of the spline. Most of the time, you can use a spline that is approximately ¾ inch wide.

You can use a router to cut the groove for a spline. Use a bit that will make a groove the correct size for the thickness of the spline you are using. When you are making the groove in the face of a board, use an auxiliary fence or a board clamped to the workpiece to guide the router. Or you can mount the router in a router table and use the fence to guide the work. To make a groove in end grain, clamp a piece of scrap to both sides of the workpiece to make a wider base for the router to sit on and then set the router fence to ride against one of the scrap boards. The router is very good for making blind grooves that don't extend to the edge of the board. You use blind grooves where you don't want the spline to show.

Spread glue on the spline and on the mating surfaces of the joint and then assemble.

The *biscuit joint* is really a variation on the spline joint. Use the biscuit joiner to cut the slots for the biscuit. Since the slots are a little longer than the splines, the parts can be shifted into alignment during assembly. Long joints require several splines. Thicker boards may require that two parallel sets of slots be made for added strength. This type of spline is very well suited for particleboard joints, because it doesn't weaken the board very much; since the slots are not continuous, it doesn't form a break line in the middle of the particleboard, as a standard spline might. Because they absorb the wet glue, the biscuits expand in the slots, making a very tight joint that is less apt to loosen than a normal spline or a dowel joint (**4–37**).

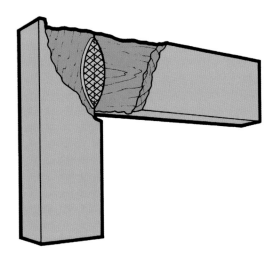

4–37. A compressed-wood spline (biscuit) expands as it absorbs moisture from the glue, making an extremely tight-fitting joint.

Edge-to-Edge Butt Joint

One of the most useful types of butt joints is the panel butt, which is used for joining two or more narrow boards into a large panel. In this instance, you are gluing long grain to long grain, which is the strongest combination. A tight-fitting glue joint of this type is so strong that further reinforcement is usually not necessary. Simply apply glue to both surfaces and clamp the boards together with bar clamps. Dowels, splines, or biscuits can be used with this type of joint to assist in aligning the board and prevent the joint from slipping out of alignment during clamping.

For this type of joint to have maximum strength, the two edges must come together tightly. The best way to ensure this is to joint both edges on a jointer (**4–38**). Make sure that you have the fence set at exactly 90 degrees. If you are using a hand plane to joint the edges, clamp the two boards together so that the edges are up and the face sides are out. Now plane both edges at the same time. When the boards are joined together, any deviation from an exact 90-degree angle will be matched by a complementary angle on the other edge. This way, there will be no gaps and the boards will lay perfectly flat. Be sure to align the faces, as shown in **4–39**.

When gluing up panels from plain-sawn lumber, reverse the direction of the annual rings, as shown in **4–40**. If the end grain does not show a pronounced ring pattern and you can't decide how to place the board, don't worry about it. Boards with the greatest tendency to cup will have a pronounced ring pattern.

Quarter-sawn lumber does not have as great of a tendency to cup, so you don't need to worry about it when you are gluing up panels. However, there is a difference in the rate of dimen-

4–38. Use a jointer to make sure that the edges are straight and square before assembling a panel butt joint.

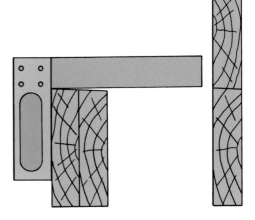

4–39. Two boards planed together with their faces out cancels any error.

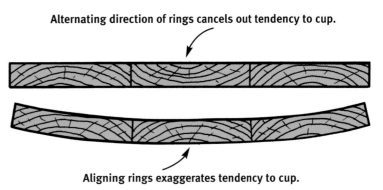

Alternating direction of rings cancels out tendency to cup.

Aligning rings exaggerates tendency to cup.

4–40. Plain-sawn lumber should have alternated growth rings when you are gluing up large panels.

sional change between old wood, where the rings are near the middle of the tree, and young wood, where the rings are near the outside of the tree. To compensate for this, some cabinetmakers glue quarter-sawn panels with old wood to old wood and young wood to young wood (**4–41**). If the curvature of the rings is difficult to determine, don't worry about the alignment.

As boards shrink and swell, the portion that is approximately 6 inches from each end changes more drastically than the rest of the board. The end grain both absorbs and loses more moisture because of the exposed fluid channels present. To compensate for this, some cabinetmakers add a little spring to an edge joint, as shown in **4–42**. After the edges have been fit to each other, take a very thin shaving from the middle of each edge. When the boards are clamped together, this puts additional pressure on the ends of the joint so that they are less likely to open up if shrinkage occurs.

Rabbet Joint

The rabbet joint, shown in **4–43**, is much stronger than the butt joint. Not only does it have a greater glue surface, but it also reduces shear forces because the lip supports the weight instead of just relying on the glue. There is no standard depth for a rabbet, but it is frequently ⅜ inch for a ¾-inch board. A rabbet cut this depth provides 50 percent more gluing surface than a butt joint (**4–44**).

It is easy to make a short rabbet with hand tools; however, for rabbets that are more than about 12 inches, it is easier if you use power tools.

Although you can cut a rabbet freehand, you will obtain more accurate results if you use guide boards clamped to the work to keep the saw square and in proper position (**4–45**). Cut a strip of wood to the thickness of the wood to be left after the rabbet is finished, and then nail it to a backing board, as shown in the photograph. Place the work on the backing board with the end resting against the strip. Clamp a scrap of wood along the cutting line, as shown in **4–46**; this will guide the saw straight and square. Make the cut to the desired depth, using either a panel saw or a backsaw.

The backsaw is a little easier to handle because the stiff back keeps the saw from whipping. Hold the saw against the thickness strip, and then make the second cut to complete the rabbet.

You can use a similar method for cutting a rabbet on a table saw. Set the fence to make the vertical cut first, as shown in **4–47**. You should set the blade height to the width of the rabbet.

There are two schools of thought on how to make the second cut. With both of these methods, the blade height is set to the depth of the rabbet. The way most professionals make the second cut is by setting the fence for the width of the rabbet, as shown in **4–47**. This method is very accurate, and you can use the same setup for boards of various sizes without any

Old wood to old wood or young wood to young wood equalizes shrinkage.

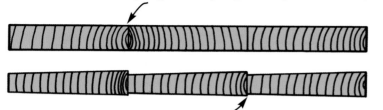

Young wood to old wood causes unequal shrinkage at joint.

4–41. You should glue quarter-sawn lumber into panels with old wood against old wood and young wood against young wood.

**Take a thin shaving from the middle.
Gap is exaggerated here for clarity.**

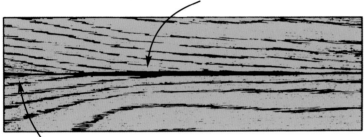

Ends are tight for 6".

4–42. Putting a little spring into a joint compensates for the greater shrinkage that occurs at the ends of the boards.

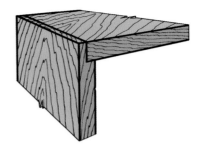

4–43. A rabbet joint is frequently used for joining the sides of a cabinet to the top and bottom.

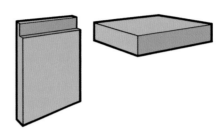

4–44. In this exploded view of a rabbet joint, the shading indicates the cutout area.

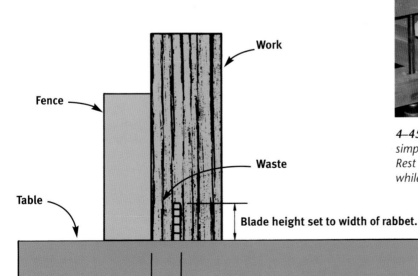

Work

Fence

Waste

Table

Blade height set to width of rabbet.

Distance from outside edge of blade to fence is equal to depth of rabbet.

4–46. Making the first cut of a rabbet on the table saw.

4–45. You can use scrap wood to make a simple backsaw guide for making rabbets. Rest the backsaw against the guide blocks while cutting to keep the cuts square.

adjustment. The only problem with this method is that there is a tendency for the waste piece to kick back out of the saw as the cut is completed. You can minimize this problem by using a push stick with a deep notch so that the push stick will push the waste through as well.

The other method of making the second cut eliminates the problem of waste kickback, but it is not as accurate, because, if the board wanders from the fence, the rabbet will be too large. This method requires a different setup for pieces of differing dimensions, and it won't work with very large boards. **Illustration 4–48** shows the setup for this method. The part is placed between the fence and the blade so that the waste isn't trapped there.

A board that is bowed may lift slightly from the table during the cut. This will leave a small piece of wood in the corner of the rabbet that must be removed. You can easily remove it with a sharp chisel, or you can run a knife blade against both edges of the rabbet so that the tip cuts into the wood to be removed.

You can also make rabbets using a table saw or a radial arm saw with an attachment called a *dado blade*. Set the blade to make a cut slightly wider than needed. You can use the miter gauge or the rip fence to guide the board. If you use the rip fence, clamp or screw a piece of wood to the fence to protect it from the blade. Lower the blade below the table, and position the fence so that the auxiliary wooden fence is over the blade. Now turn on the saw and raise the blade to create a cutout in the wooden fence. Turn off the saw and position the fence to make the proper-width rabbet (**4–49**). There is more information about the dado blade in the next section.

4–50. *Using a saw guide with an accessory router guide to make a rabbet.*

You can also use a router to make rabbets. You need an auxiliary fence or you can clamp a board or an aluminum saw guide to the work to guide the router. Set the router fence to the width of the rabbet, and set the cutter depth to the depth of the rabbet. A ¾-inch cutter will make a rabbet in one pass; if you don't have a bit this large, you can make more than one pass to cut the rabbet.

If you don't have a fence for your router, simply clamp a board to the work so that when the base of the router rubs against the board, the cutter will be in the proper position to make the joint. You can also use an aluminum saw guide for this. The type of saw guide that has an accessory router guide works well for making rabbets (**4–50**).

4–47. This method of making the second cut may kick back the waste, so use caution.

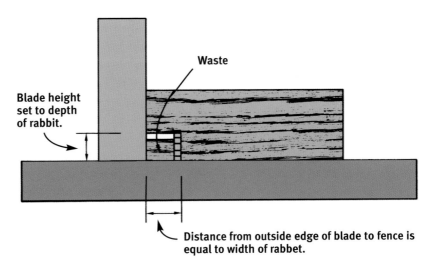

Waste

Blade height set to depth of rabbit.

Distance from outside edge of blade to fence is equal to width of rabbet.

4–48. This alternate method of making the second cut prevents kicked-back waste, but you can't use it for large boards.

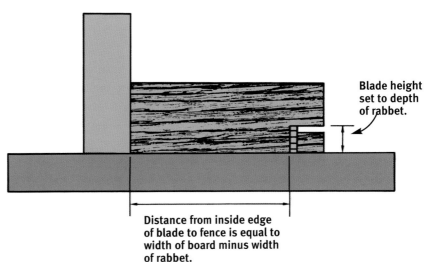

Blade height set to depth of rabbet.

Distance from inside edge of blade to fence is equal to width of board minus width of rabbet.

4–49. A dado blade makes a rabbet in a single operation. The auxiliary wooden fence prevents the metal fence and the dado blade from coming in contact with each other.

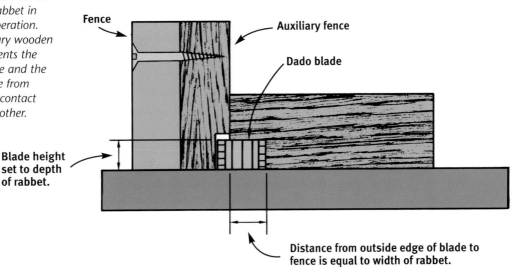

Fence

Auxiliary fence

Dado blade

Blade height set to depth of rabbet.

Distance from outside edge of blade to fence is equal to width of rabbet.

A special bit, called a rabbeting bit, makes using the router even easier. This bit has a small pin, called a pilot, that rubs against the uncut edge of the board to guide the bit. In more expensive models, a ball bearing is attached to the pilot (**4–51**). The size of the bit determines the width of the cut, but the depth can be adjusted. This type of rabbeting bit is especially useful when the rabbet is very long, as is the case when a rabbet is used to attach the back of a cabinet or when a rabbet must be cut on a curved edge.

The jointer can also cut rabbets. Most jointers have a ledge that is designed to support the uncut part of the board when making a rabbet. Set the jointer fence to the depth of the rabbet (**4–52**). If the rabbet is not too wide, you can make it in one pass by setting the depth of cut to the width of the rabbet. If the rabbet is too large to make in one pass, set the depth-of-cut adjustment to take a moderate cut. Run the board over the jointer, and then adjust the depth of cut about ⅛ inch deeper. Continue in this manner until you reach the desired depth.

When you assemble a rabbet joint, be sure to apply glue to both surfaces of the joint. A well-made rabbet that is glued and clamped will hold without reinforcement. However, rabbets are frequently reinforced with nails, as shown in **4–53**.

Dado Joint

The dado shown in **4–54** and **4–55** is a very strong joint. A dado that is cut to a depth one-half the thickness of the board provides twice as much gluing surface as a butt joint, and shear forces are totally eliminated because the board is supported on both sides by a lip. The dado is used for attaching shelves—or dividers, in drawer construction—and, in some cases, for attaching the top and bottom of a cabinet. A major advantage of the dado is that it is self-aligning; once the parts are assembled, the joint will hold the parts in alignment as the clamps are applied. The dado will also hold a slightly cupped or warped board flat, and it will help prevent boards from cupping after assembly.

In the traditional terminology of cabinetmakers, *dado* only refers to this type of joint if the joint is cut across the grain; if it is cut with the grain, it is called a groove (**4–56**). Modern materials such as particleboard and plywood have no definite grain direction, so this distinction has become somewhat obsolete. Therefore, many modern cabinetmakers use the term dado to describe any joint of this type.

To cut a dado by hand, use a saw to make cuts at each side of the joint, stopping at the proper depth. Clamping a guide block to the board will help keep the cuts straight (**4–57**). If the board is narrow enough to fit in the miter box, use it to guide the saw. Next, some people prefer to make several saw kerfs between the two sides, whereas others go straight to chiseling.

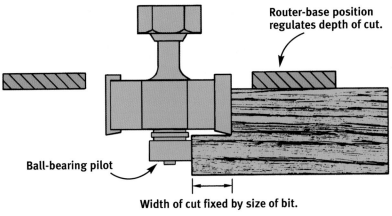

Router-base position regulates depth of cut.

Ball-bearing pilot

Width of cut fixed by size of bit.

4-51. A special rabbeting bit for the router makes a rabbet in a single operation.

4-52. Using a jointer to cut a rabbet.

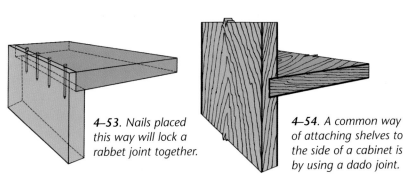

4-53. Nails placed this way will lock a rabbet joint together.

4-54. A common way of attaching shelves to the side of a cabinet is by using a dado joint.

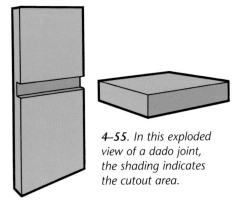

4-55. In this exploded view of a dado joint, the shading indicates the cutout area.

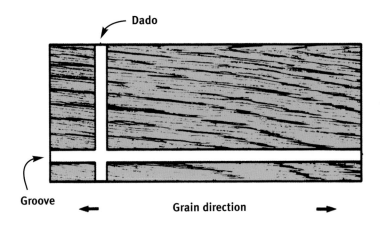

Dado

Groove

Grain direction

4-56. Adhering to the strictest definition, you can only call this type of joint a dado if it is cut across the grain; otherwise, it's called a groove.

4-57. To cut a dado by hand, make stop cuts with a backsaw. A guide block clamped to the work helps keep the backsaw square. Remove the wood between the stop cuts with a chisel.

You use a chisel to remove the wood between the saw cuts. Hold the chisel with the bevel facing the wood, and pare off the wood in fairly heavy cuts until you reach the approximate depth. Smooth the bottom and bring the dado to the exact depth by taking lighter paring cuts.

You can also use two specialized planes, the *router plane* and the *plow plane*, to remove the wood between the saw kerfs.

You may prefer cutting the dado with a portable circular saw. Set the blade depth to the depth of the dado. Use a fence or an aluminum guide to guide the saw, and make a series of cuts inside the area to be dadoed. Use a chisel to clean out the cut in the manner just described.

If you use an attachment called a *dado blade*, you can use a table saw or a radial arm saw for cutting dadoes. There are two types of dado blade available. One type actually consists of two blades that make the side cuts and a set of chippers that removes the wood between the cuts. The chippers come in several thicknesses, and can be arranged to make cuts in varying widths. You can make small adjustments in thickness by cutting out paper or cardboard washers and placing them between the chippers. There are also sets of thin brass spacers available for this purpose. When you use several chippers at once, space them equally around the circle, instead of grouping them all together.

The other type of dado blade is the wobbler. It has a single blade mounted in the middle of a set of tapered washers. Rotating the washers causes the blade to wobble on the saw arbor; the greater the wobble, the wider the cut will be. This type of dado blade is easy to adjust, because it doesn't need to be removed from the saw arbor for adjustment (**4–58**). Since it is so adjustable, it's easy to make minor variations in thickness. The cut made by a wobbler is slightly rounded at the bottom, because the blade travels in an arc from side to side. In most cases, this isn't a problem; but if you need a flat bottom, use the other type of dado blade or flatten out the cut with a chisel.

Set the blade height to control the depth of the dado, and use a rip fence or miter gauge to guide the board.

When dadoing plywood, it may be necessary to apply masking tape to the surface of the work to prevent chipping. In severe cases, score the face of the plywood with a sharp knife before cutting the dado.

4–58. A wobbler-type dado blade can be adjusted without removing it from the saw arbor; you simply loosen the arbor nut and twist the dado washer to the desired setting.

A router is very useful for making dadoes. Because you move the router instead of the board, it's easier to handle large boards with a router than with a table saw. For boards up to ¾ inch thick, you can get a cutter that will make the dado in one pass; however, to make wide or non-standard-size dadoes, you will need to make more than one cut. Since it is important for the dado to be straight on both edges, use a guide board on both sides of the router or use a track type of saw guide with an accessory router attachment to prevent the router from straying from the line (4–59).

If you don't have a track type of saw guide, you can make a simple dado guide

4-59. Using a track-type guide to cut a dado with a router.

for your router (4–60). Clamp guide boards to a scrap and make a test cut with the router. Adjust the guide boards until the cut is exactly the right width. Now screw boards across the ends of the guide boards to hold them at the correct width. Use a square to position the end blocks. With the end blocks in place, you can remove the clamps and use the guide over and over. You can place the end block against an edge to square the guide, since you used a square to position the ends. The first time you use the guide,

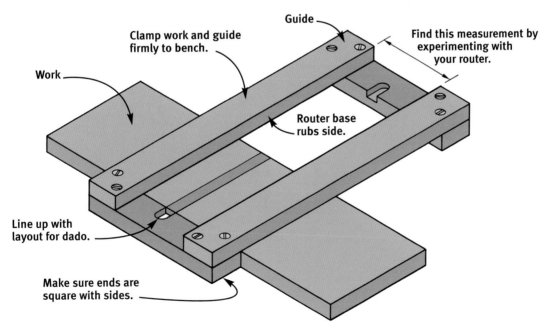

4-60. When building the guide, leave the cross pieces long. Put the router in position and clamp the guides in place. Screw the guides to the cross pieces. Then trim the cross pieces to length.

continue the cut partway into the end blocks; you can use this cut to position the guide in the future. Simply line up the cut in the end block with the layout lines on the board.

A tight-fitting dado that can be clamped while the glue dries usually doesn't require any reinforcement. If you can't clamp the joint or if the project requires additional strength, you can reinforce a dado with screws or nails. When appearance is not important, you can drive nails or screws into the end of the board through the side; however, when this isn't desirable from an aesthetic point of view, toenail or drive screws at an angle, as shown in **4–61**, so that they can't be seen from the outside of the cabinet.

Miter Joint

The miter is an attractive-looking joint that you should use when appearance is important. Since it hides the end grain of both parts, it is frequently used with plywood or particleboard. Usually you use a miter to join two boards at a right angle—in which case, you make the cut at 45 degrees. However, you can use a miter to join two boards at any angle. When you desire an angle other than 90 degrees, the miter cut is exactly one-half of the desired angle.

Even though a miter joint offers approximately 40 percent more glue area than a butt joint, it is still a fairly weak joint. In most cases, it is best to reinforce it, especially if the joint will carry a structural load.

There are actually two types of miter. One type is the face (frame) miter, which is used for joining parts such as the stile and rails of a cabinet or picture frames (**4–62** and **4–63**). With the face miter, you make the cut on the face of the board. The other type of miter is the edge (case) miter, which is used for joining parts such as the sides and top of a cabinet (**4–64**). With the edge miter, you cut along the end or edge of the board.

To cut a face miter by hand, you can simply use a combination square to mark a 45-degree angle and then you can cut the joint freehand; however, for more accurate work, you usually need a miter box. A miter box is a guide that holds the saw straight and at the correct angle. Although several types are commercially available that use various means of guiding the saw, the simplest type is made of three pieces of wood, as shown in **4–65**.

It is best to use a backsaw with a miter box, but you can also use a panel saw with the type of miter box in **4–65**. Place the miter box on the bench so that the lip hangs over the edge to stabilize it. Put the part to be cut into the box with its edge against the back of the box. Put the saw into one of the 45-degree slots and make the cut, holding the saw flat against the board so that it cuts uniformly across the entire surface at once (**4–66**).

For a miter to fit correctly, either both cuts must be exactly 45 degrees or the angles must be complementary; that is, they may not be exactly 45

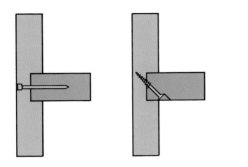

4–61. You can reinforce dadoes with nails or screws. If you want concealed reinforcement, angle the fasteners in from the bottom.

4–62. You can use a face miter to join face-frame members.

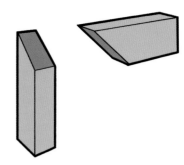

4–63. In this exploded view of a face miter, the shading indicates the mating surfaces.

4–64. You can use an edge miter to join the sides to the top of a cabinet.

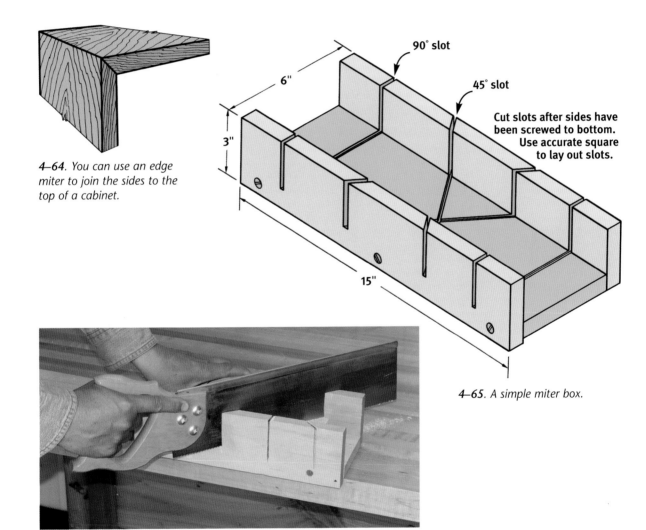

90° slot

45° slot

6"

3"

15"

Cut slots after sides have been screwed to bottom. Use accurate square to lay out slots.

4–65. A simple miter box.

4–66. To use a miter box, place it on the bench so that the front lip catches on the edge. Place the part to be cut against the rear of the box, and line up the cut with one of the slots. Put a backsaw in the slot and make the cut.

degrees, but the total of the two angles must be 90 degrees. For example, if one cut is 44½ degrees, then the complementary angle would be 45½ degrees. You can take advantage of this information when cutting miters to compensate for small inaccuracies in your miter box or in any of the other cutting devices described later. Make the first cut with the board face up; make the second cut with the board face down and on the opposite side of the saw. This procedure automatically ensures that the angles will be complementary even if they are not exactly 45 degrees.

When you are cutting both mating parts from a single board, it is sometimes possible to make both cuts at once; to do this, the board must have two good faces. Simply make one cut and turn one of the parts over. It is not always possible to use this method, because cutting a board face down can leave chips along the face of the joint. Also, irregularly shaped parts, such as moldings, can't be cut this way. In these cases, you should try to get the angle as accurate as possible and you should cut both parts face up. If the joint is slightly off, refer to the section on fitting that follows.

By far the most popular power tool for cutting face miters is the power miter saw (4–67). Similar to a portable circular saw mounted in a miter box, it can be adjusted to any angle. And it can be tilted to make compound miter cuts. Simply place the board against the fence at the back of the saw table and hold it in place. Then pull the saw down into the board.

You can use the radial arm saw to cut face miters by rotating the arm to the proper angle. Whenever possible, use the method of cutting one part face up and the other face down and on the opposite side of the blade to ensure a good fit.

You can use a table saw to make this type of miter by setting the miter gauge to 45 degrees. You can use the same method described earlier to get complementary angles, or you can make the simple accessory in 4–68 that will enable you to cut complementary angles with both parts face up.

When you use the table saw, make sure that the two sides that are used to guide the cut are exactly 90 degrees apart because all future cuts will rely on this initial setup. Check the angle with a square for accuracy. The size of the guide depends on

4–67. A power miter saw can be adjusted to the appropriate miter angle (45 degrees in most cases).

your saw; the base of the triangle should be equal to twice the distance from the blade to the outside edge of the miter gauge when the gauge is set to 90 degrees. Attach the guide to the miter gauge with screws through the holes provided for attaching an auxiliary fence. Set the miter gauge for 90 degrees, and make the first cut with the edge of the part against one side of the guide. Make the second cut with the edge of the part against the second side of the guide. You need to make both cuts with the boards face up. As long as the guide was made accurately, you will get perfect-fitting miters even if the miter gauge is slightly off.

To make edge-miter joints, you need to cut along the edge or across the end of the board (**4–69**). You can cut a narrow board in a miter box by placing it on its edge; however, for anything wider than 2 or 3 inches, you need to use a different technique.

One method of cutting edge miters by hand involves the use of a plane. This method works best with solid lumber on edge grain; it is not very effective on end grain or with manufactured materials. In these cases, or for very long joints, use power equipment. To lay out the miter, draw a line along the back of the board that is exactly the same distance from the edge as the thickness of the board. An easy way to do this is by using a scrap of the same

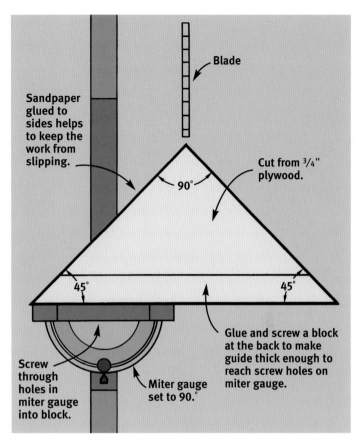

Labels:
Blade
Sandpaper glued to sides helps to keep the work from slipping.
90°
Cut from ¾" plywood.
45°
45°
Screw through holes in miter gauge into block.
Miter gauge set to 90.°
Glue and screw a block at the back to make guide thick enough to reach screw holes on miter gauge.

4–68. This simple attachment for a table-saw miter gauge produces better-fitting miter joints than the miter gauge alone. Make sure that you cut mating parts on opposite sides of the guide.

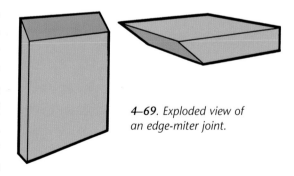

4–69. Exploded view of an edge-miter joint.

thickness to mark the line. Place the board against a bench stop with the back up; use a plane to cut away the corner of the board between the edge and the line. Hold the plane approximately 45 degrees to the surface of the board. Continue planing until the plane iron touches both the face corner and the line. This should produce a perfect 45-degree miter. Check the angle with a combination square to make sure. Fix any deviations from the correct angle with light planing strokes.

4–70. You can use a jointer to make edge-miter joints if they run with the grain.

4–71. Using a portable circular saw and a saw guide to cut an edge miter.

Since the jointer has an adjustable angle fence, you can use this same technique with the jointer. Set the fence to 45 degrees and keep cutting until you reach the corner (**4–70**).

The portable circular saw has an adjustable angle shoe, so you can cut this type of miter by setting the angle to 45 degrees and cutting along the edge of the board. Using a saw guide clamped to the work will make the cut more accurate (**4–71**). This is one of the best ways to cut long miters in sheet material like plywood or particleboard.

A table saw can be used to cut edge miters. Set the tilt arbor so that the blade will cut a 45-degree angle. When it is possible, set the fence so that the board will be between the fence and the blade and the waste piece will be on the outside. When the board is too large for you to be able to do this, add an auxiliary wooden fence to the rip fence to protect it from the blade and position the fence close to the blade. Lower the blade as you position the fence, and then turn on the saw and raise the blade until it slightly cuts into the auxiliary wooden fence. Place the edge to be mitered against the fence and make the cut. The waste piece will be trapped between the fence and the blade when you are using this method, so there is a possibility that the waste may kick back at the end of the cut. *To avoid being hit in case of a kickback, don't stand directly in line with the blade.*

Fitting Miter Joints

When you can't use the complementary angle method of cutting miters, you may have to do some fitting to get a perfect miter joint. The best way of testing a face miter is in a miter clamp. This is a special type of clamp that holds both parts exactly square. With the parts clamped, you can see how well the miter fits. The parts should make equal contact along the entire joint line. If they touch at one end of the joint and there is a gap at the other end, there are several ways you can correct the problem.

The miter clamp has a slot for a saw; place a backsaw on the joint line so that the points of the teeth on one side are lined up with one of the joint faces. Cut straight down the joint line. This will make a complementary angle cut on the adjoining part. It will also make the part approximately ¹⁄₁₆ inch shorter, so allow extra length for fitting if you anticipate that you will need to fit the joints. Reposition the parts in the clamp and they should fit well.

You can also use a block plane to fit the joint. With the parts clamped together, hold the thin edge of a square so that it lines up with the face of one of the miter cuts. Use the opposite side of the blade as a guide for draw-

ing a line on the other side of the joint. This will give you a complementary angle. Remove the part from the clamp and place it in a vise so that the miter cut is level. Use the block plane for cutting to the line. Plane from the inside corner to the outside corner to avoid tearing out the grain.

A disc sander or a stationary belt sander are excellent tools for fitting miter joints. Mark the joint in the same manner described for the block plane. Hold the part flat on the sander table, and make sure that the table is square with the sanding disk or belt; then sand to the line.

To fit an edge miter, dry-assemble the joint and use a square to hold the parts at a 90-degree angle. Examine the joint to determine where wood needs to be removed, and then use a block plane to trim the joint.

4–72. When you use blind dowels to reinforce a miter joint, you should place them at a 90-degree angle to the face of the joint (45 degrees to the edge of the board).

Reinforcing Miter Joints

When a miter joint carries a structural load in a cabinet, you should reinforce it. You can use nails or screws if they won't mar the appearance of the joint. For maximum strength, alternate sides so that the nails or screws tie the joint together from both sides. When the inside of the joint won't show, glue blocks or reinforcing blocks are often used.

Dowels are used frequently for reinforcing miter joints. Drill the holes so that they are square with the miter cut, as shown in **4–72**. To do this, clamp the dowelling jig to the joint, as shown in **4–73**.

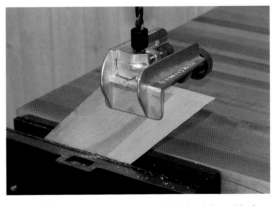

4–73. Using a dowelling jig to drill blind dowel holes in a face miter.

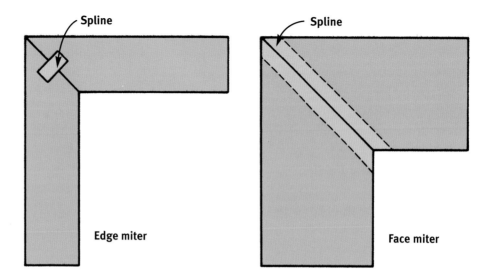

4–74. *You can use splines to reinforce both edge-miter and face-miter joints.*

Splines are very useful for reinforcing miter joints. You can use any of the previously described methods for cutting the grooves. For edge miters, you should cut the grooves square with the miter cut, as shown in **4–74**. You can reinforce face miters with two different types of spline. The spline in **4–75** is similar to the spline used for edge miters. You should cut the spline oversize and then trim it to final size and shape after the joint has been assembled and the glue has set. To install the type of spline in **4–76**, cut the parts as if a spline is not being used and assemble the joint. After the glue has set, cut the slot for the spline through the corner of the joint. Install the spline oversize, and then trim it after the glue has set.

Biscuits are a good way to reinforce both types of miter joint. They are especially useful for reinforcing long edge miters. Use the miter fence attachment on the plate joiner to align the pockets with the joint (**4–77**).

Half-Lap Joint

You can use the half-lap joint to join two narrow boards where they cross or meet at a corner. This type of joint is especially useful in building the framework of a cabinet carcass (**4–78 to 4–80**). Because of its large long-grain contact area, the half-lap joint is very strong.

You cut the end lap in much the same way as a rabbet. Make the shoulder cut first, and then cut in the other direction to remove the waste. You make the cross lap the same way as a dado. Cut saw kerfs on both sides of the joint, and then remove the waste with a chisel. You can cut half-lap joints with a router. Place scraps of the same thickness on both sides of the

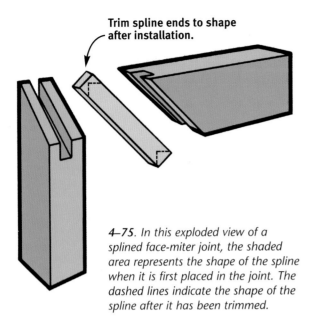

Trim spline ends to shape after installation.

4–75. In this exploded view of a splined face-miter joint, the shaded area represents the shape of the spline when it is first placed in the joint. The dashed lines indicate the shape of the spline after it has been trimmed.

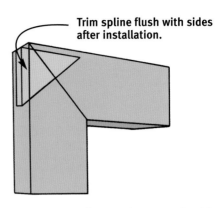

Trim spline flush with sides after installation.

4–76. You need to cut the groove for this type of spline after the joint has been assembled. You should make the spline oversize and then trim it to shape after inserting it.

4–77. Using a plate joiner on a long edge-miter joint.

4–78. You can use the half-lap joint to join face frames or for structural framing inside a cabinet.

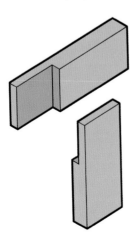

4–79. In this exploded view of a half-lap joint, the shading indicates the cutout area.

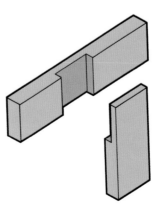

4–80. You can also use half-lap joints for joining boards that don't meet at the corner.

board to support the router base. Clamp on guide boards that will help you cut the shoulders straight.

You can also use the radial arm saw or the table saw to cut half-lap joints. Use a dado blade and make several cuts to get the correct width.

You can reinforce this type of joint with short nails driven in through the back.

Advanced Joints

IF YOU MASTER THE FIVE BASIC JOINTS, you can build almost anything you want. However, as you progress, you will probably want to try some of the more advanced joints that offer additional strength or beauty.

Mortise-and-Tenon Joint

You use the mortise-and-tenon joint in the same places that you use a dowel-reinforced butt joint, but the mortise-and-tenon joint provides much more strength because of its large long-grain contact area (**4–81**). A mortise is a rectangular hole cut into the wood, and a tenon is a projection on the mating part that fits into the mortise.

You should use this type of joint only with solid lumber; it is not suited for plywood or particleboard.

The mortise should be approximately one third of the total width of the board. So, for ¾-inch lumber, you should use a ¼-inch mortise. Try to leave approximately ¾ inch between the end of the mortise and the end of the board. Usually it's a good idea to leave the parts to be mortised slightly long and then trim them to length after the joint has been assembled (**4–82**). This provides some extra backing to prevent the wood from splitting while you are cutting the mortise. Lay out the mortise, and then drill a series of holes inside the lines to the desired depth. Use a chisel to clean out the wood between the holes and square up the corners (**4–83**).

Cut the tenons with a backsaw. Make the long cuts first, stopping at the line for the shoulder cut. Make the shoulder cut to remove the waste (**4–84**). If the tenon is too large, you can trim it with a rasp.

You can also cut tenons with a table saw. You can use a standard blade and make a series of cuts the same way as you would by hand. You should use a tenoning jig for this procedure. It is a jig that will clamp the board firmly in the vertical position while making the cut. The jig slides in the miter gauge slot in the saw table (**4–85**). You can alternately use a dado blade and do all of the cutting from the side of the board. You will have to make several passes over the blade to get the proper-length tenon.

A router accessory is available that will allow you to make both the mortise and the tenon with a router.

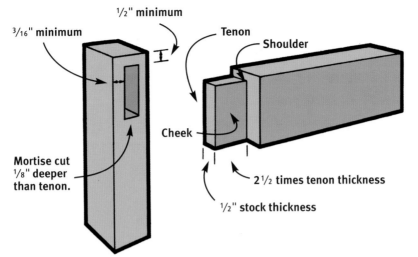

3/16" minimum

1/2" minimum

Tenon

Shoulder

Mortise cut 1/8" deeper than tenon.

Cheek

2 1/2 times tenon thickness

1/2" stock thickness

4–81. You should use mortise-and-tenon joints when a great deal of strength is required.

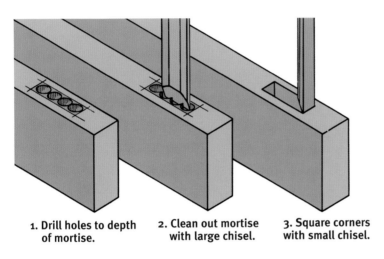

1. Drill holes to depth of mortise.

2. Clean out mortise with large chisel.

3. Square corners with small chisel.

4–82. Cutting a mortise with a drill and chisels.

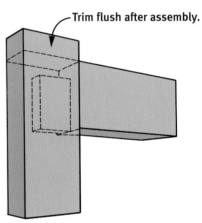

Trim flush after assembly.

4–83. When the mortise is cut near the end of the board, leave the board long during the cutting and assembly to reinforce the end of the mortise. After assembly, trim the board to length.

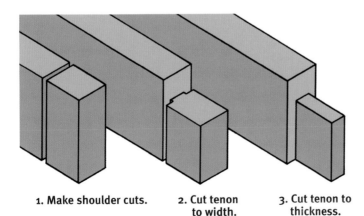

1. Make shoulder cuts.

2. Cut tenon to width.

3. Cut tenon to thickness.

4–84. Steps in cutting a tenon.

4–85. A tenoning jig holds the board safely while you cut tenons on a table saw.

Dovetail Joint

Dovetails are considered by many to be the mark of true craftsmanship. They form a strong, interlocking joint that is very useful in drawer construction (**4–86** and **4–87**). The best dovetails are cut by hand because the size of the pin can be tailored to the size of the part and the type of wood used. Softer woods require larger pins. However, today most dovetails are made with a router and a dovetail jig. Although the standard type of dovetail jig for a router does not offer any choice in pin size and the pins are often too small for softer woods, an improved type of dovetail jig allows you almost as much freedom in designing dovetail joints as hand cutting does.

Dovetails can be used with solid wood only. Pins made of particleboard will crumble and break off. The plies in plywood form a break line that will cause the pins to break. Because of consumer demand for dovetailed-drawer construction, many commercial cabinets use machine-cut dovetails with plywood and particleboard, but the resulting joint is weaker than a rabbet or dado when it is used with these materials.

When you don't want the end grain of the tails to show, you can use a half-blind dovetail (**4–88**). This joint is also called a lapped dovetail. They are often used in drawer construction and are also useful in carcass construction. Half-blind dovetails can be used to join boards that are of different thicknesses; this is usually the case in the construction of a drawer where the front will be thicker than the sides.

Half-blind dovetails can be made with a router and a dovetail jig. *I recommend that you make sure you have a full-face shield when you are using a router to make dovetails; chips will fly all over, and there is always the possibility that the bit may break or come out of the collet. Be sure to study the owner's manuals that come with the jigs before using them. The descriptions given here are meant to supplement the instructions provided by the manufacturer and to give you an idea of how the jigs operate before you purchase one.*

The router jig most commonly used for half-blind dovetails uses finger plates to guide the router. The pins and tails are cut in a single operation, and all alignment is automatically taken care of by the jig (**4–89**). The initial setup and adjustment can vary depending on the manufacturer, but they all operate essentially in the same way. The board that will have the pins cut into it (called the pin board) is placed under the finger template, on top of the jig, with the inside face of the pin board up. The board that will have the tails cut into it (called the tail board) is placed on the front of the jig with its inside face out. Adjustable guides offset the tail board so that the tails and pins line up for the cut. A template-following collar is used on the router base, and a dovetail bit makes the cut. Since the pin board acts as a backup to the tail board, there is very little splintering.

4–86. The dovetail joint is often used in drawer construction. It can also be used for joining the side to the top of a cabinet.

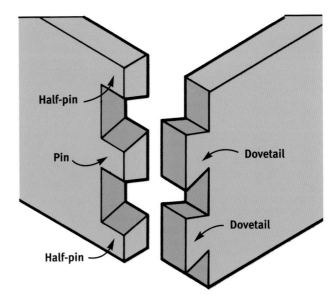

Half-pin

Pin

Dovetail

Dovetail

Half-pin

4–87. Parts of a dovetail joint.

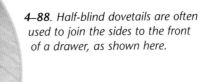

4–88. Half-blind dovetails are often used to join the sides to the front of a drawer, as shown here.

4–89. This type of dovetail jig will guide a router to cut half-blind dovetails.

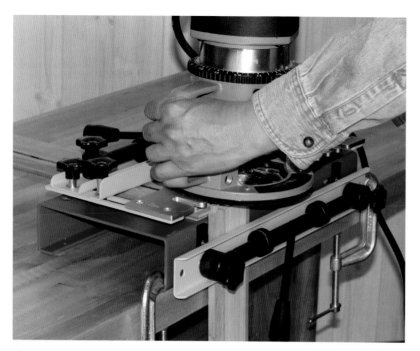

Place the router base on the template before turning on the router. The base must be flat against the template throughout the cut or the joint will not fit correctly. You will get a smoother cut with even less splintering if you make a very shallow cut across the board, just touching the ends of the fingers on the template, before you begin following the template. Next, guide the router into the first slot. Remember to keep the base flat against the template, and also make sure that the bushing rubs against the template as you

4–90. Cutting half-blind dovetails with a dovetail jig.

clean out the waste. Follow around the rounded end of the template finger and into the next slot (**4–90**). Never lift the router while it is on the template, because the bit will cut into the template and ruin it.

Before removing the boards, inspect the joint; if wood chips were collecting in the template as you worked, some of the sockets may be too shallow. If you find a socket that needs to be deeper, remove the dust and chips from the template, and cut that socket again.

The fit of the joint is controlled by the depth setting on the router. Lowering the bit tightens the joint, and raising the bit loosens the joint. Make a test joint and adjust the bit until you are satisfied with the fit; then make a gauge block so that you can easily set the router depth each time you use the jig. The gauge block is simply a scrap of wood with a rabbet cut in the edge.

The guide bushing on the router will prevent the bit from making the rabbet, so make a shallow rabbet on the board first. Then, deepen the rabbet with the dovetail bit set to the final depth setting from the test joint. Now you can return the router to the correct depth setting every time you use it by placing the gauge block on the router base and then adjusting the setting for the depth of cut until the bit just touches the bottom of the rabbet.

If the face of the tail board is not flush with the end of the pin board, adjust the depth setting on the jig. This may involve some trial and error; but, once it is set, you won't need to change the depth setting as long as you use boards of the same thickness.

4–91. An adjustable dovetail jig.

The joint produced by the jig described above will have the uniform look of a machine-cut dovetail. When you want to more closely replicate the look of a hand-cut dovetail, you can use an adjustable dovetail jig (**4–91**). With this type of jig, you can have the same degree of control over pin size and spacing that you have with hand-cut dovetails (**4–92**). This jig is capable of making through dovetails as well as half-blind dovetails. The initial setup can be time-consuming, because you adjust a separate finger for each cut, but, once set up, you can mass-produce parts quickly.

Unlike the previously described jig, with the adjustable dovetail jig two different router bits are used, and the pins and tails are cut independently. The jig automatically aligns the pins and tails, so no layout is necessary. When you are making the initial setup, use scrap wood to make a test joint. Some trial-and-error adjustments are usually necessary to get a good fit.

Once you have made the initial setup, clamp the tail board to the front of the jig and adjust the template so that the straight fingers are over the end of the board. Install the template-following collar on the router base, and chuck the dovetail bit into the router. Adjust the depth of cut, and then cut the tail by following the template fingers with the router's collar. After cutting the

4–92. Dovetails cut with an adjustable jig look more like hand-cut dovetails.

4-93. *Use a sliding T-bevel to mark the angles of the dovetails. Mark the straight cuts with a square.*

tails, replace the dovetail bit with a straight bit. Clamp the pin board to the front of the jig. Rotate the finger assembly to place the tapered fingers over the end of the board. Follow the fingers with the collar on the base of the router.

To hand-cut dovetails, use a sliding T-bevel to lay out the angles of a dovetail (**4-93**). The angle used depends on the type of wood. For softwood, use a 1:6 ratio. Hardwoods require a 1:8 ratio. To set the T-bevel to the correct ratio, place it against a square. For a 1:6 ratio, the blade of the T-bevel should be 1 inch out of square at a point that is 6 inches from the pivot. For a 1:8 ratio, use the same procedure, but the blade should be 1 inch out of square at a point that is 8 inches from the pivot.

Commercial dovetail gauges are available that are preset to the proper angles. Lay out the dovetails so that you get a half-pin at the top and the bottom. Mark the waste with an X so that there won't be any confusion as you cut.

Cut the dovetails first, and then use them to mark the position of the pins. Use a backsaw or a dovetail saw to make the side cuts, and then complete the cut by cutting across the bottom with a coping saw (**4-94**). Use a sharp chisel to smooth the cuts and trim right to the line.

There are many variations on the dovetail. You can vary the spacing of pins and tails to create decorative patterns. If you are interested in a more in-depth discussion of hand cutting dovetails, refer to my book *Wood Joiner's Handbook*.

Box Joint

The box joint is a strong joint for joining corners. It is useful for anything that resembles a box—drawers, for example (**4-95**). The box joint is a machine joint, and designed to be cut with power equipment.

You can make box joints using a router and a dovetail jig with an optional box joint template. In this case, you use a straight router bit and both boards are placed on the front of the jig. Offset one of the boards by the distance of one finger on the template. Now cut the joint by following the template fingers with the collar on the router base.

You can also make a box joint on the table saw. Add an auxiliary wooden fence that is about 4 inches high and 20 inches long to the miter gauge.

4–94. Use a coping saw to make the cut across the bottom between the pins and dovetails.

Set a dado blade to make a cut equal to the desired width of the pin (finger) of the box joint. Set the blade height to equal the thickness of the board plus $\frac{1}{32}$ inch. Cut through the wooden fence with the dado blade, and then make a wooden key block that will fit into the slot and project approximately $\frac{3}{4}$ inch from the face of the fence. Glue the key in place. Reposition the fence on the miter gauge so that the key block is separated from the side of the blade by the width of one pin.

You can cut both pieces at once by clamping them together and offsetting them by the width of one pin. Make the first cut by butting the edge of the board against the side of the key block. Reposition the work so that the cut just made is over the key block, and then make the next cut. Continue in this manner until all of the pins have been cut.

4–95. A box joint offers both strength and decoration.

⑤ Assembly Techniques

A FTER YOU HAVE CUT THE JOINTS, the parts will be ready to be assembled. Glue is often the cabinetmaker's primary fastener; other means of fastening can be used to reinforce a glued joint or to assemble a cabinet without glue. Clamping plays a vital role in producing a strong glue joint.

Glue

ALTHOUGH GLUE HAS BEEN USED for centuries, scientists are still probing the secrets of how glue actually sticks. We do know that glue bonds in two ways—physically and molecularly. A physical bond results when the glue seeps into the pores of the wood and hardens. A molecular bond occurs when molecules in the glue attach to molecules in the wood. Most wood glues exhibit both kinds of bonding to varying degrees.

The strength of a glue line between two wood surfaces depends on the type of glue, how well the joint fits, and whether end grain or long grain is being glued. A tight-fitting joint is much stronger than a loose one. Some types of glue will fill gaps in a joint, but most glues perform best when the glue line is thin. End grain does not glue as well as long grain, which is why many joints have been developed to maximize the long-grain contact. When you are gluing wood long grain to long grain, the bond is so strong that no other reinforcement is needed if the joint is tight fitting and has been properly clamped. Joints involving end grain are much weaker and usually require some type of reinforcement.

Types of Glue

Many types of glue are available and modern technology is producing new types continuously. Out of all these glues, two have emerged as the fore-most glues of the modern cabinetmaker; they are *polyvinyl acetate (PVA)* and *aliphatic resin.*

Polyvinyl Acetate Glue

Because of its milky-white appearance, polyvinyl acetate glue (PVA) is usually referred to as white glue. PVA's long-setting time is an advantage for beginning cabinetmakers. It allows them time to reposition parts and

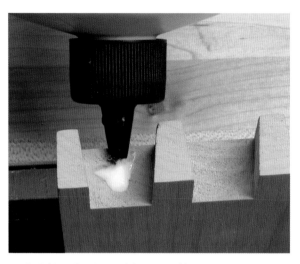

5–1. *White glue is good for assembling intricate joints, because it has a long open time that allows you to get all of the parts in position before the glue starts to grab.*

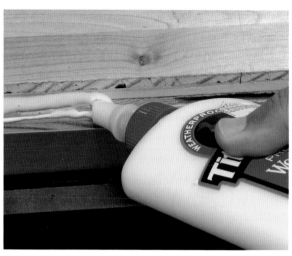

5–2. *Yellow woodworking glue is a good, all-around glue for most cabinetmaking applications.*

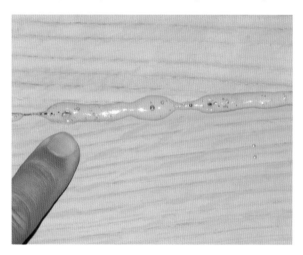

5–3. *PUR glue foams slightly as it cures. This can help to fill gaps in a joint, but is also more of a mess to clean up.*

change alignment as they assemble the cabinet. This feature also makes it a good choice when you are assembling intricate joints like dovetails (**5–1**).

Since PVA is not waterproof and heat will soften the bond, this type of glue should not be used when moisture or heat will be present.

Aliphatic Resin Glue

The professional's choice for an all around cabinetmaking glue is aliphatic resin. This type of glue is usually referred to as *carpenter's glue* or *woodworking glue* (**5–2**). It resembles white glue, except it is slightly yellow and it is stronger and more water-resistant than white glue. Aliphatic resin's faster setting time and initial tack can be advantageous for the experienced cabinetmaker, but they can also be drawbacks if parts need to be repositioned after the initial assembly.

This type of glue is very good for glue blocks, because it has a strong initial grab that will hold the glue block in place without clamps.

Since aliphatic resin sets up hard, sanding it off the surface of the wood is relatively easy. PVA glue, on the other hand, will soften from the heat generated by sanding, so it smears when you try to sand it off. Some types of aliphatic resin glue are water-resistant.

While cabinetmakers tend to use PVA and aliphatic resin most of the time, they use many other types of glue for specialized applications.

Polyurethane (PUR) Adhesives

This glue is a single-part glue that acts like a two-part glue; it uses the moisture in the wood as a catalyst. It forms a strong water-resistant bond and it sticks to a variety of surfaces. In very dry climates, it may be necessary to moisten the wood surfaces before applying the glue.

This type of glue foams slightly to fill any gaps in the joint (5–3). The added strength and water resistance usually are not needed in standard cabinet construction, but they can be important if you are making outdoor cabinets. Be sure to keep the clamps on until the glue is completely set. Because the glue foams, it can actually spread open a joint that is not clamped. The foaming property also makes it a little more difficult to clean up the joint. You can wipe off the wet glue with mineral spirits, but after you wipe it off more foam may squeeze out of the joint. You may need to wipe the joint several times before it stops foaming. The dry foam sands off quit easily, though.

Melamine Glue

This glue can be used for bonding wood, particleboard, and MDF to synthetic materials such as melamine and vinyl. This is useful when you are making cabinets out of particleboard that is covered with a melamine or vinyl overlay. It offers a fast initial tack, and a long open time that allows for accurate alignment of parts. The glue line is somewhat soft and flexible. It cleans up with water.

Contact Cement

To apply plastic laminates, veneers, and edging strips, it is best to use contact cement. Its main advantage is that it doesn't require clamping. You apply it to both surfaces and allow it to dry. As soon as the surfaces touch, they begin to bond. This means that it is necessary to pay careful attention to the initial alignment of the parts. Once the parts are in contact, you need to apply additional pressure to make a firm bond.

Contact cement can form an extremely strong bond when it is used for applying surface materials, such as plastic laminates or veneers, but it doesn't have the type of strength required for use in joints. Contact cement is water- and heat-resistant.

There are two types of contact cement available: *solvent-based* and *water-based*. The solvent-based cement is extremely flammable and produces toxic fumes. It is for professional use only. Advances in water-based contact cement technology have made the safer water-based contact cement an attractive substitute for the solvent-based glue. Many professionals have now switched to the water-based glue.

Panel Adhesive

Panel adhesive was developed for use in the building trades to attach wall paneling and plywood. It can be useful to the cabinetmaker for operations such as applying a paneling skin to a skeleton-frame cabinet. The adhesive comes in a caulking tube and it is applied with a caulking gun. Unlike most glues, it is meant to be applied in beads. It has a very high initial tack, so it will hold parts in place without clamping.

Hide Glue

This is the traditional cabinetmaker's glue, and it still offers some advantages for fine cabinetry work. It comes in dry flakes, which are first softened in water and then heated to the proper working temperature. Special electric glue pots keep the glue at the working temperature. You must apply and clamp the glue while it is still hot. Hide glue is especially good for glue blocks because it grabs so fast.

This type of glue forms a very strong bond and has exceptional shear strength. It won't stain surrounding wood, and it produces an almost invisible joint. On the other hand, hide glue is very susceptible to water and heat and certain microorganisms can destroy it.

A modern variation of hide glue is *liquid hide glue*. This liquid form requires no heating. It has many of the same advantages and disadvantages of the original hide glue, but it has a longer setting time.

Urea Formaldehyde Glue

Commonly called urea resin glue, this type of glue is frequently used in production cabinet work. It comes as a powder and must be mixed with water before use. Once mixed, it has a limited life, so it must be mixed just before use. It is highly resistant to water and produces a bond that is stronger than the wood if the joints fit well. But if the joints don't fit well, this type of glue won't fill any gaps. The glue line must be uniform and thin. A thick glue line tends to crystallize and become very weak.

Hot-Melt Glue

Hot-melt glue is a polyethylene-based plastic that softens when heated. It comes in small sticks that are placed in a special heat gun. This type of glue is especially suited for small detail work, because it sets as soon as it cools, so no clamping is needed. When you use hot-melt glue, you must assemble parts quickly before the glue begins to cool.

Resorcinol Resin Glue

When you need the greatest water resistance, you can use resorcinol glue. This type of glue is not frequently used in cabinetmaking, because it has a deep red color that makes the glue line visible. It comes in two parts, a powder and a liquid. Dust from the powder is toxic, so avoid inhaling it as you mix the two parts together. This glue has a very limited working time of three hours maximum after mixing, so mix only as much as you can use in that time.

Epoxy Glue

Epoxy glue is also an extremely waterproof glue. It comes in two parts that must be mixed immediately before use. Its main advantage for the beginning cabinetmaker is its ability to fill gaps. You can salvage a poorly fitting joint by using epoxy glue. It is rather expensive; so unless you need its gap-filling properties, you might as well use other glues.

Acrylic Resin Glue

For even greater strength and gap-filling properties, you should use acrylic resin glue. As with epoxy, it comes in two parts that need to be mixed just before use. This glue is even more expensive than epoxy, but it has unlimited gap-filling abilities. This makes it ideal for repairing broken parts because it will even fill in for missing fragments of a part.

Casein Glue

Casein glue is made from milk. It is an old product that still has some advantages. It comes as a powder that must be mixed with water before use. Although this glue is very water-resistant, it is not considered waterproof. It will adhere to oily woods, such as teak, that don't work well with other types of glue.

Applying Glue

You have two conflicting objectives when applying glue. You want to provide enough glue so that the joint will be strong, not "glue-starved," but you don't want to apply more glue than is necessary, because the glue will drip out of the joint and mar the surface of the wood.

The best way to make sure that you have just the right amount of glue is by spreading a thin, even coat on both mating surfaces. Use your finger, a scrap of wood, a putty knife, or a disposable plastic knife to spread the glue. The common practice of running heavy beads of glue and hoping that they will spread out as the parts are assembled leads to gaps where there is no glue and areas with too much glue that oozes out of the joint. On parts where you are especially concerned with the glue oozing out, stop just short of spreading the glue to the edge.

The ideal amount of glue will form a small bead along the glue line as the joint is clamped, but the glue won't spread from the bead.

The best way of removing glue from the surface is by allowing the glue to dry until it is no longer tacky but not quite set hard and then shaving it from the wood with a sharp chisel. The practice of wiping the glue while it is still wet actually tends to force the glue into the wood, sealing it. This will produce noticeable glue marks when you apply a finish. If a lot of glue is dripping out of a joint, you will probably need to wipe it, but use a damp rag to remove the glue and switch to a clean rag when the old one gets saturated with glue.

Clamping

THERE ARE MANY TYPES OF CLAMPS, but four types are the favorites of cabinet-makers; they are *C-clamps, fast-action clamps, hand screws,* and *bar clamps* (5–4). C-clamps, fast-action clamps, and hand screws are used for similar kinds of clamping. The fast-action clamps are easy to use, and hand screws are versatile, but both are also expensive; therefore, many beginners start out with C-clamps. Because bar clamps are used for joining small boards into larger panels and are used in all stages of cabinet assembly, they are almost indispensable to the serious cabinetmaker.

Hand Screws, C-Clamps, and Fast-Action Clamps

You need to use hand screws, C-clamps, or fast-action clamps to clamp parts where the distance is less than approximately 8 inches. For example, you would use them to clamp a half-lap joint together. They are also very useful for clamping boards to the workbench while you are performing operations such as planing or routing.

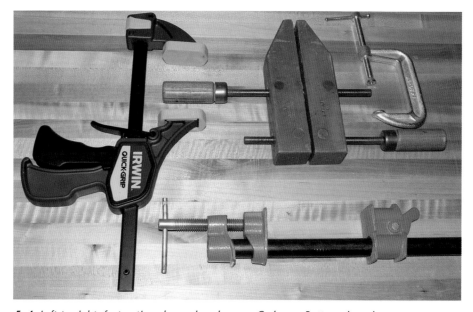

5–4. Left to right: fast-action clamp, hand screw, C-clamp. Bottom: bar clamp.

C-clamps have a C-shaped iron body and a threaded screw for exerting pressure. A small, round shoe on the end of the screw is attached by a ball joint, allowing the shoe to sit squarely. Because the anvil and shoe are so small, the C-clamp will dent most wood, even with moderate pressure, so you should always place a piece of scrap wood between the clamp and the piece being clamped.

C-clamps tend to cause parts to creep out of alignment as you tighten them. This is because the anvil and shoe are not always in perfect alignment. Watch for this as you tighten the clamps, and correct any creeping before the glue sets.

Fast-action clamps usually have padded jaws to keep them from marring the wood. A quick-release mechanism allows you to slide one jaw to the proper width; then tighten the clamp to apply pressure.

Hand screws have two threaded screws instead of one, as with the C-clamp. Because of their large maple clamping surface, hand screws are less likely to dent the wood; on important work, however, you should still put a block of wood or a piece of cork between the work and the clamp.

The two screws permit the jaws to be placed on surfaces that are not parallel, but for most work, you will want the jaws to be parallel. To get the jaws parallel, hold one handle in each hand and crank the clamp around. When one end of the jaws is closed, let that handle slip in your hand and continue spinning the clamp until the other end has closed as well. The jaws will now be fully closed and parallel.

To open the jaws and keep them parallel, hold both handles tightly again and spin the clamp in the opposite direction. The jaws will open up evenly. Stop when the jaws are far enough apart to slip easily over the parts to be clamped. To tighten the clamp, turn both handles at the same time in the same direction.

Bar Clamps

Bar clamps are very important in cabinetmaking because they are available in lengths that are long enough to use in the assembly of large cabinets. For example, you can use bar clamps to clamp both sides of a cabinet in place at the same time. Most bar clamps are very similar; their main difference has to do with the type of bar they use. Heavy industrial types have an I-beam type of bar that resists twisting and bending, but they are expensive and you are limited to certain lengths. Most beginning cabinetmakers prefer the type that employs iron-plumbing pipe as the bar. You can get the pipe in any length you want, and you can even use pipe couplings to lengthen it. This is very useful when you are building long units such as kitchen cabinets.

Edge Joining Lumber

One of the main functions of bar clamps is edge joining narrow boards into larger panels. Chapter 4 discussed how to prepare the edges for this procedure. The minimum number of clamps that you can use for joining boards into panels is three. You must have at least one clamp on the opposite side of the panel, or the clamping pressure will cause the panel to cup. Larger panels require more clamps.

Always alternate clamps on either side of the panel to even out the stresses. Place a board along each edge to protect the edges of the panel from the jaws of the clamps. If you have difficulty lining up the boards, clamp boards crosswise at the ends of the panel with C-clamps or hand screws to help hold the boards in alignment. Placing wax paper between the cross boards and the panel will prevent the cross boards from being glued to the panel by squeezed-out glue. Tighten the clamps evenly, working from the middle to the ends, until the joints are tight and a small bead of glue is squeezed out (**5–5**). Don't overtighten the clamps, or too much glue may squeeze out of the joint and weaken it, or the clamp may break.

5–5. Here, narrow boards are being joined into a wide panel. The C-clamps and plywood strips at the end help to keep the boards in alignment. The strips on the edges prevent the bar clamp jaws from denting the edge of the panel.

Assembling Cabinets Using Bar Clamps

The use of bar clamps makes cabinet assembly easier to do and stronger. Even if you are using screws or nails, hold the parts in place with bar clamps while you install the fasteners. This will ensure that all the joints are pulled in tight. Dado joints only require clamping from one direction because they have a lip on both sides. It's best to clamp rabbets from both directions to make sure they are seated firmly against the shoulder.

You can also use bar clamps to help square assemblies. To check a cabinet for square, use a tape measure to diagonally measure the distance from corner to corner. Both diagonals should be the same distance. If they are not, place a bar clamp diagonally across the corners that are the farthest apart and tighten the clamp until both measurements are equal. Leave the clamp in place until the glue has dried or until fasteners have been installed that will hold the cabinet square (5–6).

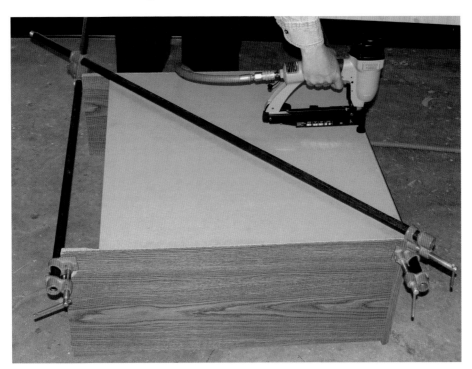

5–6. Bar clamps are very useful for assembling cabinets. The clamp running diagonally between the corners pulls the cabinet into square.

Fasteners

YOU NEED TO USE FASTENERS when joints need reinforcement or when it is impractical to clamp a joint. Out of the many types of fastener available, screws and nails are the most useful for cabinetmaking. However, special fasteners are necessary with particleboard because of its unique properties.

Nails

There are five types of nails that are usually used in cabinetmaking: *common, box, finishing, casing*, and *brads*.

Of the five types, common nails are the largest in diameter. They have large, flat heads. Common nails are only used in the roughest parts of cabinet work, such as making a sub-base for a built-in cabinet. Because of their large diameters, they tend to split the wood.

Box nails resemble common nails, but they are thinner, so you can use them in thinner wood with less chance of splitting the wood. They are used in areas where their heads won't show—attaching the back of a cabinet, for example. The large heads are especially useful when attaching thin materials, because they won't pull through as easily as the smaller heads.

Finishing nails are even thinner than box nails, and they have small heads that you can set below the surface of the wood. Finishing nails are the most common type of nail used in cabinetmaking.

Casing nails are similar to finishing nails, but they are the same diameter as box nails and their heads are tapered, giving them more holding power. Use casing nails when you need more strength, but set the heads below the surface.

Brads are the thinnest nails available. Their heads resemble the heads on finishing nails. They come in lengths from ⅜ inch to 1½ inches. The length of brads is designated in inches, whereas all other nails are designated by a penny size.

The Penny System

The length of most nails is designated by an old English system, called the *penny system*. The abbreviation for penny is d. Although no one knows exactly how the penny system originated, it may have had something to do with the cost per hundred; now it has simply become an arbitrary measure of length.

Standard nail sizes start at 2d, which is 1 inch long, and end at 60d, which is 6 inches long. There is no uniform formula for converting penny size into inches, but there are a couple of rough estimates you can make. Between 2d and 16d, each standard size is ¼ inch longer than the last, beginning at 1 inch for a 2d nail. The standard sizes run consecutively up to 10d, but then they skip to 12d and then to 16d.

Another way of estimating the length in inches of a penny size up to 10d is by dividing the penny size by 4 and adding ½ inch. Using this method to find the length of a 6d nail, you would divide 6 by 4, which comes to 1½, and then add ½, which gives you a total of 2 inches for the length of a 6-penny nail.

Nails are usually sold by the pound. Obviously, you will get a lot more small nails than large ones in a pound, so you need to estimate how many nails you will need. A pound of 3d finishing nails will contain approximately 900 nails, so a pound of these nails will last a long time. On the other hand, a pound of 16d common nails will only contain about 50 nails. Here is the approximate number of nails per pound for some finishing nails frequently used in cabinetmaking: 4d = 600, 6d = 300, 8d = 200, and 10d = 125.

Choosing a Nail

The type and length of nail you choose depend on the thickness of the lumber, the strength required, and the type of head that is needed.

The nail should not be too long, or the point will break through to the face of an adjoining board, but it should be long enough to give adequate holding power. As a general rule, a nail should be four times the thickness of the board it is driven through. For a ¾-inch-thick board, this would be 10d. Of course, if the other board isn't thick enough for a nail this size, you must use a shorter nail. Generally for cabinet work, a finishing nail is the best choice; however, for added strength, you can use a casing nail. In situations where the head won't show, a box nail is a good choice because of its greater holding power.

Driving Nails

You can usually drive a nail directly into any wood that has a specific gravity of less than 0.5. (See chapter 1.) With harder woods, you need to drill a pilot hole before you drive the nail, or the wood will probably split. The pilot hole should be slightly smaller than the nail so that the wood will grip the nail tightly.

Nails will hold better when you drive them into edge grain rather than end grain; therefore, when you have a choice, choose edge grain. Usually you don't have a choice, and you have to take what you get. If you angle nails so that they point in toward each other, they will have greater holding power. Drive one nail in straight first to keep the parts from slipping out of alignment. Use a hammer that is heavy enough to drive the nail easily; a hammer that is too light may actually bend the nail. A 16-ounce hammer is usually used for cabinet work. Hit the nail squarely with the middle of the face of the hammer. Avoid the urge to drive the nail in with one blow. Using several lighter blows will give you more control and it actually makes the nail grip better.

If you have trouble with nails bending, it could be that the work is not supported well enough. Try to place the work so that you are hammering against something solid. If it isn't possible to brace the work in some other way, hold a hammer in back of the area you are nailing (the heavier the hammer, the better). The weight of the hammer will steady the board, and the hammer will slap back after each blow, counteracting any spring in the board.

You need to use a nail set to drive the nails below the surface so that the heads can be hidden with putty (**5–7**). The set has a cup-shaped depression in its end that cuts into the head of the nail to keep it from slipping. You will need several sizes of nail sets for setting large and small nails. Don't set the nail too deep or it will lose most of its hold on the wood; approximately $\frac{1}{16}$ inch below the surface will provide enough room for the putty.

Power Nailers

There are special guns for driving nails and staples (**5–8**). Most nail guns operate on compressed air, but there are also power nailers that run on electricity. For small fasteners, there are hand-operated guns that are similar to staple guns.

For cabinet work, air-operated nail guns are the most useful. Nail guns are helpful when you will be doing a lot of repetitive nailing. Power-driven nails also tend to reduce splitting and they eliminate stray hammer marks. Power-driven staples are especially good for applying $\frac{1}{8}$- or $\frac{1}{4}$-inch backs to cabinets. The bridge of a staple resists pulling through these thin materials better than a nail head.

Nails for nail guns are sized by wire gauge and length. As with wire sizes, nails with smaller number gauges are actually thicker than the higher numbers. For cabinet work, 18-gauge and 16-gauge are the most useful (**5–9**). Thicker nails will often split $\frac{3}{4}$-inch-thick boards. Adhesive-coated fasteners are very useful for joining particleboard. The friction from driving the staple melts the adhesive, gluing the staple to the board. For $\frac{3}{4}$-inch-thick particleboard, a two-inch adhesive-coated fastener will join boards face to edge with no splitting.

Nail guns are durable and don't require much maintenance. Follow the manufacturer's recommendations about oiling. Some nail guns are oil-less, and other require oiling. To oil most guns, you drip a few drops of oil into the air inlet (**5–10**). Only use oil designated for use in air tools.

To power your nail gun, you will need an air compressor (**5–11**). Air compressors can be powered by either electric or gasoline motors ranging from smaller than $\frac{1}{4}$ hp to over 15 hp. The air is compressed by either a reciprocating piston or by a rubber diaphragm. To provide some air storage, an air tank is usually attached to the compressor. The tank can be either horizontal or vertical. There is no difference in their operation; it is simply a matter of fitting the compressor into the space available. The important factor is how much air volume (measured in cfm) the compressor can supply.

An air compressor can power a variety of tools and spray equipment. When you buy one, it's a good idea to consider future needs. If you want to be able to run all types of spray equipment and several air-powered tools, you should opt for a larger compressor that supplies over 15 cfm. Smaller

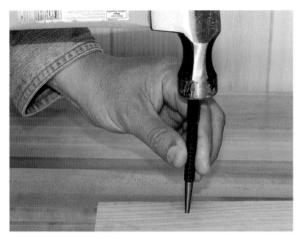

5–7. Using a nail set.

5–8. Nail gun.

5–9. Nails for nail guns are sized by gauge and length. Pictured here are 16-gauge nails in lengths ranging from 1 to 2½ inches.

5–10. To oil most guns, you drip a few drops of oil into the air inlet.

5–11. An air compressor provides the power source for air-powered nail guns.

compressors will work if you only use one piece of equipment at a time and use spray equipment rated for the lower cfm supply.

When you are using a nail gun, don't overdo it. Because this tool is easy to use, people have a tendency to put in too many nails or staples. Too many fasteners in a confined area will split the wood and make the joint weaker than if fewer fasteners were used. *Power drivers can shoot a fastener with great force, so never pull the trigger unless the gun is pressed against a board. Always follow all of the safety rules provided by the manufacturer and wear eye protection.*

Screws

Screws hold better than nails, and they will help to pull joints together. Screw sizes are designated by a number indicating the diameter of the screw and by the length of the screw in inches. The smallest screw diameter is 0, and the largest commonly found is 24. For cabinetmaking, sizes 4 through 12 are the most frequently used, and of those sizes, 6 and 8 are probably used more than any others.

Wood screws come with three basic types of head: *flat-*, *round-*, and *pan-head* (**5–12**). Flatheads are meant to be countersunk flush or below the surface. *Oval-head* screws are a variation on the flathead; they require countersinking, but their tops extend above the surface for decorative purposes. Round heads need no countersinking; their heads extend above the surface. Pan-head screws extend above the surface as round heads do, but their heads are flattened on top. Most cabinet work is done with flathead screws.

Three types of screws are commonly used with screwdrivers: the *straight-blade*, the *Phillips*, and the *square-drive* (**5–13**). When given the choice, most cabinetmakers prefer Phillips or square-drive head screws, because the screwdriver is less likely to slip out of the heads and mar the wood. Phillips and square-drive heads are also easier to drive with an electric drill or power screwdriver. The square drive is especially well suited for power drivers.

The threads on a traditional wood screw are fairly shallow, and the shank is the same diameter as the outside of the threads. This type of screw requires a two-step pilot hole. First, a hole slightly smaller than the root diameter of the threads should be drilled the entire length of the hole; then the hole should be enlarged for the length of the shank to the same diameter as the shank. There are special drills that will do this job in one operation and also countersink if needed (**5–14**). The shank allows the screw to turn freely in the outside board, while the threads bite into the inside board. This enables the screw to pull the two boards tight.

When appearance is important, you can countersink screws beneath the wood surface and put putty over them, or you can place dowel plugs or commercially made dowel buttons in the hole to cover the screw heads (**5–15**).

5–12. Types of screw head: flat, round, and pan-head.

5–14. A pilot-hole drill bit drills the thread pilot, shank clearance, and countersink for the head in a single operation.

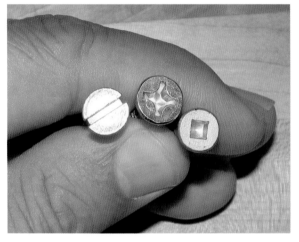

5–13. Types of screws used with screwdrivers: straight, Phillips, and square-drive.

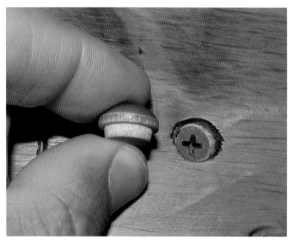

5–15. This dowel button fits in a countersink to hide the screw head.

The traditional wood screw is an old design with several disadvantages. As a result, the case-hardened, extruded-thread wood screw has been developed. This type of screw is commonly called a *drywall screw*, because it was originally developed for attaching drywall in building construction. The drywall screw is not well suited for cabinetmaking, but there are several variations that are specifically designed for cabinetmaking.

These screws have very deep, sharp threads and a much smaller root diameter than the traditional wood screw. The shank is smaller than the threads, so it doesn't require a separate clearance hole (**5–16**). This type of screw is designed to be driven into woods with a specific gravity of less than 0.5, without a pilot hole. The point is very sharp to aid in starting the screw, and the head is a modified type of flathead called a *bugle head* that will pull

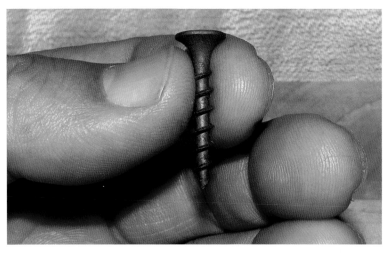

5–16. Case-hardened, extruded-thread wood screws have very deep, sharp threads and a much smaller root diameter than the traditional wood screw.

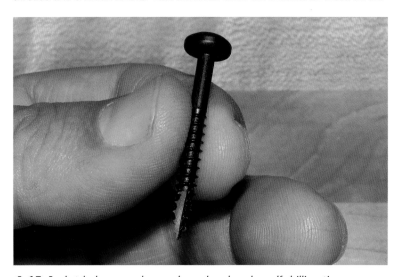

5–17. Pocket-hole screws have a large head and a self-drilling tip.

flush in these softer woods. Harder woods require a pilot hole and counter-sinking, but a shank-clearance hole is not necessary.

The *face-frame screw* is a variation on the drywall screw. With the face-frame screw, you don't have to drill a separate pilot hole in hardwoods because it has a drill-like point that makes its own pilot hole and a wafer head that doesn't require countersinking. Although you can drive these screws by hand, they were specifically designed for power drivers. Most production shops have switched entirely to this type of screw. They are usually sold by the pound, the way nails are.

Pocket-hole joinery requires a special type of screw. It is similar to a face-frame screw and has a self-drilling point, but the head is a modified type of panhead (**5–17**).

Particleboard Fasteners

Particleboard is made up of many short wood fibers; because these fibers are shorter than those in solid wood, screws and nails don't hold very well. Particleboard also has different holding characteristics on its face and edge. A fastener installed in the face of a piece of particleboard will hold approximately twice as well as the same fastener installed in the edge of the board. Although the fasteners described in this section can be used with many materials, they are most advantageous with particleboard.

Large, coarse threads hold better in particleboard than small, fine threads. For this reason, special particleboard screws have large threads (**5–18**). One type especially designed for cabinetry is the *European assembly screw (Confirmat)*. These screws require a pilot hole in both boards. The shank diameter is larger than the root diameter, so you will need to drill a larger shank clearance hole. There are special drill bits available that will drill the pilot hole, shank clearance, and countersink for the head in one operation.

Sometimes very large fasteners will weaken other parts because they require such large holes. The threaded insert solves this problem. It is a metal plug that has large, coarse threads on the outside and a small threaded hole in the middle (**5–19**). To install a threaded insert, drill a pilot hole that is slightly smaller than the insert. Use a countersink to chamfer the edge of the hole to prevent bulging around the insert.

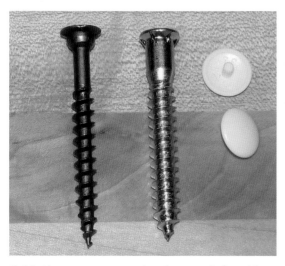

5–18. Here are two examples of screws designed for particleboard. Both have coarse threads. The one on the right has a large root diameter and a small countersunk head. This type is often used to assemble European-style cabinetry. You can hide the head with the plastic cap shown next to the screw. The other screw has a smaller root diameter. It has a wafer head that doesn't require countersinking.

5–19. A threaded insert has coarse wood screw threads around its outside diameter, providing greater holding capacity in particleboard. In the middle of the insert, there is a smaller hole threaded for a machine screw. This insert has a hexagonal hole part of the way that accepts an Allen wrench; other types have a slot that accepts a standard screwdriver.

Some inserts have a hexagonal hole for an Allen wrench; others have a slot for a standard screwdriver. Screw the insert into the pilot hole as you would a wood screw. The top of the insert should be slightly below the wood surface. You can attach the hardware or mating part with a small machine screw that fits the hole in the insert.

Since a fastener attached to the face of a piece of particleboard will hold better than one attached to the edge, particleboard fasteners are designed to be attached to the face of both boards. One such fastener is the *knock-down fitting* (**5–20**). This type of fitting has two separate parts that attach to the inside faces of boards that meet at a corner. They both have a large surface-contact area, and are attached with several screws that enter the face of the board. The plates are attached before assembly; during assembly the two parts are locked together with a screw, clip, or cam. You can assemble and disassemble knock-down fittings many times, so they are especially useful for cabinets that are moved frequently. Many commercial cabinets employ knock-down fittings to save shipping space. The cabinets are shipped flat and assembled on the job.

Another way of increasing the holding power of particleboard is by installing an insert that is stronger than the board. Two commercial fasteners that employ this principle are the *bolt-and-cross dowel* and the *cam fitting*. The bolt-and-cross dowel uses a metal dowel with a threaded hole. A hole is made in one board for the cross dowel, and a smaller hole is made through the face of the other board and into the edge of the board with the cross dowel. A metal bolt installed from the face of the outside board connects with the cross dowel, pulling the joint together (**5–21**). A shop-made substitute for this type of fastener employs a wooden dowel instead of the metal one. You need to glue the dowel into the hole and then drive a wood screw through the other board and into the dowel. Although it is not as strong as the metal version, this method provides more strength than if you simply screwed into the edge of the particleboard.

The cam fitting operates in a similar manner, but the cross dowel has a cam slot in it. Instead of twisting the bolt to tighten the connector, you twist the dowel.

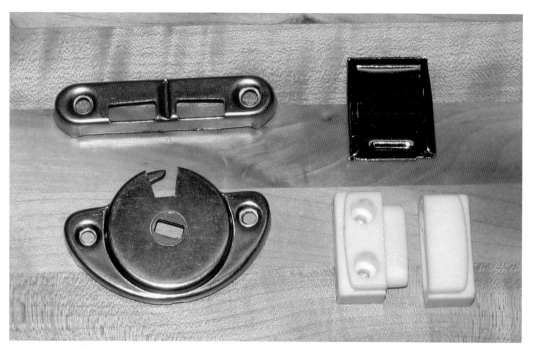

5–20. A knock-down fitting allows screws to be attached to the face of both parts and provides greater holding power than screwing into the end of a particleboard part. The one on the left locks together by twisting the cam with a screwdriver. The one on the right locks together by sliding the metal clip over the two plastic screw blocks.

5–21. The bolt-and-cross dowel fastener and the cam fastener overcome the poor screw-holding characteristic of a particleboard edge by employing a threaded-metal cross dowel or a large-diameter cam.

⑥ Carcasses

··

T HE MAIN ASSEMBLY OF ANY CABINET is called the carcass or box. Additional parts, such as doors and drawers, attach to the carcass. Backs, bases, and cornices are also considered part of the carcass. When you are building built-ins and modern-looking freestanding cabinets, you will probably want to use the case construction method described in the first part of this chapter. When you are building freestanding cabinets in a traditional style or making an antique reproduction, you may choose traditional methods such as skeleton-frame construction and panel construction, which are described later in the chapter.

Case Construction

CASE CONSTRUCTION IS PROBABLy the most widely used method of making carcasses among modern cabinetmakers. The parts of the carcass are each made from a single board. Plywood and particleboard are very well suited for this type of construction (6–1). You can also use solid lumber with this method, but in larger cabinets dimensional stability can be a problem. When you use solid lumber, the grain should be in the same direction on all of the parts in the carcass.

You should not mix solid wood with plywood or particleboard when using this type of construction. For example, if you used solid wood for the sides of a cabinet and plywood for the top and bottom, the sides would change in width with changes in humidity, whereas the top and bottom would remain stable. This would eventually cause the joints to pull apart. You can use solid wood for small parts, such as stiles and rails or reinforcing blocks, in a plywood or particleboard cabinet, because the narrow width of these small parts is not affected by dimensional change very much.

6–1. In case construction, each part of the carcass is made from a single board. This closet organizer is an example of case construction.

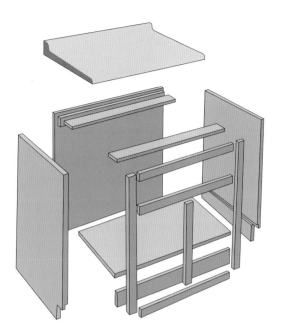

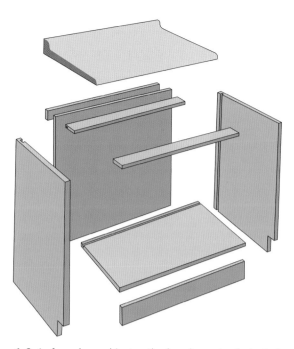

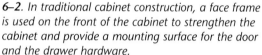

6–2. In traditional cabinet construction, a face frame is used on the front of the cabinet to strengthen the cabinet and provide a mounting surface for the door and the drawer hardware.

6–3. In frameless cabinetry, the face frame is eliminated, making construction simpler.

In traditional cabinet construction, a face frame is used on the front of the cabinet to strengthen the cabinet and provide a mounting surface for the door and the drawer hardware (6–2). Today, many cabinetmakers use *frameless cabinetry*. In frameless cabinetry, the face frame is eliminated, making construction simpler (6–3). The functions of the face frame are assumed by the sides of the cabinet, with the addition of some special hardware. Since there's no face frame to strengthen the cabinet, a very strong type of joinery is needed to attach the cabinet components. The preferred methods are dowel joints, plate joinery, and special fasteners.

Frameless construction first became popular in Europe, where it is used to make built-in cabinets. Since its introduction in the United States, the system has increased in popularity to the point where it is one of the dominant methods of making commercial cabinetry. Professional cabinetmakers often refer to it as the *32-mm system*, because the hardware that was originally developed in Europe is designed for holes that are spaced 32 mm apart.

Commercial cabinet shops usually use dowel joints or particleboard screws to assemble frameless carcasses built of particleboard. Both of these methods can speed up production in a large shop where specialized drilling machines and clamping fixtures are available. Smaller shops and do-it-yourselfers often use plate joinery. You can also use dowel joints if you have the right type of dowelling jig. You will need a dowelling jig that is capable of making T-type joints. You can also use special particleboard screws.

When making cabinets with face frames, dadoes and rabbets are still often used, but you can also use dowels, plate joinery, or special fasteners.

Plate Joinery

The plate joiner is a good way to assemble carcasses. For ¾-inch-thick material, use the large (#20) biscuits. One way to lay out the plate locations is to dry-assemble the carcass using bar clamps to hold the parts together. Mark the plate locations with a pencil on both mating parts (**6–4**).

When you are making several similar joints, it is faster to make a story stick. Cut a piece of scrap the same width as the cabinet sides. Mark the biscuit locations on the edge of this story stick. Now you don't need to dry-assemble the cabinet to lay out the locations. Simply hold the story stick in place and transfer the marks (**6–5**). Mark the centerlines for the first and last biscuit two inches in from the edges. Space the rest of the biscuits equally. The biscuits should not be more than four inches apart on center.

Now cut the biscuit slots as described in Chapter 3. In the case of shelves or a top or bottom that form a T-type joint, place the mating board and then the story stick on top of the other board and clamp them in place along the top line of the shelf location. Make sure that the mating board is in the same orientation as it will be in the finished project, except for being laid down flat against the other board. The edge of the mating board and the story stick form a guide for the base of the plate joiner (**6–6**). After you have cut the slots in the

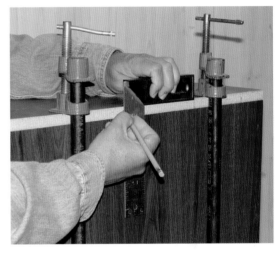

6–4. Dry-assemble the carcass and mark the biscuit locations.

6–5. Use a story stick to mark the biscuit locations when you have several joints to make.

6–6. When making T-type joints, clamp the mating board and the story stick in place to make a guide for the plate joiner.

lower board, you can reposition the plate joiner with the base down and cut the slots in the end of the mating board using the same setup (**6–7**).

After the slots have all been cut, apply glue to the joints and assemble. Be sure to get glue into the biscuit slots, because the moisture from the glue is necessary to expand the biscuits. If you are using melamine-covered particleboard, use melamine glue. Ordinary glue doesn't stick to the melamine surface very well.

Dowel Joints

The sides, the top, and the bottom of the cabinet can be joined together with dowel joints. To make these joints, get a good dowelling jig that you can place on the edge and the face of the boards. A dowelling jig that only attaches to the edge of the board won't work! The dowelling jig shown in **6–8** works well, because you can clamp both parts to the jig at once. Other jigs will also work, but you may need to drill holes in each board individually.

You'll need two drill bits to go with the dowelling jig: one that is ¼ inch and another that is ⁵⁄₁₆. A brad-point bit works best; it has a small point in the center that prevents the bit from wandering as you drill.

A depth stop is also needed for each drill bit. This is a small collar that fits around the bit. A setscrew holds the stop in place on the bit. The depth stop can be adjusted to control the depth of the hole made by the bit when you use the dowelling jig (**6–9**).

You will also need dowels that have been specially prepared for the job. For ¾-inch-thick material, use ⁵⁄₁₆-inch x 1½-inch dowels. The dowels (available at most lumberyards, hardware stores, or home-supply centers) have been cut to length, the ends are chamfered, and the sides are fluted (grooved). Fluting allows glue to be distributed evenly as the dowel is inserted in the hole, thus giving the dowel more holding power (**6–10**).

When making joints in ¾-inch-thick boards, use the ⁵⁄₁₆-inch bit. Use the ¼-inch bit when joining thinner boards. Professional cabinetmakers use a boring machine that drills all of the holes at once; the drill bits are spaced at multiples of 32 mm. Since you are drilling each hole individually, you can vary from this standard spacing as long as the dowels are never more than 75 mm apart. You can lay out each joint individually or make a story stick to mark the dowel locations.

Begin by laying out the dowel joint (**6–11**). Place the two boards together as they will fit in the finished cabinet. Make an X near the front edge of each board. Draw an arrow pointing to the outside of the cabinet on each board. Number each joint so that there won't be any confusion when it is time to assemble the cabinet. Also, label the board that will have dowel holes in the edge with an "A" and the board that will have dowel holes in the face with a "B."

6–7. *You can cut the pockets in both boards with this same setup. To make the second set of cuts, place the plate joiner base down on the lower board.*

6–8. *This dowelling jig will guide the drill for corner and T-type joints.*

6–9. *This depth stop that comes with the dowelling jig will control the depth of the dowel holes.*

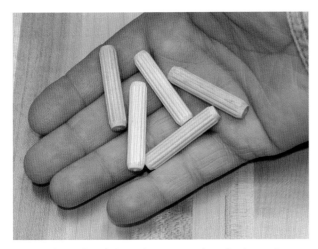

6–10. *These dowels have been cut to length, the ends are chamfered, and the sides are fluted. The fluting allows glue to be distributed evenly as the dowel is inserted in the hole, thus giving the dowel more holding power.*

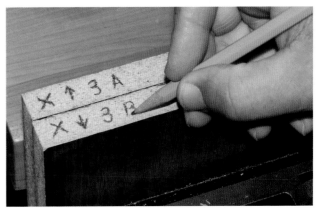

6–11. *To avoid confusion as you are making the dowel joints, make an X near the front edge of each board. Draw an arrow pointing to the outside of the cabinet on each board and number each joint. Also, label the board that will have dowel holes in the edge with an "A" and the board that will have dowel holes in the face with a "B."*

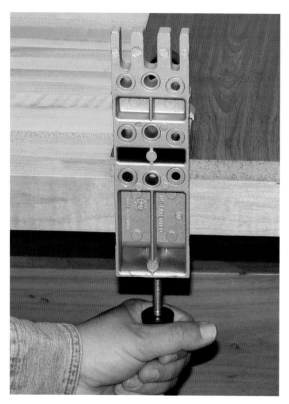

6–12. *Position the dowelling jig over the first dowel-hole location and clamp it in place.*

6–13. *Use a square to line up the edges before you clamp the jig tight.*

For boards up to 12 inches wide, use four dowels. Wider boards require more dowels. The dowels should be spaced 16 mm in from the front and back edges; the rest of the dowels should be equally spaced no more than 75 mm on center. The simplest way to lay out the joints is to make a story stick that will be used as a guide for the other boards. Make a mark 16 mm in from the front edge for the front dowel. A single dowel is placed 16 mm in from the rear. If your design calls for a rabbet or groove for the back, measure 16 mm from the front of the rabbet or groove. Next, divide the area between the holes equally so that the dowels are no more than 75 mm apart on center.

Prepare to drill the first set of holes. Place one of the parts labeled "A" on the bench top with the arrow facing up. Align the edge of the board with the front of the bench, and clamp the spacer clamp over both the board and the bench; this will keep the board firmly in place as you work. Position the dowelling jig over the first hole location and clamp it in place (6–12). Now place the mating part into the jig clamps. Line it up so that the X's are on the same side. The arrow should face away from the front of the jig (toward the clamp). Hold a square against the edges to make sure that they line up, and then tighten the clamp (6–13).

Before drilling the first hole, place a depth stop on the drill bit and adjust the stop so that 1⅛ inch of the bit will extend past the bottom of the dowelling jig when the depth stop hits the jig. Drill into the end of the "A" board until the depth stop hits the dowelling jig (**6–14**). Remove the drill bit from the dowelling jig.

6–14. Drilling the first dowel hole.

The hole in part "B" can't be as deep as the hole in part "A." To achieve this, you can reposition the depth stop on the drill bit so that ½ inch of the drill bit will extend past the bottom of the dowelling jig. However, this would mean that you would need to readjust the depth stop for each hole. A faster method is to make a stop that you can slide over the drill. Cut a piece of plastic or copper tubing to a length of ⅝ inch. Slide this stop over the drill bit, and drill the hole in part "B."

To drill the next set of holes, loosen the clamps on the drill guide jig, but leave the spacer clamp in place at the other end of the board. Slide the drill guide jig to the next hole location and clamp it tight. Drill this set of holes following the instructions above, and then reposition the guide. Continue in this manner until you have drilled the center set of holes. This time before you loosen the drill guide clamps, remove the spacer clamp and move it to the opposite side. After the spacer clamp is tight, reposition the drill guide jig. Continue drilling and repositioning the jig until all of the holes are done; then repeat the process for the other joints. I will cover making T-type joints with this jig in chapter 10.

Special Fasteners

When visible screws on the outside of the cabinet won't be objectionable, you can use European assembly screws (Confirmat) to assemble cabinets. These screws are designed to overcome the poor screw-holding properties of particleboard (**6–15**). Built-in cabinets are a typical application for this type of construction, because the outside faces of the sides are usually against a wall or covered with a decorative end cap. This method is usually not used on freestanding cabinets, where appearance is important. In these cases, you can use cam fasteners. In either case, the cabinets are assembled without glue. All of the strength comes from the fasteners. This can make assembly easier because there is no squeezed-out glue to clean up.

6–15. This screw is designed to overcome the poor screw holding properties of particleboard.

European assembly screws require a pilot hole to be drilled in both mating parts. The important thing is to ensure that the pilot holes are straight and centered on the edge of the board. Commercial shops use boring machines to drill all of the pilot holes. Do-it-yourselfers will need to drill the holes individually. Although it may seem simple to drill the pilot holes with a handheld drill as you assemble the project, it is difficult to position the holes correctly. Because of the large diameter of the screws, the joint will be weakened if the holes are off center. If the hole is not straight, the screw may break out of the joint when you drive it in.

To drill the holes correctly, you should use some type of drill guide. The guide shown in **6–16** holds the drill square with the surface, but you still must lay out the position carefully to make sure that the hole will be centered on the edge. One way to ensure that the holes are centered is to install a fence on the drill guide. Attach a piece of wood to the base of the guide as shown in **6–16**. If you make the fence 256 mm long, you can also use it to gauge the distance between holes. The holes should be 37 mm in from the edges and 128 mm on center.

6–16. This type of drill guide will keep the pilot holes straight. Attaching a piece of wood to act as a fence keeps the hole centered in the joint.

When you attach the wooden fence to the drill guide, center it in relation to the drill bit. That will make the ends of the fence 128 mm from the center of the drill bit. Also, draw a line on the fence 37 mm from the center of the drill bit. When you drill the first hole, align the 37 mm line with the edge of the board as you hold the fence flat against the end. This will position the first hole in 37 mm from the edge.

After the first hole is drilled, reposition the guide so that the end of the fence is aligned with the center of the first hole, and drill the next hole. Continue in this manner until you get close the other edge; then use the 37-mm mark to drill the last hole.

When exterior appearance is important, you can use knock-down fasteners or cam fasteners to assemble cabinets. (See chapter 5.)

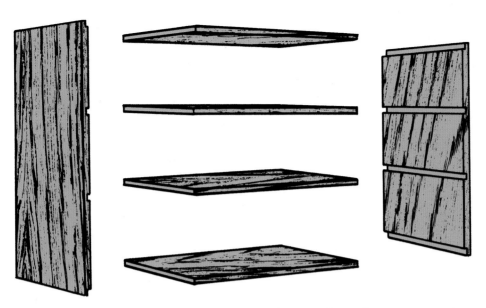

6–17. This exploded view shows how dadoes and rabbets can be used in case construction.

Dado and Rabbet Joints

The traditional way to assemble a case carcass is using dado and rabbet joints (**6–17**). You can also use miter joints when both faces will show. This method is still often preferred for fine freestanding cabinets, particularly when face frames will be used. You can make the joints using any of the techniques described in chapter 4. When the pieces are large, using a router and guide is probably the easiest method. Making dadoes on a table saw in large pieces can require help from other people to support the work.

Face Frames

DECORATIVE STILES AND RAILS ARE OFTEN used on the front edges of the carcass to cover the exposed edges and to provide a solid attaching point for hinges. Together the stiles and rails form a face frame.

Face-frame members are generally ¾ inch thick and 1½ inches wide. You can also use frame members that are 2 inches wide. You can use other dimensions for face frames, but avoid frame members wider than 4 inches to prevent problems with dimensional change.

To achieve maximum strength, the frame should be assembled with strong joints. Simple butt joints won't be strong enough, because the joint will involve end grain. To reinforce the joints, you can use dowels, plate joinery, face-frame screws, or pocket-hole screws. Follow the procedure given in chapter 4. Face-frame screws are simply driven through the edge

6–18. Pocket-hole joinery is well suited for making face frames.

6–19. Face frames can be attached to the carcass with pocket-hole screws. When the holes will be visible, you can cover them with plugs. The one shown here is made of white plastic to match particleboard covered in white melamine.

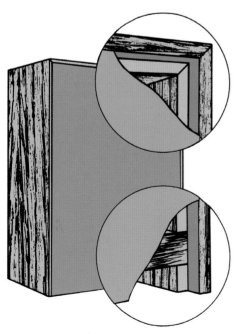

6–20. A rabbet will hide the edge of the back when it is attached to the cabinet.

of the stiles into the end of the rails. This method works well when the edges of the stiles won't show. When the edges will show, you can use pocket-hole screws. Pocket-hole joinery was originally developed for face fames and it works well in this application (6–18).

The face frame is frequently attached to the edges with a butt joint; if the sides of the cabinet are made of solid lumber, this will be a long-grain-to-long-grain joint that is fairly strong. In this case, face frames are frequently attached with glue and a few finishing nails. If you want to minimize the size of the face frame's exposed edge, you can cut a rabbet around the edge of the frame.

When you apply face frames to carcasses made of plywood or particleboard, the glue joint won't be strong enough without reinforcement. This is another place where pocket-hole joinery performs well. If the outside of the cabinet won't show, drill the pocket on the outside of the cabinet. When the outside will show, drill the holes inside the cabinet. You can plug the holes with the special plugs described in chapter 4 to improve the appearance on the interior of the cabinet (6–19). You can also use plate joinery to attach the face frames.

Cabinet Backs

THE BACK OF A CABINET is an important structural member of the carcass. It holds the entire cabinet square. If you build an open-backed cabinet, you need to include extra bracing to keep the cabinet square. Backs are usually made of ¼-inch plywood, melamine-covered particleboard, or ¼- or ⅛-inch hardboard. If the sides of the cabinet won't show, you can simply butt the back in place, but this leaves an exposed edge along the side of the cabinet. When the sides will show, a better method is to cut a rabbet along the back edges of the sides where the back can fit (6–20). Usually the back can overhang at the top and bottom, unless the top shows; then, you also need to make a rabbet at the top.

You should attach the back after you have assembled the rest of the carcass. Check the carcass for square by measuring diagonals from corner to corner. Both measurements should be equal. Use a square placed at several joints as an additional check. If the cabinet is out of square, try to rack it into square before applying the back. If you can't do this, then put the back in place and put several nails in one side but leave the other edges free. It is usually possible to apply hand pressure to the back and one side to rack the cabinet into square. If you still can't square the cabinet, then place a bar clamp diagonally across the corners that were the farthest apart and tighten the clamp until the cabinet is square. Now nail the back in place.

Backs are not usually glued. However, when you use manufactured materials, you can glue the back in place without any problem and the cabinet will be strengthened. Short box nails will hold better than brads, because their large heads won't pull through the back. When a power stapler is available, staples offer the greatest holding power, because the bridge prevents the staple from pulling through the back. Space the nails 4 to 6 inches apart around all four edges. For added strength, you can use screws instead of nails. When you need a very strong cabinet, use ½- or ¾-inch-thick material for the back and attach it with screws.

Cornices

A CORNICE IS A DECORATIVE MOLDING that is applied to the top of a cabinet. Many traditional and contemporary cabinets include a cornice (6–21). A cornice can be made from commercially available crown molding, or you can make your own.

Often contemporary designs use a simple cornice with flat surfaces. This type is usually made from the same material as the rest of the cabinet trim (6–22). If the carcass is made from a dimensionally stable material, such as plywood or particleboard, you can attach the cornice directly to the carcass. If the carcass is made from solid lumber, use the techniques described later in this chapter. If you use crown molding, you will need to cut a compound miter to join the corners.

6–21. A cornice is a decorative molding at the top of a cabinet.

6–22. Contemporary designs may use flat boards to make a simple cornice.

Because the crown molding attaches to the cabinet at an angle, the joint will have a miter angle and a bevel angle. Together, these angles are called a *compound miter*. There are two ways to cut a compound miter. The first method is the simplest, but it will only work with narrow moldings. Place the molding in a hand miter box or a power miter saw. The molding should be placed on an angle so that the bottom edge is facing up and the back angle is resting against the fence of the miter saw. The top of the molding should rest against the base of the saw. This is upside down in relation to the way it will be positioned on the cabinet. To keep the molding from slipping out of position as you make the cut, clamp a board to the saw base in front of the molding (6–23). Now make the cut with the saw set to 45 degrees.

When the molding is too wide to cut using this method, you can cut the miter with the molding flat on the saw base using the compound miter settings on the saw (6–24). Most crown molding sold in the United States has a standard angle of 52 degrees at the top and 38 degrees at the bottom (6–25). The compound miter settings for this type of molding are a miter angle of 31.6 degrees (6–26) and a bevel angle of 33.9 degrees (6–27). Many power miter saws will have detents at these angles to simplify the setup. However, if your cabinet is out of square, these angles may need to be adjusted. Always make a test joint on scrap first.

When you make your own crown molding, you may choose to use a different angle. For example, 45 degrees works well for shop-made molding. To produce a molding like the one shown in 6–28, set a table saw to cut a 45-degree bevel as you would to make a miter joint. Rip one edge of the board at the 45-degree angle; this will form the surface that attaches to the front of the cabinet. Next, move the fence ¼ inch further away from the blade, flip the board over, and make another 45-degree cut. This will form the flat edge at the bottom. Finally, reposition the board and make another 45-degree cut to make the flat edge at the top. To cut a compound miter for 45-degree molding, the miter setting should be 54.75 degrees and the bevel setting should be 30 degrees.

Cabinet Bases and Legs

A CABINET THAT RESTS on the floor needs some type of base or legs. Bases, also called *plinths*, can be an integral part of the carcass or a separate part. You can create a simple base by installing the bottom of the cabinet in a dado that is spaced approximately 3 to 4 inches above the bottom of the side and by using a filler board, called a *toe-kick*, across the front, to complete the base.

6–23. You can cut a compound miter with the saw set for a simple 45-degree cut if the board is narrow enough to be placed on the saw, as shown here.

6–24. When the molding is wide, you can cut a compound miter with the molding flat on the saw base using the compound miter settings on the saw.

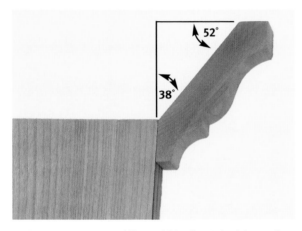

6–25. Most crown molding sold in the United States has a standard angle of 52 degrees at the top and 38 degrees at the bottom.

6–26. Setting the compound miter angle to 31.6 degrees. Note the detent stop that this saw has for this setting.

6–27. Setting the bevel angle to 33.9 degrees.

6–28. This contemporary design cornice molding can be made by ripping the edges of the board at a 45-degree angle.

In some designs, the toe-kick may have a decorative shape along its bottom edge (**6–29**). Frequently, the toe kick is recessed into the cabinet approximately 2 to 3 inches. This creates a toe space that allows people to stand closer to the cabinet without bumping their toes against the toe-kick (**6–30**). You can notch back the sides to meet the toe-kick, or you can leave them full-width. To attach the toe-kick, you can use butt joints, rabbets, or miters (**6–31**). In some designs, the toe space extends around the sides as well. This gives the impression that the cabinet is floating above the floor. The effect is heightened if you paint the toe-kick black. To achieve this effect, you must use a separate assembly for the base (**6–32**).

A separate base also makes it easier to add additional bracing in the middle and at the back of the base. Bases can be made from ¾-inch-thick lumber, plywood, or particleboard. If the base may get wet, don't use particleboard. Some traditional designs employ a separate base that extends past the carcass, instead of being recessed. If it is not visually objectionable, you can attach the base with nails or screws driven down through the bottom of the cabinet. Otherwise, add screw blocks to the base and attach it from underneath.

A base with a flat bottom will tend to rock if the floor has any minor irregularities. The base should only contact the floor at the corners. To achieve this, you can attach small feet, called floor glides. If you don't use floor glides, remove a small amount of wood from the middle of the bottom of each part of the base. An easy way to do this is by using a jointer (**6–33**). If the jointer has an adjustable outfeed table, set the infeed table for approximately a ⅛-inch cut and adjust the outfeed table so that it is level with the infeed table. Hold the board slightly off the table for the first 4 inches so that no cut is made, and then lower the board to the table and push it through until the cut is 4 inches from the other end. Lift the board from the jointer.

If you can't adjust the outfeed table, then two passes over the jointer will be necessary. Follow the procedure just described for the first cut. This will produce a tapered cut, because you haven't lowered the outfeed table. Next, turn the board end-for-end and follow the same procedure again. This may still leave a high spot in the middle of the board; if this is objectionable, you can remove it with a hand plane.

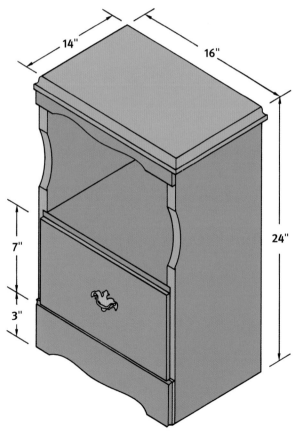

6–29. This nightstand uses the simplest type of base. The bottom is dadoed into the sides, and the toe-kick is attached to the front.

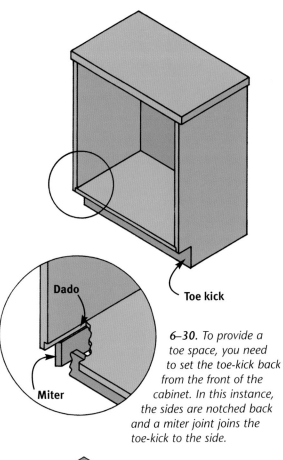

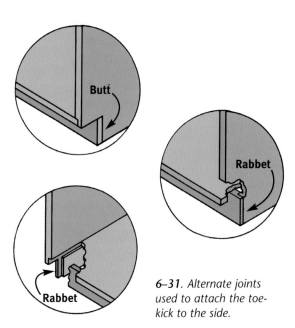

Butt

Rabbet

Rabbet

Dado

Toe kick

Miter

6–30. To provide a toe space, you need to set the toe-kick back from the front of the cabinet. In this instance, the sides are notched back and a miter joint joins the toe-kick to the side.

6–31. Alternate joints used to attach the toe-kick to the side.

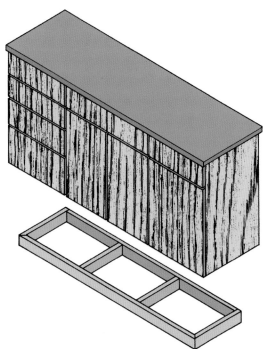

6–32. A separate base is frequently used for large cabinets.

6–33. To keep the base from rocking, you can cut away a small amount from the middle of the bottom edge of the base with a jointer. (The guard has been pulled back for clarity in the photo; you should keep the guard in place as you perform this operation.)

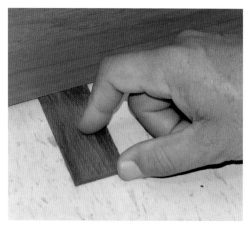

6–34. Using shims to level a built-in cabinet base.

6–36. When using leveling legs, you can add a toe-kick with clips that come with the legs.

6–37. To give built-in cabinets a more furniture-like appearance, decorative legs can be added in the toe-kick area.

6–35. Commercial legs are usually attached with a threaded plate screwed to the bottom of the cabinet.

Bases for built-in cabinets are usually left flat on the bottom, and shims are used to compensate for irregularities in the floor (6–34).

Factory-made legs are available in many sizes and styles—from simple, tapered legs to cabriole legs. Commercial legs can be very useful for the beginning cabinetmaker. They are usually attached with a metal plate that is threaded to accept a threaded bolt in the leg. The plate attaches to the bottom of the cabinet with screws (6–35).

You can purchase mounting plates similar to the type used on commercial legs for attaching shop-built legs to a cabinet. If the load the legs must carry won't be too great and if the bottom of the cabinet lends itself to this type of attachment, the use of mounting plates can be an effective method.

When making frameless built-in cabinets, you can use European leveling legs instead of a base. These legs attach to the bottom of the cabinet with screws. They can be adjusted to compensate for irregularities in the floor. The legs can be left exposed in utility cabinets or you can add a toe-kick with clips that come with the legs to make the cabinets look more finished (6–36).

To give built-in cabinets a more furniture-like appearance, legs can be attached to the front of the base cabinet. The cabinet can sit on a base and the decorative legs can be added in the toe-kick area, as shown in **6–37**, or you can eliminate the base by hanging the cabinet from the wall like an overhead cabinet and adding legs to the front, as shown in **6–38**.

6–38. This cabinet hangs from the wall like an overhead cabinet and has legs in the front to give it a furniture look.

Traditional Carcass Construction Methods

IN THIS SECTION I will discuss some traditional carcass construction methods that are not typically used by production cabinet shops but are still useful for custom work and antique reproductions. They include exposed joinery, skeleton-frame construction, panel construction, special procedures for solid-lumber tops and cornices, and traditional back construction.

Exposed Joinery

When you use solid lumber for the carcass, you can use the joinery as a design detail. Using through dovetails and mortise-and-tenon joints can add an interesting detail to both contemporary and traditional cabinet designs. The basic construction is still case construction, but you use exposed joints instead of blind dowels or other hidden joinery methods. Through dovetails work well for attaching the top to the side of a freestanding cabinet. For a wall-hung cabinet, you can use them for the bottom too (6–39). Through tenons can be used for shelves and to attach the bottom of a freestanding cabinet.

6–39. This Southwestern-style cabinet uses exposed joinery as a design feature.

You can cut the joints by hand or use a router template. The adjustable dovetail jig described in chapter 4 works well for this (**6–40**). There is also an accessory tenon guide available for this type of jig that will make the through tenons.

Skeleton-Frame Construction

Skeleton-frame construction is similar to the framing of a house. The framework is made of small parts put together in the shape of the cabinet; then the framework is covered with a thin "skin" that hides all of its details (**6–41**). From the outside, the cabinet looks that same as if case construction was used. Skeleton-frame construction was often used in factory-made furniture before the advent of furniture-grade particleboard. It is still useful when you want to decrease the weight of a cabinet. The framework is made of solid wood, usually an inexpensive species. The skin is usually plywood, but you can also use particleboard or hardboard.

To assemble the framework, you can use dowel joints, mortise-and-tenon joints, or half-lap joints. Mortise-and-tenon joints and half-lap joints are stronger than dowel joints. Since the framework isn't visible in the finished cabinet, half-lap joints are often used because they are easier to make than mortise-and-tenon joints. Frame members are usually 1½ inches wide; avoid widths greater than 4 inches to prevent problems associated with dimensional change in the frame members.

You can build frames individually, and then treat them as solid boards for subsequent operations. For example, you can make the side frames of a cabinet with rails placed wherever a joint with another part of the

6–40. This adjustable dovetail jig is capable of making through dovetails in wide boards, so it is well suited for cutting exposed joinery in carcass construction.

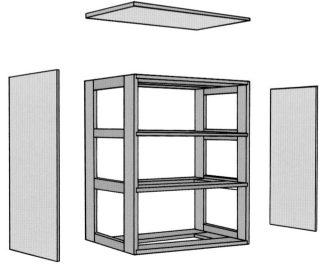

6–41. Skeleton-frame construction uses a thin skin that covers an inner framework.

6–42. This cabinet uses panel construction.

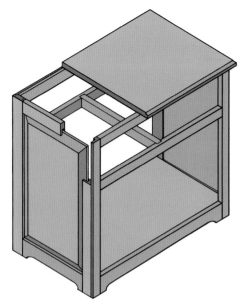

6–43. Panel construction is one of the best methods in terms of accommodating for dimensional change in solid wood.

cabinet will be made. Once you have built the side frames, you can cut rabbets and dadoes in them for the top, bottom, and shelves or drawer guides, as if the frames were solid pieces. The frames that fit into these joints can also be constructed beforehand, and the frames can be assembled into a carcass as if each frame were a solid board.

Once you have assembled the frames, skin them over with a thin (usually ¼- or ⅛-inch) sheet of plywood, particleboard, or hardboard. You can glue on the skin without using any fasteners if sufficient clamps are available, or you can glue the skin and then nail it with small brads. You can also use contact cement or panel adhesive to apply the skin.

The skin adds rigidity to the frame. Complex corner joints are not necessary when skinning the frames. Simple butt joints are usually used; however, if both faces will show, you can use a miter joint. When an edge of the frame will show around a drawer or door opening, you can cover the frame with decorative stiles and rails. Stiles are the vertical members of the frame, and rails are the horizontal members. You can also use one of the edge treatments described in chapter 1, such as edge banding.

Panel Construction

One of the most stable methods of carcass construction using solid wood is panel construction (6–42). This form of carcass construction has evolved over many years to accommodate the dimensional changes that are constantly occurring in solid wood. As with skeleton-frame construction, the carcass is made of many small parts joined into a framework, but in this case, the framework is visible (6–43).

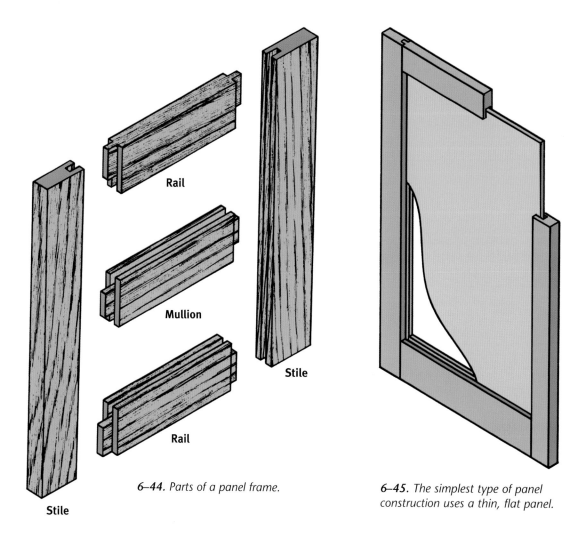

Rail

Mullion

Stile

Rail

Stile

6–44. Parts of a panel frame.

6–45. The simplest type of panel construction uses a thin, flat panel.

As previously mentioned, the vertical members of the frame are called *stiles* and the horizontal members are called *rails*. A frame member between two panels is called a *mullion* (**6–44**). Frame members are usually 1½ to 2 inches wide, but you can use any dimension up to 4 inches. Stiles and rails wider than 4 inches are subject to dimensional change, so they should be avoided in most cases.

A groove cut into the inside edge of the frame holds a panel. The panel is slightly smaller than the space allowed, and it is not glued in place. This leaves the panel free to expand and contract without distorting the carcass. The frame members are always long and narrow, with the grain running with their length, so there is little dimensional change in the frame. The result is a very stable carcass. Because of this stability, you can mix plywood and solid wood in the same carcass. You can make the top and bottom of plywood and the sides of solid wood in panel construction without any problems.

The simplest type of panel construction is shown in **6–45**. The frame has no decorative edge, and a thin, flat panel is used. Besides solid wood, you

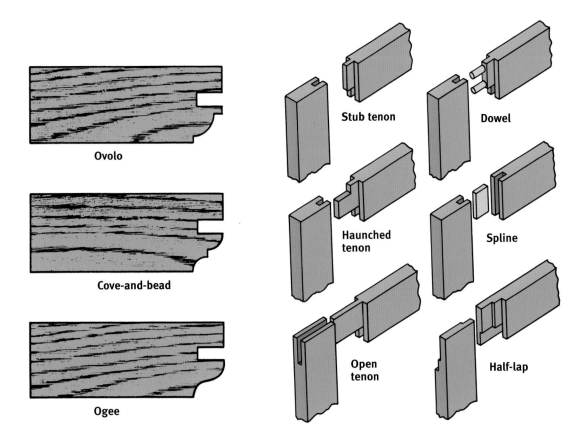

6–46. Decorative sticking.

Ovolo

Cove-and-bead

Ogee

6–47. Joints used for panel construction.

Stub tenon

Dowel

Haunched tenon

Spline

Open tenon

Half-lap

can use plywood, particleboard, or hardboard for the panel. The manufactured materials can be glued in the groove. In this case, dimensional stability is not the main concern; the frame is simply used to strengthen a panel that would not be strong enough on its own.

You can cut the groove on a table saw using a dado blade or with a router or shaper. You can cut short grooves by hand using the methods described in chapter 4 for dadoes. To cut a long groove by hand, you need to use a plow plane.

Frequently, a decorative edge, called *sticking*, is added on one or both sides of the groove. *Ovolo*, *cove-and-bead*, and *ogee* are three popular designs (6–46). A shaper or router is usually used to cut the sticking. In the past, special planes were used for making sticking. Some molding planes are still available, though not as many as in the past. Cabinetmakers who prefer to use only hand tools still use molding planes for this purpose.

The frame members are usually joined with mortise-and-tenon joints (6–47). A short tenon that fits into the groove made for the panel is called a stub tenon. The stub tenon is acceptable when a great deal of strength is not required, but a full-length tenon provides greater strength. You need

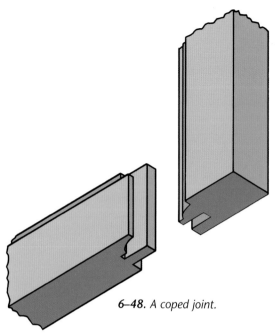

6–48. A coped joint.

to use a haunched tenon so that the exposed end of the groove will be filled. If the groove will not show, then it is not necessary to use this tenon.

It is easier to cut an open tenon than a mortise, so an open tenon is sometimes used when the edges of the frame are concealed. You can also use dowel joints, in which case, you will still cut a stub tenon on the end of the rail to fit into the groove on the stile. A spline joint offers about as much strength as a stub tenon and is simpler to make. To cut a groove in the ends of the rails, use the same saw setup that you used to cut the grooves for the panels. Exercise care when making this cut on a table saw. *Be sure to keep your fingers well away from the blade.* Using a tenoning jig that clamps the board in place is the safest way to handle cuts on the end of narrow parts.

You can use half-lap joints, but they are not as simple as those normally used, because an added step is necessary to make the projection that fills the groove.

When you use decorative sticking, the end of the rail must have an opposite matching cut to fit over the edge of the stile. This is called a *coped joint* (**6–48**). To accomplish this, you should use special matched pairs of router bits or shaper cutters. I will cover these matched router bit sets in more detail in chapter 8 when I cover panel doors.

You may use a raised panel both for appearance and to give the added strength available from a thicker board. The panel can be beveled on both sides or only on the front. When both sides are beveled, you can use a full ¾-inch-thick panel and it will still be flush with the frame. If only one side is beveled, then you need to use a panel that is ½ or ⁷⁄₁₆ inch thick to keep the front surface flush with the frame. You can use a ¾-inch-thick panel if you don't mind having the panel extending past the frame.

You can cut the bevel on a table saw. Set the blade to a 10-degree tilt and raise it 1¼ inches above the table. Position the fence ³⁄₁₆ inch away from the blade. Hold the panel upright with its back against the fence. *This operation must be done without the guard, so use caution and keep your hands well clear of the blade.* It will be easier to keep the panel from rocking if you attach a board to the fence that extends higher than the fence to help support the panel.

Another method of guiding the panel is by cutting a spacer that is the same width as the rip fence; sandwich this spacer between the back of the panel and a scrap board approximately the same size as the panel. If you place the spacer in the middle of the panel, you can make two cuts on opposite sides of the panel before you have to reposition the spacer. Clamp this assembly together and place it on the saw so that it straddles the fence. This method will practically eliminate any rocking or wandering from the fence.

A bevel cut on a table saw will usually require a lot of hand sanding to remove the saw marks. Using a planer blade will help to minimize the marks. A special type of blade that has an abrasive coating on the side will further reduce the marks left by the saw.

A shaper is often used to produce the bevel on a panel. Shaper cutters can produce a curved bevel or a bevel with a dual angle. For the do-it-yourselfer, a panel-raising router bit is a good option. These bits are discussed further in chapter 8.

You can use a plane to cut the bevel by hand. Planes are the original tool used for this operation, and have been used for centuries. Although you can use special panel-raising planes, you can produce a simple raised panel with a block plane. Lay out lines on the panel to indicate the thickness of the edge and the end of the bevel on the face. Cut the cross-grain bevels first so that any tear-out will be removed when you cut the other bevels. Hold the plane at the approximate angle of the bevel and chamfer the corner. Keep cutting down the corner until you are near the layout lines. Hold the plane at the angle necessary to meet both lines, and clean up the bevel with a few fine cuts.

Whenever possible, stain the panels before assembly; that way, if they shrink, there won't be a noticeable light line at the joint between the panel and the frame. Since the panel is loose in the frame, it can sometimes shift too far out of alignment. This is not noticeable with flat panels, but with a raised panel there may be a noticeable difference in the width of the exposed bevel from one side to the other or the panel may tilt slightly. To prevent this, put a one-inch-long bead of silicone caulking in the middle of the top and bottom grooves. The caulking will glue the panel in place, but it is also flexible enough to allow panel movement. By gluing only the middle of the end-grain part of the panel, the panel will expand and contract evenly on either side of the glued section, maintaining an equal exposure on both side bevels.

Solid-Lumber Tops

When you use solid wood for a cabinet top, there is a tendency for the top to cup. Changes in humidity can cause large dimensional changes in the wide panels used for tops. A 12-inch-wide top can change as much as ¼ inch in width as a result of changes in moisture content. Therefore, you must pay special attention to keeping the top flat and allowing for dimensional change.

You can use cleats to help keep the top flat (6–49). Don't glue the cleats to the top. Attach the cleats with screws placed in slotted holes to allow for expansion and shrinkage. Use round-head screws with a washer to keep the screw head from pulling through the slot. If you don't allow for dimensional change in this way, the top is apt to crack as the wood shrinks.

You can also use end caps to keep the top flat (6–50). A tongue cut on the end of the top fits into a groove cut into the end cap. End caps can cause the top to split if you attach them incorrectly. You should only glue the cap to a section approximately 4 inches wide in the middle of the top. You need to leave the rest of the tongue and groove free to move as the top shrinks and expands.

Traditionally styled cabinets usually have a top that is not an integral part of the cabinet. A subframe is integral to the carcass, and the top is screwed from underneath to the subframe. If the top is solid wood, it should not be glued and the screw holes should be enlarged in the subframe or slot-shaped to allow for dimensional changes in the top (6–51).

Instead of attaching the top to a subframe, you can use small brackets to attach the top. The brackets can be made from wood or metal. You make the wooden type (6–52) by cutting a ¼- x ½-inch rabbet on the edge of a two-inch-wide strip of wood. This strip should have the grain running across its width, instead of along its length as is usual.

After you have made the rabbet, cut the strip into 1½-inch lengths. Drill a hole in the middle of each bracket for a screw. Cut a ¼- x ¼-inch dado ½ inch down from the top-inside edge of the sides of the cabinet. Position the top on the sides, and place the brackets so that the projecting tongue fits into the dado in the side. Attach the bracket to the top with a screw. You can glue the brackets to the top, but don't let any glue get on the parts that touch the sides. Space the brackets four to six inches apart, all along the dado.

You can use the same type of brackets to attach the top to the front and back rails, but you need to make the tongue longer and the dado deeper. Position the bracket so that the tongue is only halfway into the dado. This will allow the tongue to move in and out of the dado as the top shrinks and swells.

The metal type of bracket (6–53) works in exactly the same way, but the dado is narrower and usually a saw kerf is all that is necessary. You can purchase the metal brackets ready-made, or you can make your own by bending strap iron in a vise.

Some contemporary designs call for a top that is integral with the carcass. Case construction is usually used for the rest of the carcass when an integral top is needed. An integral top usually doesn't overhang the edges, so miter joints are usually used to hide the end grain. Sometimes the joinery is used for decorative effect; should this be the case, you can use exposed dovetails or box joints to attach the top.

Don't glue cleat to top.

6–49. *Screw holes in the cleat should be slotted. Use a washer on the screw to keep the head from pulling through the slot.*

Only apply glue to middle area.

6–50. *When you use end caps, apply glue only to the middle area of the tongue so that the top can freely expand or contract freely.*

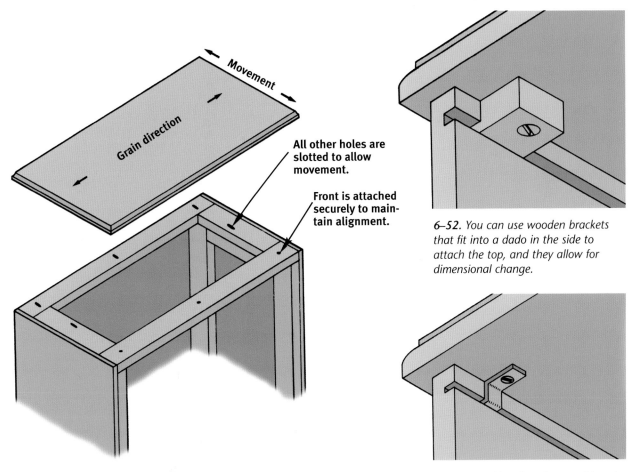

Movement

Grain direction

All other holes are slotted to allow movement.

Front is attached securely to maintain alignment.

6–52. *You can use wooden brackets that fit into a dado in the side to attach the top, and they allow for dimensional change.*

6–51. *When a solid wood top is attached to a subframe, use slotted holes for the screws everywhere except along the front. Attach the front securely to maintain proper alignment.*

6–53. *Metal brackets for attaching the top are available commercially, or you can make them by bending strap iron.*

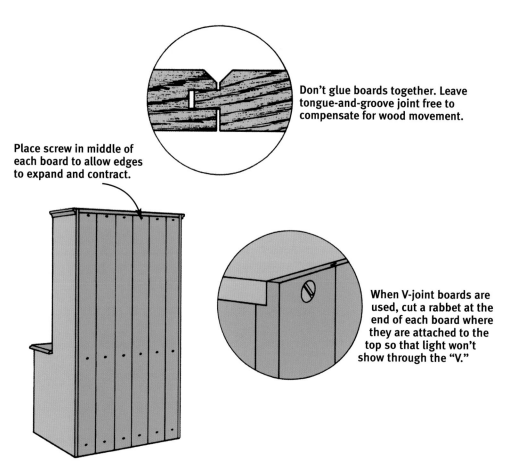

Don't glue boards together. Leave tongue-and-groove joint free to compensate for wood movement.

Place screw in middle of each board to allow edges to expand and contract.

When V-joint boards are used, cut a rabbet at the end of each board where they are attached to the top so that light won't show through the "V."

6–54. On an authentic antique reproduction, you can use tongue-and-groove boards for the back.

Cabinet Backs

If you are building an antique reproduction and you want it to be authentic, you can't use manufactured materials for the back. Several types of back were used before the advent of plywood. You can assemble tongue-and-groove strips, which are similar to the type used as flooring, into a large panel for a back (**6–54**). Screw or nail the boards only in the middle of their widths, and don't use glue on the tongues or grooves.

Another type of back, called a *muntin back,* uses thin pieces of solid wood joined together by muntins, which are narrow uprights made of thicker wood and grooved on both edges (**6–55**). You can also use muntins for joining manufactured materials when the back is too large to be cut from a single 4-foot x 8-foot sheet.

A tongue-and-groove back or a muntin back won't hold the carcass in square as rigidly as a back made from a single sheet of plywood or hardboard. A type of antique back that does add rigidity to the carcass is the *panel back* (**6–56**). It is made the same way as the paneled sides discussed earlier. Usually flat panels are used, but beveled panels will also work.

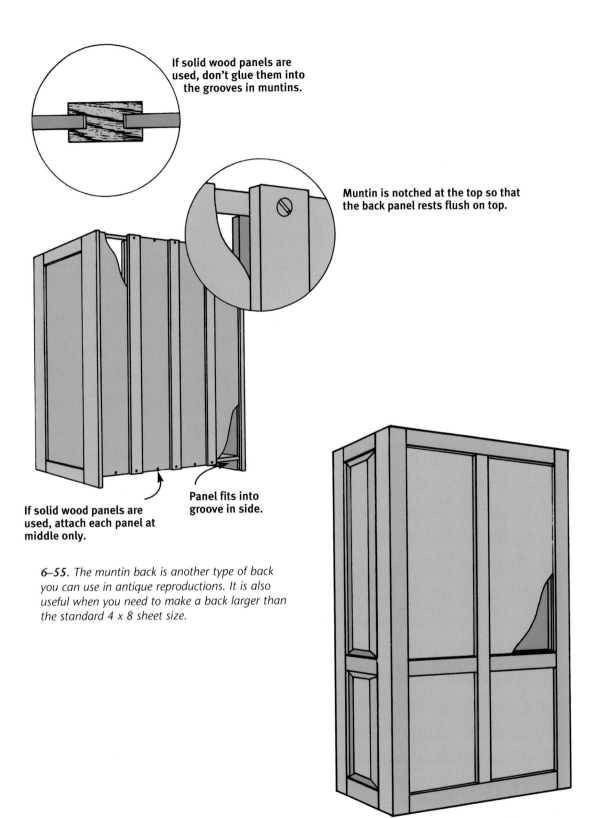

If solid wood panels are used, don't glue them into the grooves in muntins.

Muntin is notched at the top so that the back panel rests flush on top.

If solid wood panels are used, attach each panel at middle only.

Panel fits into groove in side.

6–55. The muntin back is another type of back you can use in antique reproductions. It is also useful when you need to make a back larger than the standard 4 x 8 sheet size.

6–56. The paneled back offers more rigidity than the muntin back.

6–57. When the weather is humid, the solid-lumber sides and top of this cabinet become wider, but the cornice stays about the same length. Notice that the end of the cornice is even with the rear edge of the cabinet.

6–58. This photo taken in dry weather shows how much the cabinet sides and top have shrunk in relation to the length of the cornice. If the cornice were firmly attached to the cabinet, the sides and top may have split at this point.

Cornices

6–59. Here, you can see the slotted hole for one of the screws that attach the cornice.

When you use panel construction, you can attach the cornice directly to the top rail as described above. This method will also usually work with solid lumber if the sides are not wider than approximately eight inches. Since the grain direction of the molding is 90 degrees to the grain direction of the side, differences in expansion will create problems when the sides are wider than eight inches. **Illustrations 6–57** and **6–58** show the amount of expansion from the wet season to the dry season in a cabinet with sides 15 inches wide. This cornice is attached with slotted-hole screws so that the sides won't split (**6–59**).

Another way to solve this problem is to attach the cornice to a separate part, called a *frieze* (**6–60**). The frieze is a box-shaped unit, shown in **6–61**. The grain direction is indicated by arrows. Apply the cornice molding to the frieze. Since the grain of the frieze runs in the same direction as the cornice molding, no problems will result from dimensional change. Apply a thin strip with a rounded edge to the bottom of the frieze assembly so that the rounded edge projects slightly past the rest of the carcass. This strip is called a frieze molding, and it hides the joint between the carcass and the frieze.

Attach the frieze assembly to the carcass with screws, but do not use glue. The screw holes should be slotted, or wooden brackets similar to the ones described for attaching tops should be used to allow for shrinkage and swelling.

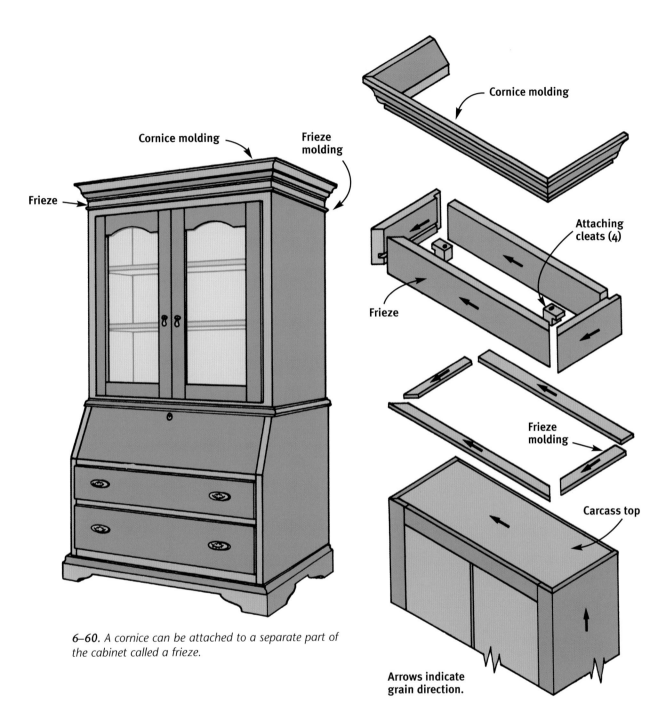

Cornice molding

Frieze molding

Cornice molding

Frieze

Frieze

Attaching cleats (4)

Frieze molding

Carcass top

Arrows indicate grain direction.

6–60. A cornice can be attached to a separate part of the cabinet called a frieze.

6–61. This type of cornice construction allows for dimensional change when you use a solid-wood case type of construction for the carcass.

Cabinet Legs

When a cabinet is designed to sit more than a few inches above the floor, legs are usually used. Simple, tapered, lathe-turned legs are frequently used in modern designs, whereas ornamentally turned legs are often used with period cabinets. Many modern designs use a square leg or a square, tapered leg. The square leg is simple enough to make; the square, tapered leg is more difficult.

One method for tapering the legs involves using a jointer. Determine the amount of taper per foot required, and set the jointer depth of cut to that figure. Make a mark on the leg that is one foot from the end. With the jointer turned off, move the guard back and place the leg over the cutters so that the mark is in the middle of the cutter head. The part of the leg to be tapered should be on the infeed table.

Lift the end of the leg on the outfeed table so that the leg is not touching the knives, but it is still holding the guard open. Use a push block on the infeed side. Turn on the jointer and lower the leg until it touches the knives, and then push the leg through. Repeat this process on all sides of all of the legs, and then change the depth of cut to approximately 1/16 inch. Place the leg with the small end facing the cutter and the tapered section flat on the infeed table. Push the leg through the jointer, keeping the taper flat against the table. Continue taking cuts in this manner on all sides of the leg until the entire leg is tapered (6–62).

6–62. *Tapering a leg on the jointer.*

You can make custom-turned legs on a lathe. To attach the legs, turn a round tenon at the top of the leg. The tenon fits into a corresponding hole bored into the base. You can bore the hole at an angle if you plan on angling the legs. You can simply glue the tenons into the hole; however, for a stronger joint, cut a slot in the tenon and drive a wooden wedge into the slot from above when the leg is in place.

If you don't want the top of the tenon to show through the bottom of the cabinet, you can make a blind hole if you stop boring before the bit emerges from the base. A Forstner bit is best for this operation because it doesn't have a long middle spur that will break through the wood before the hole is at an adequate depth. You can wedge this blind joint with a foxed wedge. You need to place the point of the wedge into the slot before inserting the leg in the hole. As you insert the leg, the end of the wedge will hit the top of the hole, and it will be forced into the slot as you drive the leg home. You may need to experiment with scrap to get the proper size for the wedge. If it is too long, you won't be able to drive the leg all the way in; if it is too short, the wedging won't be effective.

If you use a skeleton frame, you can incorporate the legs into the frame. For square legs, simply extend the corner frame members past the bottom of the cabinet. When turning round legs, leave a square section at the top that can be attached to the frame before you apply the skin.

You can also make a separate base where you can attach the legs. The legs can be attached to the rails with dowels or mortise-and-tenon joints.

Bracket feet are sometimes used in place of a base (6–63). They resemble the corners of a base with the middle part cut away, and are usually cut in a decorative pattern.

A glue block inside the corner of the bracket foot actually carries the weight of the cabinet. The glue block should extend slightly past the bottom of the foot; if you use a floor glide, it should be attached to the glue block. This block must be constructed in a special way to prevent cross-grain shrinkage and swelling from splitting the foot. The block is glued up in segments. The first segment is positioned with its grain running in the same direction as the grain in one side of the foot, and every other segment is turned 90 degrees to the grain of the last segment. The resulting block is similar to plywood with very thick plies. This procedure provides long-grain gluing surfaces for both sides of the foot, while keeping the grain in the block running in the same direction as that in the foot.

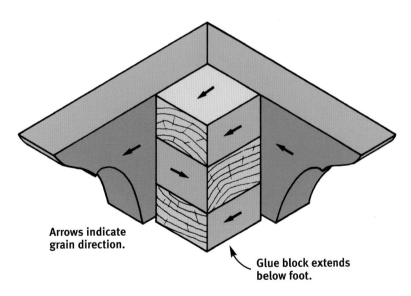

Arrows indicate grain direction.

Glue block extends below foot.

6–63. Bracket feet are supported by a glue block in the corner. Laminating the block, as shown here, prevents problems caused by cross-grain expansion and provides long-grain gluing surfaces on both parts.

⑦ Shelves

S HELVES ARE AN IMPORTANT PART of most cabinets (**7–1**). Shelves may be attached permanently to a cabinet, or they may be adjustable. Fixed shelves form a part of a cabinet's structure and add more strength to the cabinet. Adjustable shelves, on the other hand, add little strength to a cabinet, but you can move them to accommodate different-size objects.

7–1. Shelves are an important part of cabinet construction whether they are open shelves, as seen here, or interior shelves covered by cabinet doors.

Design Considerations

SHELF SIZE SHOULD BE DETERMINED by the type of objects that will be stored on the shelf. You can place small paperback books on 6-inch-wide shelves with 8-inch spacing between the shelves. CDs and DVDs will fit comfortably on 6-inch-wide shelves spaced 6 inches apart. A common size for a bookshelf that will accommodate a variety of books is 8 inches wide with a 10-inch spacing. Very large books and loose-leaf binders require shelves that are 12 inches wide and 14 inches apart. Overhead food-storage shelves are usually 12 to 14 inches wide, whereas below-counter shelves are approximately 24 inches wide.

When you use fixed shelves, be sure to measure the things you intend to store on the shelves before you lay out the shelf spacing. It's frustrating to find that the item you had intended to place on a shelf is ¼ inch too tall to fit between the shelves. That is why adjustable shelves are so popular; you can adapt the shelves to fit new items at any time.

Materials differ in terms of their stiffness and load-carrying capacity, so the material you use will affect the way you design the shelves. In cabinet-making, most shelves are made of ¾-inch-thick material. The thicker the material, the greater will be the load-carrying capacity.

The distance between supports is a critical factor in shelf design. When a middle support is not desirable, the length of the shelf is limited by the maximum distance the material you are using can span without support. Solid lumber is the stiffest material that is used for building shelves.

The actual load-carrying capacity varies among wood species. For light loads, ¾-inch solid-wood shelves can be up to 48 inches between supports. Generally, 36 inches between supports is best. Plywood is not as stiff as solid wood. Although ¾-inch plywood can span 48 inches if the load is very light, 36 inches is usually considered maximum. For a heavy load, 30 inches between supports is best.

Particleboard is the least stiff of the products that are used for making shelves. The maximum distance that particleboard can span without deflecting under load is approximately 30 inches. In most cases, supports should be spaced 24 inches apart. **Illustration 7–3** shows the results of a test using 12-inch-wide shelving. A load was placed on each shelf and the deflection was measured. The actual measurements will vary depending on wood species and other factors, but this chart will give you an idea of the amount of sag to expect.

7–2. A 1½-inch-wide facing strip applied to the front of a shelf increases the shelf's load-carrying capacity and also hides plywood or particleboard edges.

You can increase the load-carrying capacity of a ¾-inch-thick shelf by applying a 1½-inch-wide facing strip to the front edge of the shelf, as shown in **7–2**. The strip can be applied using a simple butt joint reinforced with nails, dowels, or biscuits, or you can use a rabbet or

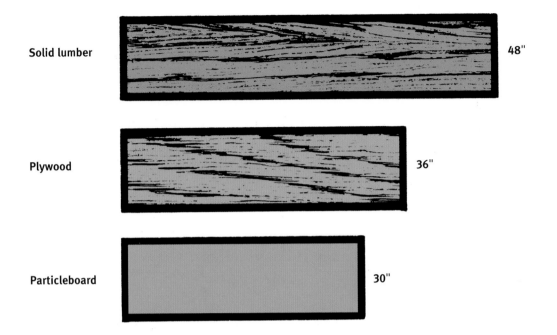

Load	25 lbs.				50 lbs.			
Shelf length (inches)	24	30	36	48	24	30	36	48
Solid lumber	*	*	*	*	*	*	$\frac{1}{16}$	$\frac{1}{8}$
Plywood	*	*	$\frac{1}{16}$	$\frac{1}{8}$	*	$\frac{1}{16}$	$\frac{1}{8}$	$\frac{1}{2}$
Particleboard	*	$\frac{1}{16}$	$\frac{1}{4}$	$\frac{3}{8}$	*	$\frac{1}{8}$	$\frac{1}{4}$	$\frac{5}{8}$

* no significant sag

7–3. Recommended maximum length for ¾-inch-thick shelves with no middle support. This chart gives the deflection obtained when sample shelves were loaded with 25-pound and 50-pound weights.

miter joint (**7–4**). You can achieve even greater strength by applying a similar strip to the rear of the shelf. You can increase the load-carrying capacity of fixed shelves if you attach the shelf to the back of the cabinet. Nail through the back into the shelf, spacing the nails about four inches apart.

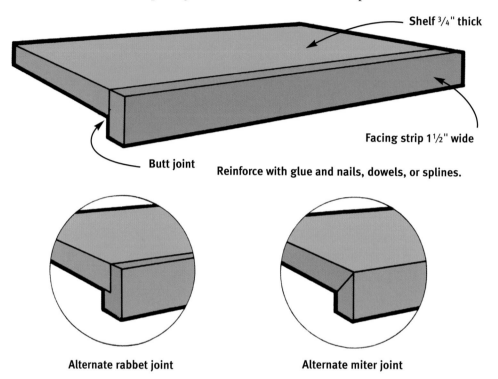

Shelf ³⁄₄" thick

Facing strip 1¹⁄₂" wide

Butt joint

Reinforce with glue and nails, dowels, or splines.

Alternate rabbet joint

Alternate miter joint

7–4. Joints for attaching facing strip to shelves.

Fixed Shelves

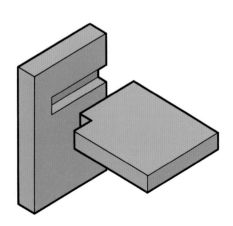

7–5. A stopped-dado joint can be used to conceal the shelf-to-side joint in solid lumber construction.

FIXED SHELVES ARE USUALLY attached with dowels, biscuits, or dado joints. The dado provides a lip to support the shelf and plenty of glue-surface area. When you use plywood or particleboard, you should usually conceal the joints with face frames or edging strips. (For more details, refer back to the section on edge treatments in chapter 1.) The end of a dado joint in solid lumber can be quite attractive, and, in most cases, there is no need to conceal it; however, if you prefer having the joint not show on the front of the cabinet, then you can use a stopped dado instead (**7–5**).

The easiest way to cut a stopped dado is with a router because you have greater control. You can also cut a stopped dado with a table saw, but you have to make a mark on the fence that indicates the front of the blade and a mark on the side of the board opposite the dado that indicates where to stop the dado. Stopping before the end of the cut can be difficult when the parts are large. Turn off the saw and wait for the blade to stop before you remove the board from the saw. If you remove the board with the saw running, there is a chance that the board will move out of line with the saw and, at the least, the dado will be enlarged and an unsightly gap will result. In extreme cases, the blade may bind and kick back the board.

The end of the dado is rounded at this point. You can use a chisel to square up the end, or you can simply make the cutout in the shelf large enough to miss the rounded section. However, if this will result in a large cutout, it is better to square up the dado because the cutout section only has the strength of a butt joint.

You can use butt joints for shelves, but they must be heavily reinforced. To reinforce a butt joint, you can use screws driven through the side into the end of the shelf. The screws should be at least two inches long and spaced approximately 3 inches apart. You can also use nails, but they won't be as strong. You need to use 10d nails, spaced 3 inches apart. Dowels or biscuits can also be used for reinforcing butt joints. Regardless of how you reinforce a butt joint, remember that the weight is being carried mostly by the reinforcement because the force on the joint is almost entirely a shear force.

Adjustable Shelves

ADJUSTABLE SHELVES ARE attached to the side of the cabinet with some type of bracket. One type has a metal standard with a series of rectangular slots spaced approximately ½ inch apart. A small metal clip fits into the slots and supports the shelf (7–6). One of the most important things to remember when installing this type of shelf standard is that the standard should extend down to a solid support, such as a fixed shelf or the bottom of the cabinet. In an attempt to save money, some people don't start the standard at the bottom, because they think that there is no need for a shelf that low; however, if the standard doesn't extend to a solid support, all the weight must be carried by the fasteners that are used to attach the standard.

7–6. Metal standards and brackets offer a wide range of shelf positions.

The fasteners are actually designed to only keep the standard in place, not to support the weight of everything placed on the shelves. Three types of fastener are usually used, and two types of fastener hole are found in the standard. One type of fastener hole is a countersunk hole that will accept a flathead screw or a special nail. You must use very short screws in order to avoid going through the other side of the board. Instead of screws, you can use special nails that have heads that resemble the heads on flathead screws.

Another type of fastener is a special type of staple that is usually only used in production shops. A second set of holes in the standards accommodates the staples; the standards have two small holes side by side with a recessed area between them for the bridge of the staple. You need to use a special type of staple gun that has a positioning finger that fits into one of the notches in the standard, to ensure that the staple will line up with the holes.

You can cut the standards to length with a hacksaw. Production shops use a special nipper to cut the standards. It produces a very clean square end that is similar to the factory cut. Whenever possible, leave a factory end at the bottom of the standard and cut it to length at the top. This will ensure that all of the slots will line up. If the slots are out of alignment, then the shelf will slant or rock.

If you have to cut the bottom end of a standard, make sure that you keep the same distance from the first slot to the end on all of the standards. The slots are marked with a small embossed number. This helps to line up the clips when you are installing the shelves. As long as you keep a factory end at the bottom, the numbers will always line up. If you cut a long standard into smaller ones, the numbers won't always line up. It's a good practice to try to line up the numbers even if it involves some waste.

Different types of standard are available for surface or recessed mounting. If you use the surface mount, there will be a small gap between the end of the shelf and the side of the cabinet, unless you cut a notch in the end of the shelf to fit around the standard. The recessed type fits into a groove cut in the side of the cabinet. Use a dado blade on a table saw or a router to make the groove. The standards are usually placed approximately 1½ to 2 inches away from the front and back of the sides. Since the shelf is free to slide from front to back with this type of bracket, you shouldn't place the standard too near the back. If it is too near the back, a slight forward movement of the shelf will cause it to fall off the clips. On very narrow shelves, the spacing is decreased to approximately 1 inch. A decorative stile that is wider than the side can help keep the shelf in position. Usually a 1½-inch stile is placed on a ¼-inch-thick side so that the extra width extends into the area for shelves. The shelves are made to fit behind the stile. This eliminates any front-to-back movement.

Another popular type of adjustable shelf bracket consists of a small pins or L-shaped metal brackets that have a short metal pin attached to it. This type of bracket doesn't need a standard. The pin fits into a hole drilled into the side of the cabinet (7–7). If you use the pin type, the shelves can be cut to fit the opening; however, if you use the metal L brackets, you must cut the shelf slightly smaller than the distance between the sides to accommodate the thickness of the metal bracket. The bracket hangs with the lower part of the L facing down so that it supports the shelf, while the shelf presses against the side of the L, holding the dowel firmly in its hole. This type of bracket is almost completely concealed when installed; only the bottom of the L is visible from the bottom of the shelf. There is also a plastic version of this type of shelf bracket. It will fit in the same-size holes as the metal bracket. The plastic version has a larger exposed area under the shelf, so it is more visible.

Since you drill the holes for the brackets in the sides, you can determine how much adjustability you want. You may decide to make a continuous row of holes spaced 32 mm apart as is done in commercial cabinetry, or you could drill three or four holes on either side of a shelf position to allow for some adjustment. You could simply drill holes in one position for each shelf, and then drill more holes later if you need to move a shelf. Regardless of the way you choose to drill the holes, it is important for the holes to line up or the shelves will rock or slant. Use a depth stop on the drill bit to keep the hole depth uniform and prevent drilling though the side of the cabinet.

If you will be making many shelf holes, it is a good idea to buy a commercial hole guide. These guides have steel bushings at each hole location to guide the drill bit. If you are only going to drill a few holes, you can use a story stick to lay out the holes or make a template from a strip of hardboard and drill holes in it to act as a drilling guide.

A piece of pegboard can also be used as drill guide (7–8). Cut a piece that is the same size as the side of the cabinet, and draw lines that indicate which row of holes to use. Keep front-and-back spacing the same so that the template

7–7. These adjustable shelf pins fit into holes drilled into the side of the cabinet.

can be reversed for use on both sides. Always position the template with the same end at the bottom. You can make a drill guide from a piece of 2 x 4. Use a drill press or drill guide to drill the holes. That way, the holes will be perfectly straight and they can be used to keep the drill bit square with the face of the board as you drill the shelf holes. Be sure to label the top and front of the guide so that you can orient it correctly in each location (7–9).

Adjustable shelves may seem to be a fairly modern development, but actually they have been used for a long time. If you are building an antique reproduction and you want to use adjustable shelves, you can make wooden brackets that will be appropriate for the time period. One of the simplest types of wooden brackets is very similar to the metal pins just described. It uses a series of holes drilled into the sides, but the shelves rest on wooden pegs instead of metal brackets. You can use a short length of dowel to support the shelf. The dowel can be exposed on the underside of the shelf, or you can conceal it by cutting a stopped groove where it can fit on the underside of the shelf. Following the same concept, you can whittle brackets from wood that will fit into the holes.

Another form of wooden bracket uses strips applied to the front and back of the sides, which have notches cut into them. A wooden cleat fits

7–8. Pegboard makes a good drill guide when you are making multiple holes in the cabinet side for adjustable shelf brackets. A drill stop on the drill keeps the holes a uniform depth.

into the notches, and the shelf rests on the cleat (**7–10**). You may need to cut the ends of the shelves to fit around the strips or simply make the shelves narrower to fit between the strips.

You can cut the notches in several ways. Square notches are easy to cut with a dado blade. You can make rounded notches by drilling a set of holes in the middle of a board and then ripping the board down the middle. A V-notched strip is easy to make with hand tools, because each notch can be made with only two cuts of a handsaw. For perfect alignment of the notches, clamp both strips together back-to-back while making the cuts.

7–9. This drill guide is made from a piece of 2 x 4.

7–10. Using notched, wooden standards is an authentic way of providing adjustable shelves for antique reproductions.

⑧ Doors

W HEN YOU APPLY DOORS to a cabinet, the doors often become the dominant visual feature (**8–1**). For this reason, the type of door you use is very important to the overall look of a cabinet.

8–1. In this kitchen, the cabinet doors are the dominant visual feature.

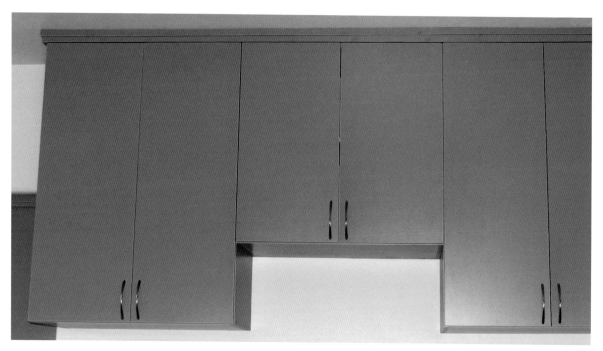

8–2. The slab door is easy to make and install. It is often used in utility cabinets like these garage storage cabinets.

Slab Doors

THE SIMPLEST TYPE OF CABINET door you can make is the slab door. It is merely a single piece of wood cut to the correct size for the door (8–2). Plywood and particleboard are usually used for slab doors because of their dimensional stability, but you can glue solid lumber into slabs that are large enough for doors also.

Slab doors are often used in utility applications where visual appeal is not of prime importance. However, slab doors can also be used in high-style applications. They can give cabinets a sleek, contemporary look; in these cases, the material that covers the door becomes the dominant visual feature. Frequently, wood with a prominent grain is used for slab doors, and, when more than one door is involved, the doors may be grain-matched. A simple way to grain-match plywood doors is to lay them out on the sheet the same way they will appear on the cabinet. Number the doors with an inconspicuous pencil mark so that you can install them in the correct order.

The slab door is generally usually used with modern-looking cabinets; to adapt the slab door to other styles, some type of decoration is usually applied to it. A type of decoration that is frequently used simulates a panel door. You can make a simulated panel door by applying moldings to the door or by cutting a beveled edge on the door.

Another method involves cutting a decorative groove in the face of the door with a router. Special bits are available for this purpose. An adjustable metal guide is available that guides the router around the door. It has several attachments that will make an arched top cut or various corner designs.

You can make your own template that does the same thing, but it won't be quite as versatile. Cut a piece of ¼-inch hardboard the same size as the door, and then cut the desired shape out of the middle. Use a template-following collar on the router. Clamp the template to the door at the top and one side. Make the cuts across the bottom and the other side; then reposition the clamps to the areas that you have already cut and make the remaining cuts. With this type of template, you need a different one for each size of door.

Panel Doors

A RAISED-PANEL DOOR is frequently used for traditionally styled cabinets (8–3). Since the construction details of the door are the main visual focus, wood with a more subdued grain is usually best for this type of door. A flat-panel door can give the cabinet a traditional look, but contemporary cabinets may also use a flat-panel door (8–4).

8–3. These raised-panel doors give a traditional look to built-in cabinets.

8–4. Flat-panel doors can give a cabinet a contemporary look.

Panel doors can be constructed using any of the techniques described in chapter 6, but for do-it-yourselfers the most popular method is to use a matched set of router bits (**8–5**). The bit set will come with specific instructions. You should always follow all of the safety rules given by the router and bit manufacturers and follow the specific procedures for the particular type of bits that you buy. Here, I will give a generalized description of the procedures so that you will have an idea of what to expect before you buy the bits. You will need a powerful router, usually over 3 hp. The router should have a variable speed-capability because the large bits involved must be used at a reduced speed. You will also need a router table; bits this large cannot be used freehand.

Panel doors consist of the same parts as described in chapter 6 for panel carcass construction. The stiles are the vertical sides of the frame, the rails are the horizontal fame members at the top and bottom of the frame, and the panel is the board in the center of the frame.

There are two bits used to make the frame; the first is called the stick bit. It produces the decorative sticking and the panel groove on the edges of the stiles and rails. The second bit is the coping bit. It produces the reverse profile of the sticking bit. It is used to make the coped cut on the ends of the rails that joins the rails to the stiles.

You should cut the coping on the ends of the rails before you cut the sticking. This helps to prevent tear-out in the sticking. Insert the bit in the collet of a router mounted in a router table. Make sure that whenever you install any of these router bits that you insert at least 80 percent of the shank into the collet, but don't bottom out the shank.

The bit has a guide bearing, but you should also use the router table fence to guide the work. In addition, you will need a miter gauge or a coping sled to support the rails and keep them square with the fence. A coping sled is a shop-made accessory made from a piece of ¼-inch-thick plywood or hardboard approximately 10 inches by 12 inches.

8–5. This set of router bits is used to produce raised-panel doors.

8–6. A coping sled holds the rail securely and guides the work.

8–7. Cutting the coped joint.

8–8. Cutting the sticking.

A ¾-inch-thick backup board is attached the plywood and a clamp attached to the backup board (**8–6**). The rails are clamped in place against the backup board, and the edge of the sled rests against the fence (**8–7**).

This gives you a large surface to guide the work. The router table miter gauge will perform the same function, but always place a backup board between the work and the fence; this will help to prevent tear-out as the rail exits from the bit.

Once all of the coping cuts are made, you can cut the sticking. Change to the sticking bit and adjust it so that the groove lines up this the tongue of the coped joints. Using a test board that is the same thickness as the finished stock is a good idea for setting up the cuts, because you may need to do a little trial-and-error adjusting. Adjust the router table fence to guide the cut. Now you can cut the sticking on the stiles and rails (**8–8**).

At this point, you can dry-assemble the frame and make sure that the joints line up (**8–9**). If you are making a flat-panel door, the next step is to cut a flat piece of plywood to fit in the frame. If you are making a raised-panel door, you will need to use a panel-raising bit next.

There are two types of panel-raising bit; the first type only cuts on one side of the panel. When you use this type, the back of the panel will be recessed in the frame. If the panel is the same thickness as the frame, the panel will be proud (raised above the surface of the frame); this may be used as a style feature, or you may want to use thinner wood for the panel to keep it flush with the frame.

The second type of cutter cuts away a small area on the back as well as raises the panel on the front. This leaves a tongue

8–9. Dry-assemble the frame to make sure that the joints line up properly.

8–10. *Raising the panel with a router bit.*

that fits into the groove in the frame. With this type of bit, you can use a panel that is the same thickness as the frame and still have it flush with the frame.

The panel-raising bit is the largest of the three bits. Be sure to observe the router speed recommendations that come with the bit and follow all of the safety procedures recommended by the manufacturer. To minimize tear-out, make the first cut on the end grain of the panel, rotate the panel one-fourth turn, and make a cut on the edge grain. Make another one-quarter turn and cut on the other end of the panel. Finally, make another one-quarter turn and cut on the remaining edge (8–10).

Now you can dry-assemble the entire door and check it for fit. The panel should not be glued in place, because it must be free to expand and contract with changes in humidity. Because the panel will shrink and swell, it is a good idea to finish the panel before assembly. If you finish the door after assembly, the panel may shrink later and expose a small section of unfinished wood. Don't get any finish on the coped joints before assembly or the glue won't adhere well to the joints.

After the finish on the panel is dry, assemble the door. Glue the copped joints, but try not to use too much glue. If glue squeezes into the panel groove, it may glue the panel in place. This could result in a split panel later when the panel shrinks. Use bar clamps to clamp the joints until the glue dries.

Glazed Doors

A GLAZED DOOR IS VERY SIMILAR to a panel door, except you use a piece of glass or plastic instead of a panel (8–11). From a safety standpoint, acrylic plastic is better than glass because it won't shatter into sharp pieces. The only problem with acrylic plastic is that it is not as hard as glass, so it tends to get scratched easier. Tempered glass combines the safety of plastic with the hardness of glass, but it must be special-ordered to size and it can't be cut into smaller pieces once it is tempered.

A glazed door can have a single pane or several small panes. When you use the smaller panes, you can assemble them with lead channels—in which case, the wood frame is the same as for a single pane—or you can place the panes in a wood frame consisting of small muntins. You can simulate the look of small panes without the complications of

8–12. The glass fits into a rabbet cut in the door. In this example, it is held in place by a bead of silicone caulk.

8–11. The glazed doors on this cabinet protect the contents, while also allowing them to be seen.

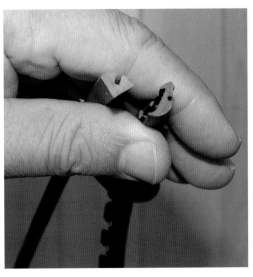

8–13. A plastic stop can be used to secure glass in a door frame. The one on the right has a barbed spine that fits into a kerf cut in the frame. The one of the left is meant to be stapled in place; the groove in the center hides the staples.

installing many small panes of glass by making a decorative framework, called a muntin grill, that is attached in front of a large piece of glass.

Constructing the door is similar to constructing a frame for a panel door, but rather than using a groove for the panel, you need to make a rabbet for the glass. The best way to do this is to buy a matched set of router bits designed for glass doors. Follow the instructions that come with the bits. The procedure is very similar to the one described above for panels doors. The rabbet is open to the back of the door and, once the door is assembled, the glass is held in place by using one of several methods.

The simplest method is to apply a bead of silicone caulk around the perimeter of the glass (8–12). You can also use a small strip of wood, called a stop. You need to attach the stop with very small brads driven parallel with the glass. Use a small tack hammer or a special brad driver, and drill pilot holes to avoid breaking the glass as you drive the brads. A plastic stop is available that makes glass installation easier. There are two types: One has a barbed spline that fits into a kerf cut around the edge

8–14. *Thumb screws can be used to secure glass when ease of replacement is a consideration.*

of the rabbet. The other type is meant to be stapled in place (**8–13**). You can also use special glass fasteners that use thumb screws to hold in the glass. This makes glass replacement easy (**8–14**).

There are several ways to make a decorative muntin frame. If you are using a set of router bits, you can use them to make the muntins and assemble the frame with coped joints. Because the parts are small, you should cut the sticking before cutting the piece from a larger board. After the sticking has been routed, you can then rip the piece to thickness. *The router bits will come with specific instructions; follow them precisely, because this can be dangerous operation if done incorrectly.*

If the door and muntins will have square edges, you can use half-lap joints (**8–15**). Since the muntin strips are so thin, you must take great care when making the joints. A router table is a good option. Attach an auxiliary wooden extension to the miter gauge and clamp a hold-down block to it (**8–16**). Cut the joints for smaller pieces before you cut the parts to length. When the parts are too short, they will be hard to handle safely.

The ends of the grill fit into gains made with a router in the rabbeted area of the frame (**8–17**). You can either round the ends of the muntins or square up the cutouts with a chisel. Cut the gain on a router table, and use a miter gauge to guide the work. Make a mark on the table where the edge of the work will be when the cut is deep enough, or clamp a stop block to the table.

Cleated Doors

FOR A RUSTIC LOOK, a cleated door is frequently used. This type of door is made of several pieces of solid lumber held together with cleats. You can place the cleat on the back of the door, or you can use it as a decorative detail on the front.

Tongue-and-groove lumber is often used in this application. The edges of the boards may be beveled to form a V-groove along the joint (**8–18**). Sometimes this effect is simulated on a plywood slab door by making a series of straight cuts across the door with a router.

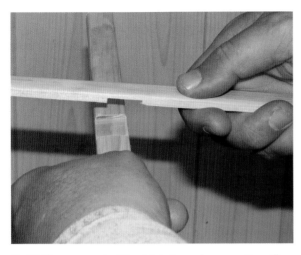

8–15. You can use half-lap joints to make a muntin grill.

8–16. When using a router table to make the half-lap joints, guide the work with a miter gauge and clamp a hold-down block to the miter gauge extension.

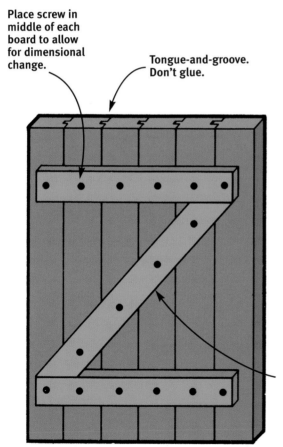

Place screw in middle of each board to allow for dimensional change.

Tongue-and-groove. Don't glue.

Diagonal brace keeps door from sagging.

8–18. Cleated doors are often used when a rustic look is desired.

8–17. A half-lap joint on the end of the muntin fits in a gain cut in the door frame. The cut made by a router will be rounded; you can shape the end of the muntin to fit or chisel the gain square.

Door Applications

IN ADDITION TO THE WAY it is constructed, a door is also classified by the way it is applied to the cabinet. There are three ways cabinet doors are usually applied: *overlay, lipped,* and *flush.* You can use all of these methods with any of the types of door previously described.

Overlay Doors

The overlay door is one of the easiest to make and fit. It fits over the front of the cabinet, and since it is larger than the opening, there is no problem in fitting it to the opening. The overlay door is the standard used with fameless cabinetry. Because all of the edges of an overlay door show, you will need to use some form of edge treatment for plywood or particleboard. (See chapter 1.)

You need to use a special type of hinge on an overlay door. You can apply this kind of door to a stile, or you can eliminate the stile and attach the door directly to the side of the cabinet. Different types of hinge are required for each application. Overlay doors without stiles but with concealed hinges are frequently used in built-in cabinets to give a sleek, modern look (**8–19**).

8–19. Overlay doors are easy to attach and align. In this example of a frameless cabinet the hinges attach directly to the side of the cabinet.

Lipped Doors

The lipped door has a rabbet cut around the edge so that half of the edge is inside the opening and half overlaps the outside. This type of door is difficult to use with frameless cabinetry; it is usually applied to a cabinet that has a face frame (8–20). It offers the same ease of fitting as the overlay door, but it does not project as far from the front. Since the entire edge doesn't show, as it does with the overlay door, it is not always necessary to cover the edge of the plywood.

8–20. Lipped doors work best when used with a face frame. They can give the cabinet an old-fashioned look.

You can leave the edge square or you can round it. You can do the rounding with a shaper or router. This type of door was used extensively on kitchen cabinets in the mid-twentieth century. Many of these cabinets were built on-site by the finish carpenter. A lot of these old-time cabinetmakers rounded the edges by beveling the edge with a jointer or hand plane, rounding it with coarse sandpaper, and then smoothing it with finer grades of sandpaper. You could use the same technique when you want to duplicate the look of these old cabinets.

When two lipped doors meet without a stile between them, they are usually given a 2-degree bevel. Another method involves making a rabbet on one door and cutting a tongue on the other door to project into the rabbet. If you use this method, the doors won't work independently; you must always open the door with the tongue last and close it first.

The hinges used with lipped doors are made to fit into the rabbet. Buy the hinges before you cut the rabbet so that you can cut the rabbet to fit the hinge.

Flush Doors

A flush door fits inside of the face frame of the cabinet, and the door front is flush with the stiles and rails that surround the door (8–21). The flush door is the most difficult type to fit because a gap shows all around the door. To look good, the gap must be even. To keep the gap as small as possible, you should bevel the edges of the door about 2 degrees to the inside. This allows the door to fit tightly and still

8–21. This cabinet uses flush doors with butt hinges.

open. If the edges are square, you will need a larger gap for the rear corner to clear as the door opens.

A flush door is usually attached with butt hinges. You need to set the hinges into cutouts, called gains. Cut the gains with a chisel or a router. In some cases, a decorative type of hinge, such as a butterfly hinge, is face-mounted. Hinge placement is not too critical; the hinges should be a short distance away from the top and bottom. For a shortcut, some professionals use the hinge itself as the measuring tool. Place the hinge so that it is touching the top or bottom edge, and make a mark at the other end of the hinge. Now position the hinge so that its top is on the mark. This method seems to provide a visually pleasing amount of space for a hinge of any size, and it ensures that all of the hinges will be equally spaced.

A flush door requires some type of stop to prevent it from being pushed too far into the cabinet. On small doors, it may be sufficient to simply allow the door to hit the inside shelves, or a door catch may be all that is necessary. However, larger doors need a stop applied to the inside of the stile to keep the door in position.

Sliding Doors

SLIDING DOORS ARE ALSO CALLED *bypass* doors. You can open them without having the door project out from the cabinet, which can be an advantage when you want to leave the door open for some time; however, only one side can be open at a time, which can be a disadvantage. Sliding doors are good when you want a door directly behind a counter, because the doors won't interfere with items on the counter (**8–22**). Sliding cabinet doors are usually made from ¼-inch plywood, hardboard, or glass, but ½-inch plywood doors are also used. The doors should be slightly wider than one-half of the opening so that there will still be about a 1-inch overlap when the doors are closed.

There are several types of commercial track available to accommodate different-size doors and different degrees of usage. For light usage, a *plastic track* works well. Heavy use requires a *metal track with ball-bearing rollers*. Metal ball-bearing tracks can also be used with sliding glass doors in display cabinets (**8–23**).

You can easily make your own wooden tracks for sliding doors that will receive moderate use. One way involves cutting two parallel grooves with a router or dado blade. The grooves should be slightly wider than the doors so that they won't bind. Make the top grooves deeper than the bottom grooves so that you can install and remove the doors after assembling the cabinet. Cut the doors so that when the top of the door is pushed all the way into the top groove, the bottom of the door will just clear the top of the bottom track. When the door is in place, it will come partway out of

8–22. You can open these sliding doors without interfering with items on the countertop.

8–23. Metal ball-bearing tracks can be used with sliding glass doors in display cabinets.

the top track; however, since the bottom track is not as deep, it will not come all the way out.

The grooves can't be much closer together than ¼ inch; otherwise, the strip of wood separating them will be too weak. This results in a gap between the two doors. You can eliminate the gap by using ½-inch doors and cutting a ¼-inch rabbet along the top and bottom of the back. The lip that is formed will fit in the ¼-inch groove, and the rabbeted-out section will straddle the strip of wood between the two doors.

Tambour Doors

The type of door used in a roll-top desk is called a *tambour door.* It can be used vertically or horizontally. A tambour door is composed of many small strips that are hinged together with a canvas or plastic backing. The tambour door rides in a track as does a bypass door, but the track curves so that the door opens all the way and is stored inside the cabinet (**8–24**).

Although some tambour doors are made from strips that have overlapping rabbets and tongues, most are simply made from flat strips

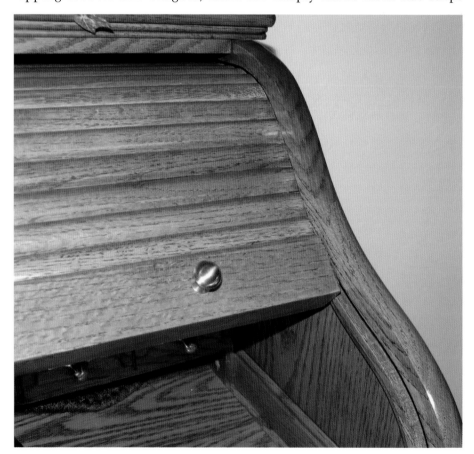

8–24. Tambour doors are also called a roll top, because they are associated with roll top desks. However they are well suited to built-in applications as well as freestanding cabinets.

with slightly rounded edges. If the strips have overlapping joints, the tongue must be very short and the rabbet must have plenty of clearance for the door to bend correctly. Factory-made tambours may have a plastic backing, but most shop-made tambours still use canvas for the backing (8–25).

The strips are generally ¾ inch wide and ¼ inch thick. This size enables you to rip them from a ¾-inch-thick board. Set the rip fence to make a ¼-inch cut. If you have a jointer, joint the edge of the board after each cut so that you have a good face for the strip. It is also easier to round the edges before cutting

8–25. Tambour doors usually have a canvas backing glued to the strips.

off the strip. Keep ripping strips from the edge of the board until you have enough to make the tambour. If you number the strips consecutively as they come off the saw, you can assemble the tambour so that the grain matches closely.

You make the pull strip from a thicker piece of wood. Cut rabbets on the ends to fit into the track. You can use a router to cut finger pulls in the strip, or you can attach knobs or pulls to the pull strip.

Lay the strips in position face down on a piece of scrap plywood. Place the pull strip at the edge of the plywood so that it is level with the rest of the strips. Nail some scrap strips to the bench around all four sides of the door to hold the strips in position. Apply contact cement to the back of the strips and to a piece of canvas slightly larger than the door. When the cement is dry, apply the canvas to the back of the strips. With a sharp knife, trim the canvas to fit the door.

You can cut the track directly into the side of the cabinets with a router. You must do this before assembling the cabinet. Make a template out of ¼-inch hardboard and clamp it to the side. Use a template-following collar on the router.

You can determine the proper radius for the corners by bending the completed door around different curves until you find one that works best. The width of the individual slats in the tambour determines the minimum corner radius. To make a sharp bend, the track groove needs to be wider than is necessary for straight parts of the track. You can widen the track at a sharp bend by slightly repositioning the template and

8–26. You can purchase a commercial tambour door and track. The track is made of plastic and is attached to the side of the cabinet. A roller mechanism that fits at the top of the track rolls up the tambour the way a window shade rolls up.

taking a second pass over the curved sections of the track. This is better than cutting the entire track wide because it avoids a loose fit in the straight parts of the track.

Depending on the size of the opening, the tambour may fit entirely in the side of the cabinet or the track may have to extend around the back of the cabinet to fit the open door. False sides and a false back are sometimes used to hide the tambour when it is open. Unlike the tracks for bypass doors, both tracks should be of equal depth. You must install the door during assembly.

Another way to install a tambour door involves an applied track. You can use this method to install a tambour door in a cabinet that has already been assembled. Purchase a commercial tambour door and track. The track is made of plastic and is attached to the side of the cabinet. A roller mechanism that fits at the top of the track rolls up the tambour the way a window shade rolls up (**8–26**).

Door Hardware

CABINET DOORS NEED SOME TYPE of hardware to enable them to function. Pulls, hinges, catches, and locks are all types of door hardware

Door pulls are available in a wide range of styles, but they can be divided into three general categories: knobs, *surface-screw pulls,* and *rear-screw pulls*. Knobs used for cabinets are usually small and attach with a machine screw through a hole in the door from the rear, or the knob has a threaded shaft that screws directly into the face of the door (**8–27**).

Surface-screw pulls use wood screws to attach the pull from the face side. They are often used for rustic or period cabinets (**8–28**). Probably the most widely used type is the rear-screw pull; it mounts with two machine screws that come from the rear of the door through holes drilled in the door. The screws are concealed with the doors closed (**8–29**). Carved, wooden pulls are popular for both modern and traditional cabinets. They usually are

8–27. Knobs used for cabinets are usually small and attach with a machine screw through a hole in the door from the rear, or the knob has a threaded shaft that screws directly into the face of the door.

8–28. Surface-screw pulls use wood screws to attach the pull from the face side. They are often used for rustic or period cabinets.

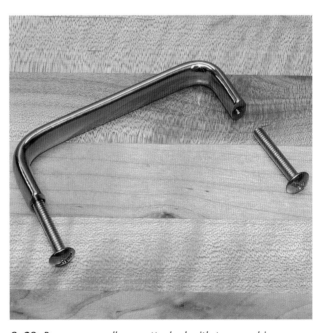

8–29. Rear-screw pulls are attached with two machine screws that come from the rear of the door through holes drilled in the door.

8–30. Carved, wooden pulls are popular for both modern and traditional cabinets. They usually are attached with screws from the rear.

attached with screws from the rear (8–30). Many styles of carved pulls are available commercially, or you can make custom pulls of your own design. A router is very useful when you are making your own pulls.

There is no standard for the placement of door pulls; a lot depends on the size and style of the pull. It is common practice to place pulls near the top on low doors and near the bottom on high doors; however, in some instances, the pulls are placed in the middle in both cases. A common placement would be 1½ inches in from the edge and 2 inches from the top or bottom.

The type of hinge you use largely determines the function of the cabinet doors, so carefully choosing the correct hinge is an important part of applying cabinet doors.

When using full overlay doors, European-type hinges work well. They are available for both frameless cabinets and those with face frames (8–31). When the door is closed, the hinges are completely concealed. The hinges incorporate a self-closing mechanism that eliminates the need for separate door catches.

This type of hinge requires a 35-mm hole drilled partway through the back of the door. You can buy a special bit for this purpose from the place you buy the hinges (8–32). The hinge attaches to the side of the cabinet with a separate base plate. The base plate has elongated holes that allow you to adjust the door position after the hinges are installed (8–33). This is a good feature

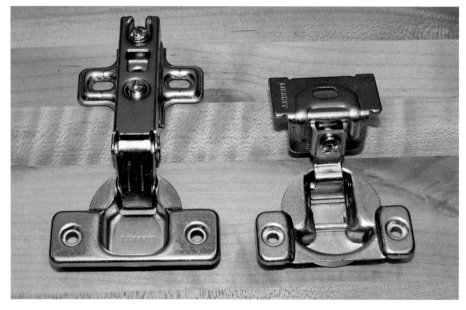

8–31. European type hinges are available for both frameless cabinets (left) and those with face frames (right).

8-32. European-type hinges require a 35-mm hole drilled partway through the back of the door. You can buy a special bit for this purpose from the place you buy the hinges. Some bits will also come with a marking template like the plastic one shown here.

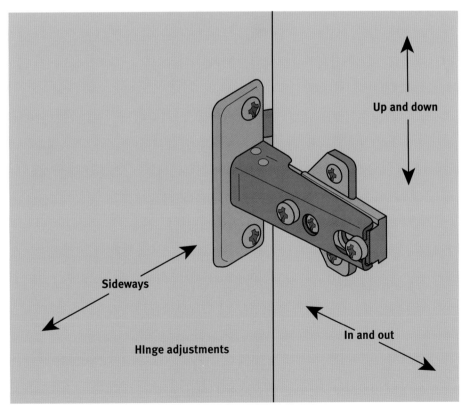

Up and down

Sideways

In and out

Hinge adjustments

8-33. This hinge can be adjusted in three directions, allowing you to align the doors after the hinges are installed.

when you have a row of doors on a built-in cabinet. After the cabinets are installed, you can adjust the hinges so that all of the doors line up.

Another type of hinge designed for overlay doors that are applied to face frames has the screws that mount to the stile exposed (**8–34**). This makes door alignment easier, since you can hold the doors in place in the closed position as you install the screws. Lipped-door hinges have a bent leaf that fits into the rabbet around the door (**8–35**). The butt hinge is the type usually used on flush doors (**8–36**). You can mount it on the face of flush doors or cut it into gains on the edge of the door.

Self-closing hinges have made door catches unnecessary in many cases; they have a built-in spring mechanism that holds the door closed. When installing self-closing hinges, it is usually necessary to allow more clearance on the opposite side of the door than usual; as you tighten the screws, the spring action of the hinge forces the door slightly away from the hinge side. If you don't allow for this, the doors will bind.

You must use catches if you don't use self-closing hinges. One type is the *roller catch*, which is referred to as a *friction catch* because it holds the door shut with the friction between a spring steel clip and the plastic rollers. The *bullet latch* is another type of friction catch. You install the bullet latch in a hole drilled in the side of a flush door. The small *spring-loaded latch* fits into a strike plate mounted on the side of the stile. The *magnetic catch* uses magnetism instead of friction to hold the door closed. A small, powerful magnet mounts on the cabinet, and a steel plate mounts on the door.

To position a catch, mount the magnet or roller on the stile or a shelf. Attach the other part of the catch to the magnet or roller in its proper position; then shut the door. Small points on the catch will make dents in the door where you should mount the catch.

There are several types of lock that you can apply to cabinet doors (**8–37**). One type requires a single hole through the door, and it is attached with two wood screws. This type of lock is designed to be used with flush doors. The bolt extends from the lock flush with the back of the door, and it will lock against a stile of the same thickness as the door. You can also use this type of lock on lipped doors or flush doors with a thicker stile if you cut a mortise into the stile for the bolt to enter. Whenever two doors meet without a stile between them, this is the type of lock to use. You mount the lock on one door, and you secure the other door with a barrel bolt inside. You can't use this type of lock with overlay doors unless the two doors meet and one is secured with a barrel bolt.

Another type of lock that you can use on doors is the *cam* lock. This type of lock requires a single hole through the door, and it is secured with a nut that threads onto the body of the lock. A washer with spurs that bite into the wood keeps the lock from rotating in the hole. This type works better on overlay and lipped doors, because it is available in several lengths, so you can get one that is long enough to reach behind the stile.

When traditional styling is more important than security, small *mortise* locks are used. The lock fits into a mortise cut in the back of the door. You cut a keyhole through the door and then place a small metal plate over the hole.

8–34. This type of hinge is designed for overlay doors that are applied to face frames. It has the screws that mount to the stile exposed. This makes door alignment easier since you can hold the doors in place in the closed position as you install the screws.

8–35. Lipped doors require special hinges that are bent to fit the rabbet cut around the door.

8–36. The butt hinge is the type usually used on flush doors. You can mount it on the face of flush doors or cut it into gains on the edge of the door.

8–37. You can add a lock to a cabinet door when it is necessary to secure the cabinet.

(9) Drawers

Since Drawers Have a Reputation for being very difficult to build because of the many complex joints used in fine drawer construction, many beginning cabinetmakers are often reluctant to tackle them. But strong, good-looking drawers can actually be built quite simply. Intricate drawer construction has always been a source of pride among master cabinetmakers, and the drawers are beautiful and will last for centuries. However, for many applications, much simpler construction practices will suffice. Later in this chapter, I will cover some of the more complex types of drawer construction, but first I will show you how to make some simple yet functional drawers.

Drawers are classified by the way they fit into the cabinet. As with cabinet doors, the drawer front can be *overlay*, *lipped*, or *flush*. In most cases, you will use the same style as the cabinet doors.

Overlay drawers have a front that is larger than the drawer opening, and the full thickness of the front overlays the face of the cabinet (9–1). They are the simplest type to make and fit, and they work well with frameless construction. Lipped drawer fronts are also larger than the drawer opening, but a rabbet cut around the perimeter of the drawer reduces the thickness of the exposed edge that overlays the cabinet face (9–2). The edge of the lip may be left square, shaped, or rounded. The front of a flush drawer is slightly smaller than the opening in the cabinet, and the

9–1. Overlay drawers have a front that is larger than the drawer opening and the full thickness of the front overlays the face of the cabinet.

9–3. *The front of a flush drawer is slightly smaller than the opening in the cabinet, and the front fits flush into the opening.*

9–2. *Lipped drawer fronts have a rabbet cut around their perimeter that reduces the thickness of the exposed edge that overlays the cabinet face.*

front fits flush into the opening (9–3). They have a traditional look, but they are more difficult to fit because the gap around the drawer is visible.

Drawer fronts are usually made from ¾-inch-thick material, whereas the sides and back are generally made of ½- or ⅜-inch material. The sides are thinner to give the maximum amount of space inside the drawer and to save weight, but there's nothing wrong with using ¾-inch-thick material for the sides and back.

Drawer Hardware

THERE ARE MANY TYPES of commercial drawer pull that are similar to the door pulls described in chapter 8. Sometimes the drawer pull is incorporated into the design of the drawer front, and a commercial pull is not used. The simplest way is to cut the bottom edge of an overlay front at a 45-degree angle. This provides a fingerhold all along the bottom of the drawer.

A slightly better grip is provided if you use a router or shaper to cut a cove along the bottom. You can also use this method with flush drawers if you cut a cove along the top of the rail between drawers. This makes a space that allows you to get your fingers into the cove along the bottom of the drawer.

Most modern cabinets use some type of commercial roller guide. Several types of commercial drawer slide are available. The most popular type is the *side-hung* type; the slides are made of metal and incorporate ball-bearing rollers (9–4). This type is very strong and will support the most weight of any type of drawer slide. It also allows the drawer to be extended to the full length of travel without tipping. The drawer must be smaller than the opening to allow for this type of slide. Usually ½-inch clearance is needed on each side of the drawer, but check the instructions that come with the drawer slide for specific measurements. Using this type of slide can simplify the cabinet construction considerably. There is no need for

9–4. Side-hung drawer slides are made of metal and incorporate ball-bearing rollers; they will support the most weight of any type of drawer slide.

any type of frame or divider between drawers. When you use overlay fronts, you don't even need a rail between the drawers.

The *center slide* is another type of commercial drawer slide. This type is less expensive than the side-hung type, but it is not as strong and it requires a front rail between drawers. The slide consists of a steel channel, which fits between the front rail and the back of the cabinet, and a roller, which fits into the channel and attaches to the back of the drawer. The sides of the drawer rest on the front rail; sometimes a roller or a plastic glide is supplied to attach to the front rail for the sides to ride on.

False-Front Drawers

A SIMPLE WAY TO MAKE a drawer is to construct the drawer box; then, using screws driven in from the rear, attach a false front that is wider than the box (9–5). The extra width of the front allows clearance for metal side-hung drawer slides. This type of construction is used widely in commercial built-in cabinets. It allows the drawers to be mass-produced without individual fitting, and the fronts can be adjusted to compensate for slight errors in drawer alignment. The fronts are usually of the overlay type, but they can be made lipped or flush also.

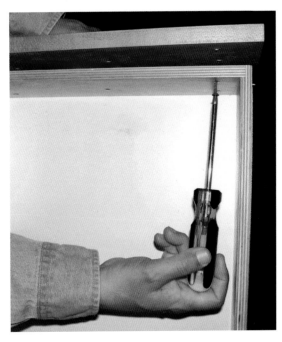

9–5. This type of drawer has a false front that is attached to the drawer box with screws driven in from the rear.

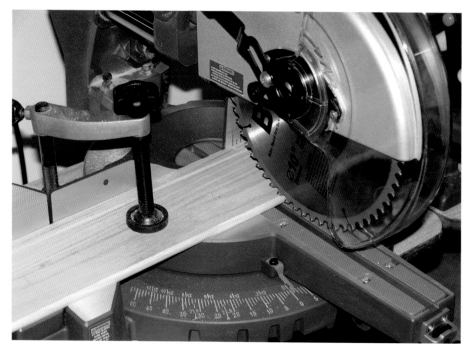

9–6. *Premanufactured drawer sides reduce the time involved in making large numbers of drawers. They come in several standard widths, and the groove for the bottom is precut. Simply cut the parts to length and assemble the drawer.*

The front should be made of the same material as the outside of the cabinet. The sides and ends of the drawer box are usually made of a different material. In the highest-quality cabinets, solid oak or another hardwood is sometimes used for drawers, but in most cases today plywood and particleboard are predominately used for drawer construction.

Premanufactured drawer sides are available that cut down the time involved in making large numbers of drawers. They come in several standard widths, and the groove for the bottom is precut. The tops are rounded and in some cases prefinished.

Manufactured sides made of hardwood are available from some mail-order woodworking-supply companies. Another type of manufactured drawer side is made of a fiberboard that is similar to hardboard; the surface is covered with an imitation wood grain (9–6). Commercial shops use this material extensively, but it is not widely available to the general public. If you will be building a lot of drawers and would like to use this material, contact a cabinet shop in your area and they may sell you some of their stock.

The drawer bottom is usually made of ¼-inch-thick material. Vinyl- or melamine-covered particleboard is the usual choice. For very high-quality work, use a hardwood-veneer plywood. Another good choice is ¼-inch hardboard. You can also use ½-inch-thick material, if you choose the European assembly screw option.

Dowel or Biscuit Construction

ILLUSTRATION 9–7 SHOWS A SIMPLE yet strong drawer design that uses dowel or biscuit joints. This design is especially well suited to plywood and particleboard, because these materials don't work well with the more intricate type of drawer joints. The drawer box described here is made from ½-inch-thick plywood or particleboard. The bottom is made from ¼-inch-hardboard or melamine-covered particleboard. Make the overlay front from the same material that you use for the doors.

You can cut the groove for the bottom with a dado blade on the table saw, or you can use a router. You can mount the router in a router table to cut the groove (9–8). The router table is a good choice for drawer construction, because it can handle the small parts of a drawer better than other methods.

You can also use a fence or a clamp-on aluminum guide to guide the router. If you use a clamp-on aluminum guide, it will be easier if you cut the groove for the bottom before you cut the box

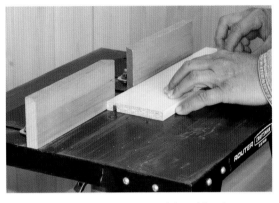

9–8. *A router table is a very useful tool for drawer construction. You can use it for making the groove for the bottom as shown here or rabbets, dadoes, and dovetail dadoes described later.*

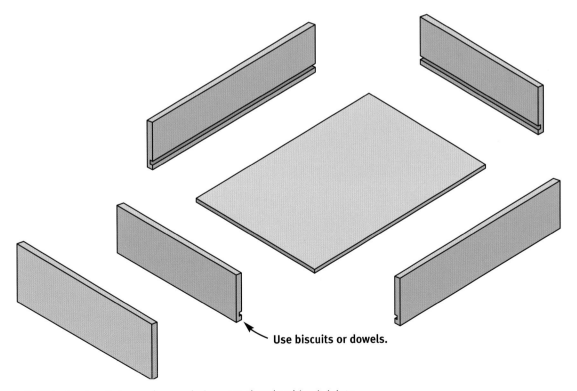

Use biscuits or dowels.

9–7. This simple yet strong drawer design uses dowel or biscuit joints.

parts from the larger sheet. If you wait until after the parts are cut to size, there won't be enough room for you to clamp the router guide. Cut the groove all along the length of the sheet to make several drawers. The groove should be ¼ inch deep and ⅜ inch up from the bottom edge of the drawer sides.

Cut off a strip from the sheet that is the width needed for the drawer sides and back, and then cut the parts to length. The length of the sides is determined by the length of the drawer slide. Measure the distance inside the cabinet from the back to the front; then choose a standard slide size that is smaller than this measurement.

When determining the width of the drawer, consider the thickness of the sides and the clearance needed for the drawer slides. Most drawer slides will need some clearance on each side of the drawer. Measure the distance from the inside edge of one side of the cabinet to the other inside edge. For example, if the drawer slides require ½-inch clearance and you are using ½-inch-thick material for the drawer sides, you would make the front and back parts of the drawer box two inches smaller than interior measurement of the drawer opening. The 2-inch space allows for two ½-inch-thick sides and two ½-inch-thick drawer slides.

Cut the drawer bottom from ¼-inch-thick material. The width of the drawer bottom is equal to the length of the end board plus ½ inch. The length of the drawer bottom is equal to the length of the side board minus ½ inch.

Cut the overlay front from ¾-inch-thick material that matches the outside of the cabinet. The front overhangs the sides. Measure the distance between the outside edges of the cabinet to get the length of the overlay front.

Make a trial assembly of all the parts. Number both sides of each joint for later reference when you make the joints.

Next, make the joints; you can use either biscuit joints or dowel joints. If you choose to use biscuit joints, use the medium-size #10 biscuits. For small drawers less than 4 inches high, use two biscuits per joint. On larger drawers, space the biscuits 64 mm on center all along the joint (9–9).

If you choose dowel joints, use dowels that are ¼ inch in diameter and 1⅛ inches long to assemble the drawers. Position the top dowel 16 mm down from the edge. The bottom one should be 16 mm up from the top of the groove. For small drawers

9–9. Using a plate joiner to make drawer joints.

less than 4 inches high, space the rest of the dowels 32 mm apart. On larger drawers, space the dowels 64 mm apart all along the joint.

Place the drawer parts in the dowelling jig, and line up the ¼-inch hole with the layout mark (**9–10**). Clamp the dowelling jig in place. Set a depth stop on the drill bit to make a hole that is ⅞ inch deep. Drill the holes in the ends; then change the depth setting to ⅜ inch before you drill the holes in the sides. You can slip a piece of plastic or copper tubing over the drill, as described in chapter 6, to change the depth setting. Repeat the procedure on to the opposite end of the board.

9–10. Using a dowelling jig to make drawer joints.

Begin assembly by applying a bead of glue on the joints on the side boards. Drip some glue into each biscuit slot or dowel hole until each hole is approximately one-third full. Using a sliver of wood, spread the glue around inside the holes. The ½-inch sides may split if you drive the dowel in without first spreading the glue. Insert the biscuits or dowels into the side, and drive the dowels all the way in, using a hammer.

Next, apply glue to the mating board. Drip glue into the biscuit slots or dowel holes until they are one-third full of glue, and spread the glue around. Assemble the joint and drive the joint tight with a hammer. Use a scrap of wood against the side to keep the hammer from marking the side. Put glue into the grooves for the bottom piece. Insert the bottom into the grooves (**9–11**). Then assemble the joints to attach the other side. Put glue into the groove for the bottom piece before putting the side in place.

After assembly, measure the diagonals of the drawer to check its squareness (**9–12**). Square it quickly before the glue has a chance to set. If necessary,

9–11. The drawer bottom fits in a groove.

9–12. After assembly, measure the diagonals of the drawer to check its squareness.

clamp diagonally from corner to corner to align the drawer so that it is square. Apply clamps to the drawer to hold the joints tight as they dry. Leave the clamps in place for at least one hour.

European Assembly Screws

DRAWERS CAN BE ASSEMBLED using European assembly screws (**9–13**). In this case, no glue is needed. The screws in the side will show, so you should cap them with plastic caps. In this type of drawer, the bottom is made from ½-inch-thick material and is attached with screws. The edges of the bottom will be visible along the side of the drawer, but you can hide them with the drawer slide if you use a bottom-mounting type of slide (**9–14**).

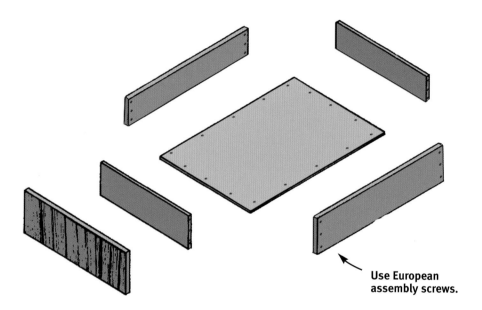

Use European assembly screws.

9–13. This plan shows how drawers can be assembled using European assembly screws.

9–14. You can hide edges of the bottom with a bottom-mounting type of drawer slide.

Traditional Drawer Designs

ALTHOUGH THE DRAWERS described above are strong and functional, when building fine cabinets or reproductions of antiques you may want to use more traditional joinery (**9–15**). The instructions below give you several options using traditional joinery, beginning with simple rabbet and dado joints. As you progress to more advanced projects, you may want to try some of the traditional drawer joints used in fine cabinetmaking. You should only use these joints when the drawer components are made of a solid hardwood such as oak. If you try to use dovetails or locked joints with

9–15. When building fine cabinets or reproductions of antiques, you may want to use more traditional drawer joinery.

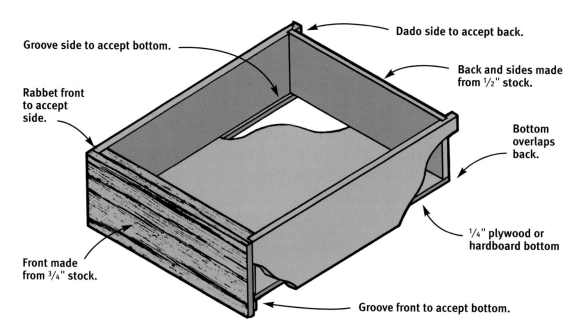

Groove side to accept bottom.

Dado side to accept back.

Back and sides made from ½" stock.

Rabbet front to accept side.

Bottom overlaps back.

Front made from ¾" stock.

¼" plywood or hardboard bottom

Groove front to accept bottom.

9–16. This simple type of drawer construction uses rabbet and dado joints.

plywood or particleboard, the small projections will crumble off, leaving a very weak joint. You can use dovetails with softwood, such as pine, but the dovetails should be coarser than the ones used in hardwoods. (See chapter 4.)

Illustration 9–16 shows an easy way to make a flush drawer that uses rabbet and dado joints. The first step in constructing this type of drawer is to measure the opening. Even if you are going to make several drawers the same way, it's a good idea to measure all of the openings and custom-fit each drawer. Cut all the parts to rough size, and then cut the groove for the bottom in the front and sides. Round off the top corners of the sides with a block plane, router, or shaper.

Notice that the back is not as wide as the sides; it stops at the top of the groove, so no groove is cut in the back. Leave ½ inch between the bottom of the groove and the bottom of the sides so that there will be plenty of support for the bottom of the drawer. This groove will carry all of the weight of the drawer's contents. The depth of the groove should be approximately one-half the thickness of the side; therefore, for a ½-inch side, the groove would be ¼ inch deep. Cut the groove wide enough for the bottom to slide in it without being too loose.

This type of drawer fits flush inside the drawer opening, so the next step is to make sure that the front fits the opening; then cut the rabbets in the ends of the front. A router mounted in a router table is a good tool for making drawer joints. Next, cut the dadoes for the back in the sides. Leave at least ½ inch between the dado and the rear of the side. Now cut the back to length and begin assembly. Since a drawer is submitted to a lot of stress as you open and close it, you need to reinforce the joints. You can use nails, screws, and dowels for this type of drawer construction. The fasteners are driven through the side into the front and back. The joints between the front and back and the sides are all glued, but the bottom is not glued. You should cut the bottom to fit snugly in the groove. The bottom overhangs the back and should be flush with the ends of the sides.

It is very important for the drawer to be square. Place the drawer bottom up on the bench with the front facing you. Place a

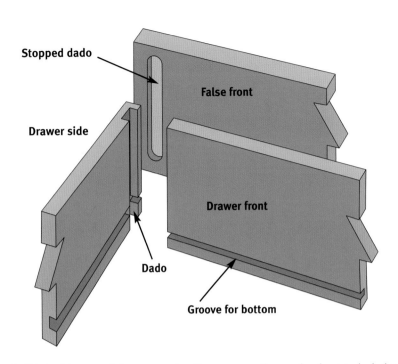

9–17. *In this type of drawer construction, you use the overlay front to lock the dadoes on the sides. You use a router to cut the stopped dado in the front.*

square in the corner formed between the front and one side. Place your hands on the back of the drawer and pull the drawer against your body. In this position, you can easily twist the drawer until it is square. When the drawer is square, make sure that the bottom is tight against the front and then nail it in place along the back. Use box nails, because their heads will hold better than the heads on finish nails. Space the nails approximately 2 inches apart.

High-quality drawers should have a groove for the bottom cut in the back. This makes the bottom stronger but also more difficult to assemble and square. The bottom must fit snugly in all four grooves or it won't be able to hold the drawer square.

You can use the same basic construction to make a lipped drawer. A lipped drawer is easier to fit, because the drawer front overhangs the drawer opening, hiding the gap around the drawer. The drawer is made in exactly the same way, except the front is larger than the opening. A ⅜-inch lip on all sides is usual. Cut a ⅜-inch-wide rabbet along the top and bottom of the front, and make the rabbet for the sides ⅜ inch wider than the side so that the sides will be recessed in from the sides of the front. The front edges can be rounded, as described for lipped doors in chapter 8, or left square, depending on the style of the cabinet.

A variation on this type of construction is shown in **9–17**. The joint between the front and the sides is a dado set in ½ inch from the end, the

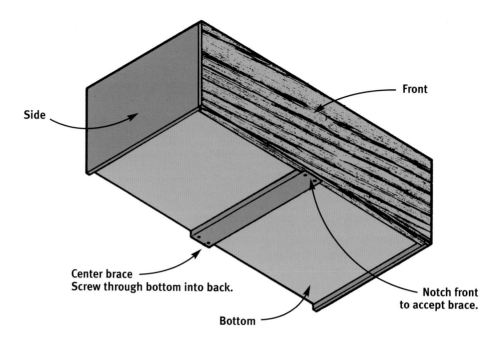

Side

Front

Center brace
Screw through bottom into back.

Notch front
to accept brace.

Bottom

9–18. Wide drawers require a center brace to support the bottom.

same way as the back joint. The ends of the sides fit into stopped dadoes in the false front. This is a very strong type of construction, because once the false front is screwed in place, the sides are locked. The extra strength provided by the dadoes helps to resist the stresses placed on the front joints during heavy use.

This type of drawer is easy to make if you have a router, and it adapts well to mass production. You can use the same dado setup for both the front and back joints, and since the sides are reversible, you don't need to worry about making the correct amount of right and left sides. Make the stopped dado in the false front with a router. If you are making a number of drawers, make a template that will guide the router and position the dado.

Very wide drawers, like those commonly found in a chest of drawers, require a center brace that helps support the bottom. To install the brace, cut a notch in the middle of the front, as shown in **9–18**. The brace should be as thick as the distance between the drawer bottom and the bottom of the sides so that it will be flush with the sides. Screw the brace in place after installing the bottom. The screws should go through the bottom and into the front and back.

The dovetail is the traditional favorite for drawer construction. Except in cases where the joinery forms a decorative part of the cabinet, half-blind dovetails are used so that they won't show from the front. An exception to this is when you use overlay false fronts. When this is the case, open dovetails can be used and hidden by the false front. Router-cut dovetails are often used in drawer construction, but hand-cut dovetails are still the mark of the highest-quality construction. Making dovetails is discussed in detail in chapter 4.

Most drawer dovetails are made with a router jig (**9–19**). The dovetail jig can be set to make three types of drawer fronts (**9–20**). The flush joint is used when the drawer front is flush with the cabinet and no side clearance is needed for drawer slides. The small lip is used when more side clearance is needed, but the drawer front will be flush with the cabinet. The full-lipped type allows side clearance for drawer slides or it can be used for a lipped overlay.

9–19. Here, you can see a half-blind dovetail joint still in the router dovetail jig after being cut. There is also an assembled dovetail joint sitting on top of the jig.

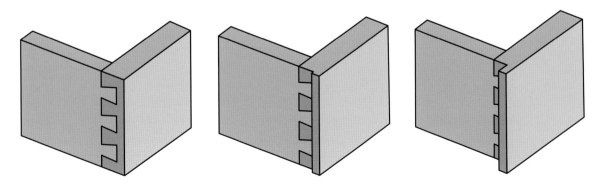

9–20. The dovetail jig can be set to make these three drawer fronts.

The tongue-and-lap locked joint is simpler to make than the dovetail, but it is not as strong. You can make this joint easily on a table saw. **Illustration 9–21** explains the procedure. This joint will be stronger if it is pegged with small dowels. You can also make this joint with a special router bit.

You can use a dovetailed dado joint (**9–22**) to attach the sides directly to an overlay front, with no need for a false front. Don't use this joint with pine, plywood, or particleboard. You cut the dado with a router and a dovetail bit. The dado must be open at the bottom of the front and stopped at the top. You can make the dovetail on the front end of the sides on the table saw. Set the tilt arbor to the same angle as the dovetail bit and cut the angles on both sides. Set the angle back to 90 degrees and lower the blade to make a square shoulder. You can also use this type of joint in place of the dado to join the back to the sides.

Another method of attaching the back involves using the tongue-and-dado joint (**9–23**). First, cut a rabbet on both ends of the back. The tongue formed should be one-half as long as the thickness of the sides. Next, cut a dado in the sides that will fit the tongue.

You can also attach the back with open or blind dovetails, in which case the sides do not overhang past the back.

Traditional Wooden Guides

WHEN YOU ARE MAKING TRADITIONALLY styled cabinets or antique reproductions, you may want to use wooden drawer guides. In its simplest form, a drawer guide is a shelf where the drawer rests. For very small drawers, such as the ones found in the small compartments of a roll-top desk, the drawer guide is usually just a thin shelf. When the sides of the cabinet are made of panel construction or from a dimensionally stable material such as plywood, the guides can be made of strips put together into open frames.

Use mortise-and-tenon, half-lap, or dowel joints to put the frames together. The best-quality construction also incorporates dust panels made of thin material such as ⅛-inch hardboard (**9–24**). The dust panel fits into a groove in the frame. Dust panels not only keep things from falling from one drawer opening into another, but they also help keep the drawer guides square and add rigidity to the entire carcass.

Flush drawers need some type of stop that will prevent them from being pushed too far back into the opening. Small blocks placed at the rear of the frame that will hit the ends of the drawer sides are the best form of stop. To use this method, the drawer needs to be made at least ¾ inch smaller than the depth of the opening. A great deal of pressure can be placed on the stop blocks when a drawer is shut, so attach them with glue and screws.

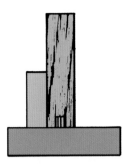
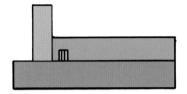
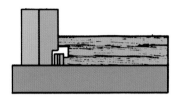

1. Cut $^1/_4$"-wide groove $^9/_{16}$" deep in middle of both edges of drawer front.

2. Cut $^1/_4$"-wide dado in drawer side $^1/_4$" deep. Set fence $^1/_4$" away from blade.

3. Attach auxiliary fence. Trim lower tongue to $^1/_4$" from inside groove.

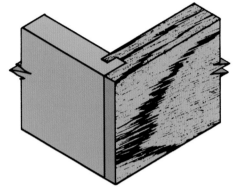
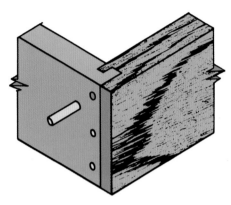

4. Assemble joint.

5. Add small dowels for extra strength.

9–21. The tongue-and-lap locked joint is stronger than a simple rabbet for connecting the sides to the front of a drawer.

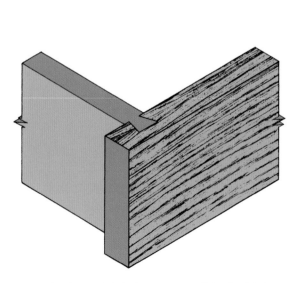
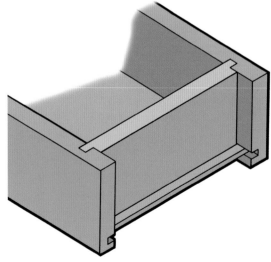

9–22. The dovetailed dado is a strong joint for joining an overlay drawer front directly to the sides.

9–23. The tongue-and-dado joint is sometimes used to attach the back of the drawer to the sides.

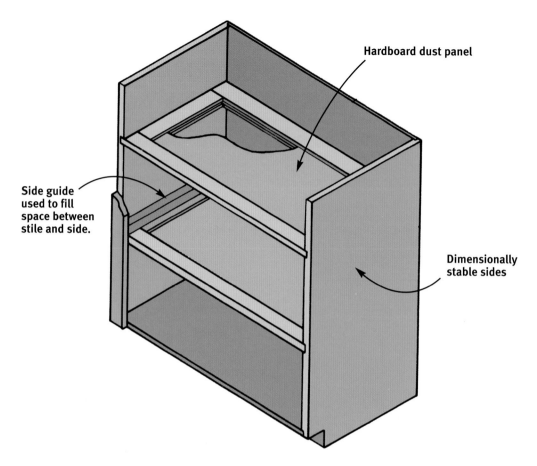

Hardboard dust panel

Side guide used to fill space between stile and side.

Dimensionally stable sides

9–24. You can use this type of frame and dust-panel drawer guide when you use dimensionally stable sides, such as sides made of plywood or particleboard, in case construction. You can also use it in panel-construction carcasses.

It is customary to let the front of a lipped or overlay drawer stop the drawer, but this is not a good practice, because when a fully loaded drawer is slammed shut, a tremendous stress is placed on the joint between the front and sides. So, even though the front will stop these drawers, a stop placed at the back will prolong the life of the drawer.

When the cabinet sides are made of solid wood, a different type of dust-panel construction is necessary to prevent cross-grain shrinkage and swelling from splitting the sides or loosening the joints. **Illustration 9–25** shows the proper way to construct the dust panel for use with solid wood. Instead of using a frame, you only use a ¾-inch-thick front rail. The dust panel is made of ⅜-inch-thick solid wood.

A ⅜-inch-thick strip, called a *kicker*, fills in the lower part of the dado below the dust panel. The kicker should extend past the side far enough for the top of the drawer below to ride against it. You should only glue the

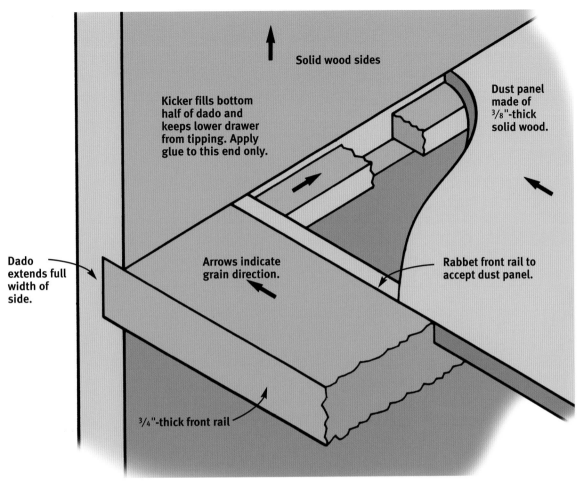

Solid wood sides

Kicker fills bottom half of dado and keeps lower drawer from tipping. Apply glue to this end only.

Dust panel made of ³⁄₈"-thick solid wood.

Dado extends full width of side.

Arrows indicate grain direction.

Rabbet front rail to accept dust panel.

³⁄₄"-thick front rail

9–25. When you use solid-wood sides, you should use this type of dust-panel construction. It allows for dimensional change in the sides.

kicker in place at the front in an area approximately 4 inches long. The rest of the kicker is left free to slide in the dado as the sides shrink and swell. Leave the kicker approximately ½ inch short of touching the back of the cabinet. If the kicker touches the back, it may push the back off as the sides shrink.

When the sides of the drawer are separated from the sides of the cabinet by a face frame, you need to add side guides to keep the drawer from twisting when you pull it open. You can use a center guide instead of side guides (9–26). A hardwood runner with a wide groove is attached to the middle of the bottom of the drawer, and a guide that fits into the groove is attached in the middle of the frame. When the drawers won't be carrying a lot of weight, you can use the center guide alone, without the frame. In this case, the center guide is attached to the front rail and the back of the cabinet.

For wide drawers, the frame type of guide is recommended; however, narrower drawers up to about 24 inches wide can be side-hung (**9–27**). Side-hung drawers have a cleat that rides in a groove. You can place the cleat on either the drawer or the cabinet. If you attach the cleat to the cabinet, then you cut a groove into the side of the drawer to fit the cleat. When you attach the cleat to the drawer, you make a dado in the side of the cabinet to fit the cleat.

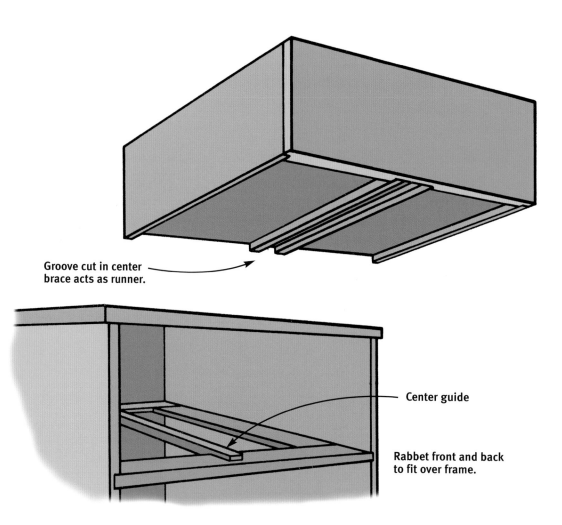

Groove cut in center brace acts as runner.

Center guide

Rabbet front and back to fit over frame.

9–26. The center guide is particularly useful for wide drawers, because it prevents binding caused by twisting the drawer as it opens.

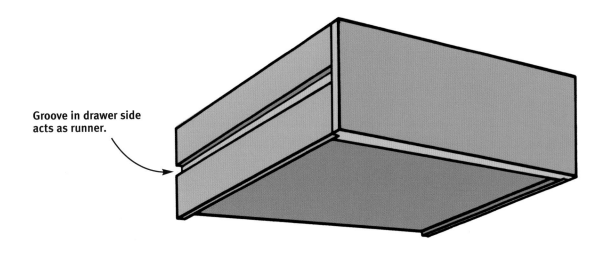

Groove in drawer side acts as runner.

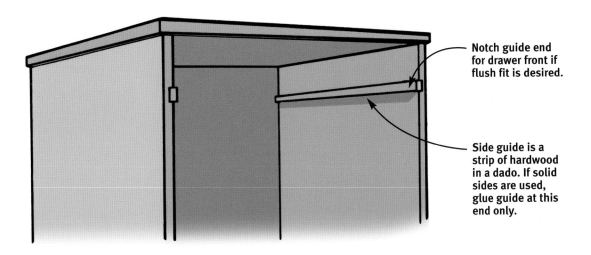

Notch guide end for drawer front if flush fit is desired.

Side guide is a strip of hardwood in a dado. If solid sides are used, glue guide at this end only.

9–27. Side guides are often used for smaller drawers.

⑩ Freestanding Modular Cabinets

NOW THAT YOU HAVE LEARNED all of the basic techniques of cabinetmaking, it is time to start making some projects. In this chapter I will show you a system of modular cabinet plans that can be used to make practically any type of freestanding cabinet you want. You can build anything, from a small bookcase to a china hutch, using the same construction (**10–1**). This system can also be used to build entertainment centers; however, some additional considerations are needed in order to accommodate the electronics that I will cover in the next chapter.

WITH THIS SYSTEM, large projects are made from smaller modules. By varying the size of the modules and the way you combine them, you can make many designs.

Three basic modules are used in this system of freestanding cabinets: the *base module*, the *shelf module*, and the *tall module*. The base module is designed to rest on the floor. It can be used alone to make a TV stand or a small bookcase. A base module can have doors, or you could add drawers to make a dresser or a night table (**10–2**). The shelf module is not designed to stand alone on the floor; it is used as the upper section of projects like a china hutch,

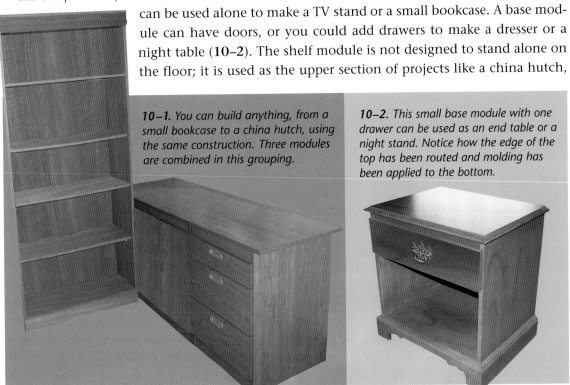

10–1. You can build anything, from a small bookcase to a china hutch, using the same construction. Three modules are combined in this grouping.

10–2. This small base module with one drawer can be used as an end table or a night stand. Notice how the edge of the top has been routed and molding has been applied to the bottom.

10–3. The shelf module is not designed to stand alone on the floor; it is used as the upper section of projects like a china hutch, a large bookcase, or an entertainment center.

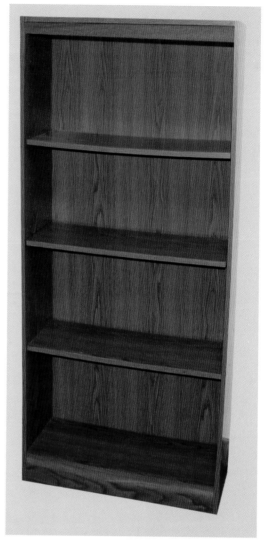

10–4. The tall module design is used when a module must be taller than 4 feet. It includes a fixed shelf in the center to add rigidity to the cabinet.

a large bookcase, or an entertainment center (**10–3**). The tall module design is used when a module must be taller than 4 feet. It includes a fixed shelf in the center to add rigidity to the cabinet (**10–4**). Modules can be placed side-by-side to make wide projects, or they can be used individually (**10–5**).

This system is designed to be used with both solid lumber and manufactured materials like plywood and particleboard. The only constraint is that you should not mix solid lumber and manufactured materials in the same project. There are three exceptions, however. The back can always be made of manufactured materials even if the rest of the cabinet is made of solid lumber. You can use small trim pieces of solid lumber in a cabinet that is otherwise made entirely of manufactured materials. And you can use a different material for the base top if you use slotted holes to attach it to the sub-top.

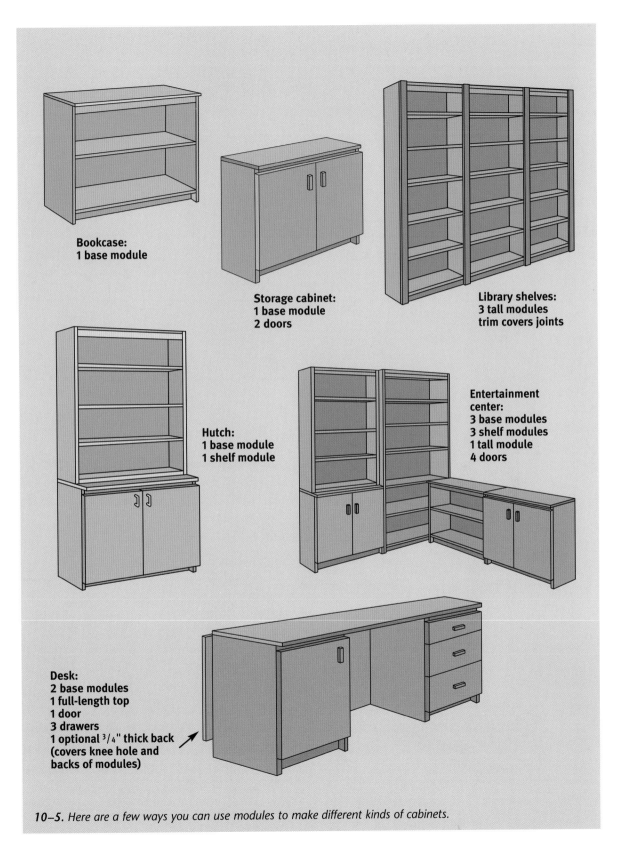

Bookcase:
1 base module

Storage cabinet:
1 base module
2 doors

Library shelves:
3 tall modules
trim covers joints

Hutch:
1 base module
1 shelf module

**Entertainment
center:**
3 base modules
3 shelf modules
1 tall module
4 doors

Desk:
2 base modules
1 full-length top
1 door
3 drawers
1 optional 3/4" thick back
(covers knee hole and
backs of modules)

10–5. Here are a few ways you can use modules to make different kinds of cabinets.

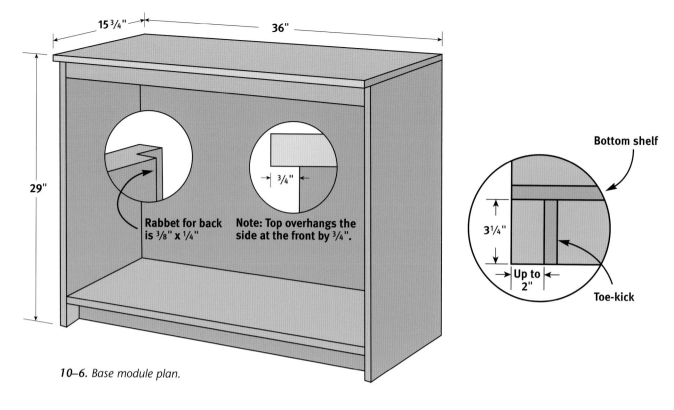

10–6. Base module plan.

Rabbet for back is ³/₈" x ¹/₄"

Note: Top overhangs the side at the front by ³/₄".

Bottom shelf

Toe-kick

The reason why you should not mix materials is that the solid lumber will shrink and swell more than manufactured materials. If you used solid lumber for the sides and plywood for the top and bottom, the sides may eventually split. Because the cabinet is designed to avoid cross-grain construction, you can safely use solid lumber as long as all of the parts are solid lumber.

Base Module

A BASE MODULE RESTS ON THE FLOOR. The height of a base module can be varied. The width of the module should not be greater than 36 inches. If you need a wider cabinet, build two modules and place them side-by-side. The modules that I show are 29 inches high, 15 inches deep, and up to 36 inches wide (**10–6**). This is a good size for many uses. If necessary you can make the cabinet deeper; 24 inches is a good size for desk components and cabinets for large pieces of electronic equipment.

The top is attached to cleats with screws from below. This allows you to combine several modules

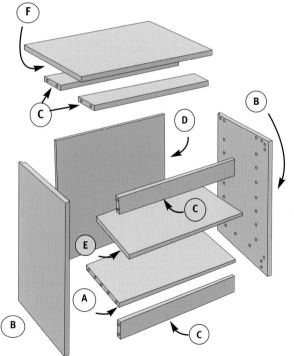

10–7. Base module (exploded view).

into a unit and attach a single top across all of the modules. A trim strip called an *apron* fills in the area below the top on the front of the cabinet (**10–7**). The plans show a 3¼-inch apron, but the size can be varied to suit your design. The apron can be as small as 1½ inches.

The bottom shelf is raised off the floor 4 inches. The space below the shelf is boxed in by a board called the toe-kick (**10–8**). The toe-kick can be recessed up to 2 inches, or it can be flush with the front. If the toe-kick is placed flush with the front, you can add a base molding that is attached with screws from the rear. Tack furniture glides (**10–9**) to the bottom of the sides; they will protect the floor, keep the bottom of the cabinet from getting chipped, and prevent rocking on an uneven floor.

10–9. Tack furniture glides to the bottom of the sides; they will protect the floor, keep the bottom of the cabinet from getting chipped, and prevent rocking on an uneven floor.

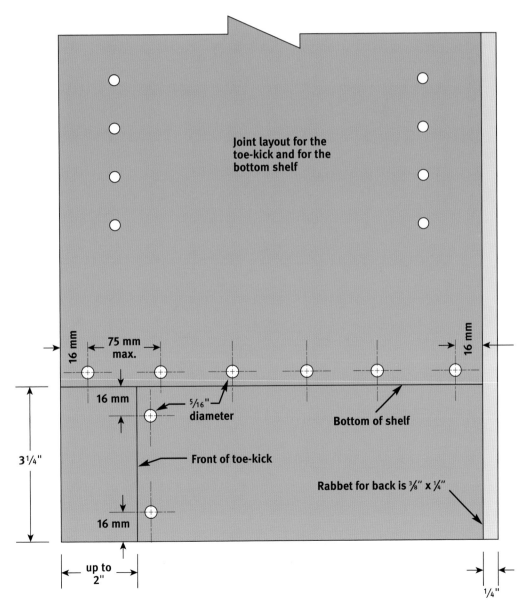

Joint layout for the toe-kick and for the bottom shelf

16 mm

75 mm max.

16 mm

16 mm

⁵⁄₁₆" diameter

Bottom of shelf

Front of toe-kick

Rabbet for back is ⅜" x ¼"

3¼"

16 mm

up to 2"

¼"

10–8. Joint layout for toe-kick area. The toe kick can be recessed up to 2 inches or it can be flush with the front. Dowel joints are shown here, but you can also use plate joinery.

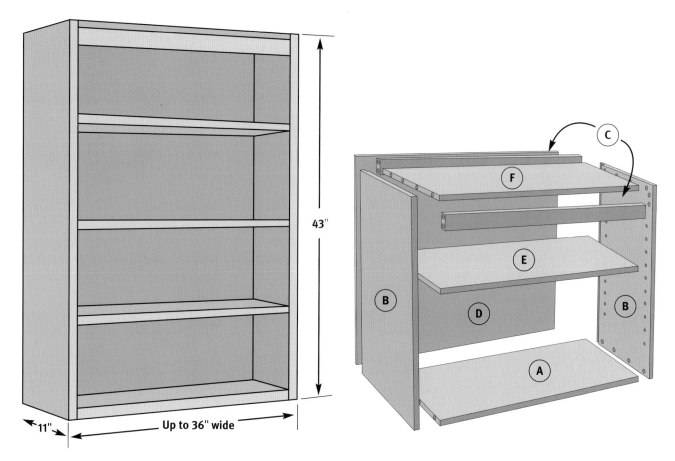

10–10. Shelf module plan.

10–11. Shelf module (exploded view).

Shelf Module

A SHELF MODULE can be attached atop a base module. The shelf can be the same width and depth as the base module, or you could make it smaller. The modules described here are 43 inches tall, 11 inches deep, and up to 36 inches wide (**10–10** and **10–11**).

After constructing both modules, place the shelf module atop the base module resting on the top. Use clamps to temporarily hold them together. Drive screws up through the cleats and top of the base module into the bottom of the shelf module (**10–12**).

The shelf module includes a stabilizing cleat. When the module is used atop a base module, this cleat is used to provide additional stability. A loaded tall cabinet can sometimes be top-heavy and become unstable. By driving screws through the cleat into wall studs, you can improve the stability.

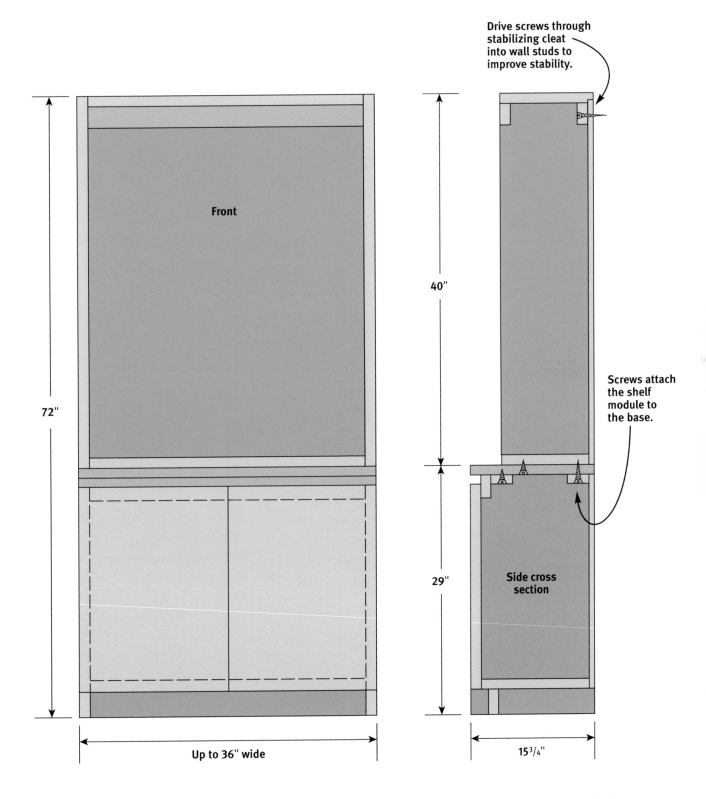

Front

72"

Up to 36" wide

Drive screws through stabilizing cleat into wall studs to improve stability.

40"

Screws attach the shelf module to the base.

29"

Side cross section

15³/₄"

10–12. A shelf module attached atop a base module makes a bookcase or hutch. Drive screws up through the top of the base module into the bottom of the shelf module.

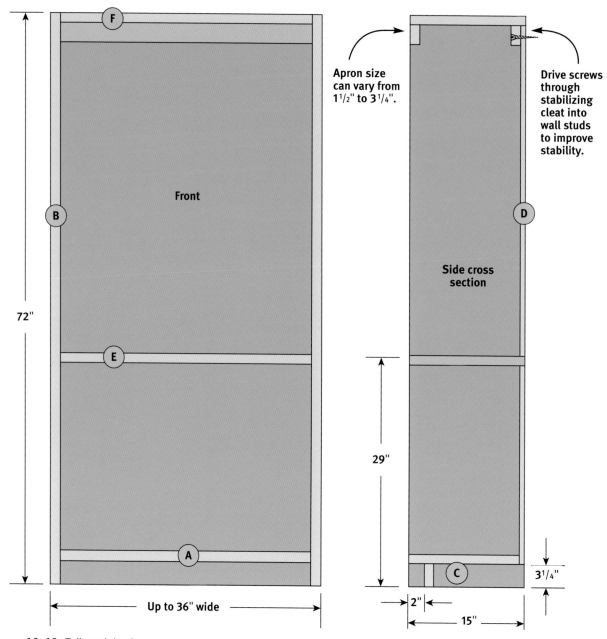

Apron size can vary from 1¹⁄₂" to 3¹⁄₄".

Drive screws through stabilizing cleat into wall studs to improve stability.

Front

Side cross section

72"

29"

Up to 36" wide

2"

15"

3¹⁄₄"

10–13. Tall module plan.

Tall Module

WHEN A MODULE THAT stands on the floor must be taller than four feet, it needs a fixed center shelf to add rigidity. The tall module described here is 72 inches tall, 11 inches deep, and up to 36 inches wide (**10–13**). This is a good size for a book shelf or shelf units used in an entertainment center. The bottom includes a toe-kick, and you should tack furniture glides to the bottom of the sides. The top includes a cleat, as with the shelf modules. Attach the cleat to wall studs with screws before loading the shelves.

Style Variations

THE BASIC MODULES PRODUCE the clean, simple lines of European-style cabinets. Slab doors and simple door pulls, as used on the cabinets shown in **10–1**, keep the lines simple. Adding different types of door and trim can transform the cabinet. Changing the style of the doors can have a dramatic effect on the style of the cabinet. One of the most effective ways to give the cabinet a traditional look is to use panel or glazed doors (**10–14**). Follow the instructions given in chapter 8 to build the doors.

Adding trim to the top and bottom of the cabinet can also help change the style. A cornice molding added to the top gives the cabinet a traditional look (**10–15**). The cornice is made from standard crown molding that's available at most lumberyards. Cut the cornice molding as described in chapter 6. Attach the cornice molding to the top of the cabinet, using screws driven from the back through the cabinet sides and the front apron (**10–16**).

The top apron and the toe-kick can also be used as a mounting for front trim pieces that will give the cabinet a different style. The trim pieces are as wide as the full width of the cabinet and attached with screws driven through the apron or toe-kick from the rear. If the trim has cutouts, you may need to reduce the size of the apron so that it won't show behind the cut outs.

10–14. Adding different types of door and trim can transform the cabinet. This cabinet is made from a base module and a shelf module. Panel doors on the base and glazed doors on the shelf module change the look dramatically. This cabinet also has a simple cornice added.

10–15. A cornice molding added to the top gives the cabinet a traditional look. This cornice is made from standard crown molding.

10–16. The apron can be used as an attachment point for a cornice or other trim; use screws driven from the back.

10–17. To create a "mission" look, add trim that has been cut in an arch shape.

To create a "mission" look, add trim that has been cut in an arch shape (**10–17**). For an Early-American-style cabinet, you can add some "gingerbread" to the top of the cabinet. A board with a fancy edge is called *gingerbread*. You could change the look of the cabinet depending upon the type of gingerbread you choose (**10–18**).

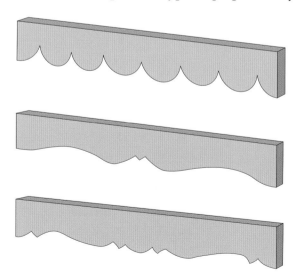

10–18. For an Early-American-style cabinet, you can add some "gingerbread" to the top of the cabinet.

Transfer the pattern to the board. The patterns shown in **10–19** are sized for a 36-inch-wide cabinet. Enlarge the pattern onto a piece of paper. Fold the paper in half, and draw the pattern so that the centerline is on the fold. Then cut out the design and unfold the paper. This will give you a full-length pattern. Each square on the drawing is equal to a 1-inch square on the full-size pattern. To enlarge the pattern, follow the directions given in chapter 2.

Use a jigsaw to cut the "gingerbread." Study the jigsaw's operating manual to find and follow complete directions. Make relief cuts (straight cuts in from the

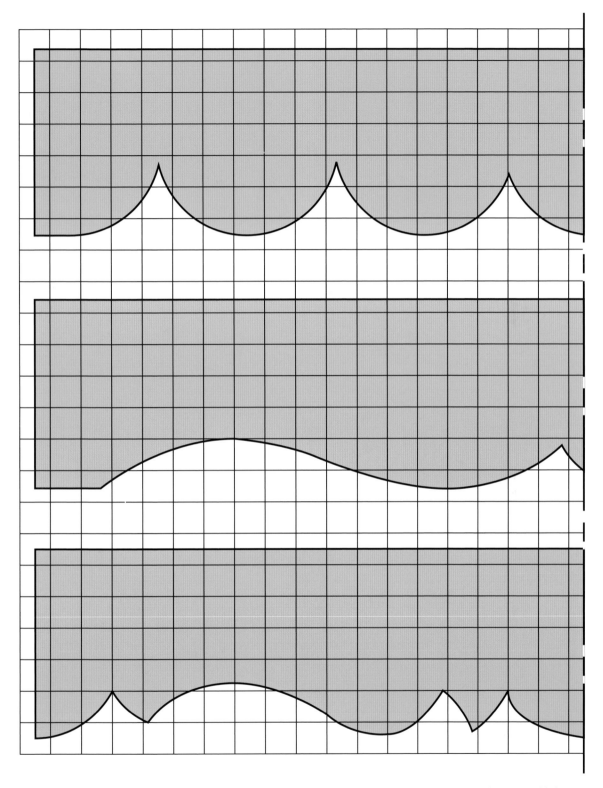

10–19. *These patterns are sized for a 36-inch-wide cabinet. Enlarge the pattern onto a piece of paper. Fold the paper in half, and draw the pattern so that the centerline is on the fold. Each square on the drawing is equal to a 1-inch-square on the full-size pattern.*

10–20. Use a jigsaw to cut the "gingerbread." Make relief cuts (straight cuts in from the edge of the board through the waste) for some of the tight angles. After making the relief cuts, follow the drawn line with the jigsaw.

10–21. To change the look of a base cabinet, you can cut out part of the sides to create the effect of legs.

edge of the board through the waste) for some of the tight angles. After making the relief cuts, follow the drawn line with the jigsaw (**10–20**).

To change the look of a base cabinet, you can attach molding to the bottom, as shown in **10–2**. You can also cut out part of the sides to create the effect of legs (**10–21**).

You can combine several modules together to create a single larger unit. Use screws through the sides to attach the modules (**10–22**). You can add face trim to hide the joint between modules. This is not a true face frame, but it gives the same look. Cut a strip of wood 1½ to 2 inches wide. Attach this to the front of the modules after they are assembled to hide the front edges of the sides (**10–23**).

Construction Techniques

YOU CAN USE ANY OF THE assembly methods described in previous chapters to build these modules, but I will focus on a few methods that work particularly well. Using dowel or biscuit joinery, you can build these modules with a minimum of tools. For a more traditional approach, you can use rabbets and dadoes. And if you want to show off your joinery skills, you can use exposed dovetails and mortise-and-tenon joints.

The modules can be built any width up to 36 inches. In the Bills of Materials, the length of parts that are dependent on the width of the cabinet is indicated by a "W." If necessary, there may also be an amount to subtract from the width to get the length of the part; for example, the length of the shelves may be listed as W–1½ inches. In this case, if the width of the cabinet is 30 inches, the shelves would be 28½ inches long. Cut the parts to size using a table saw or a portable circular saw and a saw guide (**10–24**).

10–23. *A piece of face trim can be added to hide the joint between modules.*

10–24. *Start construction by cutting out the parts. I'm using a portable circular saw and a saw guide, but you can also use a table saw.*

10–22. *You can combine several modules together to create a single larger unit. This unit is made from two equal-size shelf modules on top of one two-door base module and one single-door base module. Notice the trim strip that hides the joint between the two shelf units.*

10–25. Dowel holes for both parts of the corner joints can be drilled at the same time when using this type of dowelling jig.

10–26. When making T-type joints, such as for the bottom of a base module or the center shelf of a tall module, you must make the joint in two steps. First, clamp the shelf into the jig and drill the dowel holes in the ends of the shelf.

Dowel Construction

Most of the construction follows the same procedures described in chapter 6 (10–25). However, because they use a T-type joint, the instructions for the bottom, the toe-kick, and the fixed middle shelf are different. To make these dowel joints, begin by marking the location of the shelf on the inside face of the sides. Draw a line indicating the bottom of the shelf. Number the joints on both the side and the shelf, make an X on each part to indicate the front edge, and draw an arrow on the end of the shelf pointing toward the bottom. Label the shelf "A" and the side "B."

Clamp the shelf (part "A") into the dowelling jig, as described in chapter 6, but the side (part "B") is not placed in the jig at this time. Drill the dowel holes in the ends of the shelf, as usual (10–26). Next, temporarily place dowels in the holes in the ends of the shelf. Place the shelf on top of the side, and align the front edges. Remove the auxiliary clamp from the dowelling jig. Place the slot in the jig over the-first dowel.

Now, slide the shelf back and forth until the mark on the side of the dowelling jig is on the line (10–27). Then clamp the boards together. Adjust the drill stop to drill a ½-inch-deep hole. Using the dowels to position the jig, drill the holes (10–28).

The toe-kick board and the apron are attached to the sides using dowels. The board can be flush with the front of the cabinet, or recessed back, up to 2 inches. If you recess the toe-kick, you will need to follow the procedure given above for T-type joints.

After drilling the holes in the ends of the toe-kick board or apron, temporarily put dowels in the holes and use the toe-kick or apron as a guide for the dowelling jig when drilling the mating holes in the side. Place the toe-kick or apron on the side. Then remove the auxiliary clamp from the dowelling jig, and place the slot in the jig over the first dowel. Slide the toe-kick or apron back and forth until the mark on the side of the dowelling jig lines up with the lay-out line that indicates the location of the front of the toe-kick. Clamp the toe-kick or apron to the side. Now drill the holes in the side (10–29).

Assembly procedures are similar to those described in chapter 6. Make sure to put the toe-kick and apron in before you attach the second side (10–30). If you are using melamine-covered particleboard, be sure to use melamine glue. Clamp the carcass together with bar clamps and let the glue set (10–31).

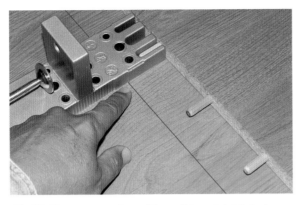

10–27. The next step in making a T-type joint is to temporarily place dowels in the holes in the ends of the shelf. Place the shelf on top of the side, and align the front edges. Place the slot in the jig over the first dowel, slide the shelf back and forth until the mark on the side of the dowelling jig is on the line, and then clamp the boards together.

10–28. Adjust the drill stop to drill a ¹/₂-inch-deep hole. Using the dowels to position the jig, drill the holes in the side of the module.

10–29. The toe kick board can be flush with the front of the cabinet, or recessed back, up to 2 inches. If you choose to recess it, you will need to follow the procedures for a T-type joint. After drilling the holes in the ends of the toe kick board, temporarily put dowels in the holes and use the toe kick as a guide for the dowelling jig when drilling the mating holes in the side.

10–30. Make sure to put the toe kick and apron in before you attach the second side.

10–31. Use bar clamps to apply pressure to the joints as the glue dries.

10–32. You can use a plate joiner to make the joints for the modules. To make the corner joints, cut the slots on the parts separately.

10–33. To make a T-type joint with the plate joiner, clamp the parts together. I'm also using a story stick, as described in chapter 6.

Biscuit Construction

Using a plate joiner is another good way to assemble the modules. The construction follows the same procedures described in chapter 6 (**10–32**). Use the instructions given there for T-type joints to cut the slots in the bottom, the toe-kick, and the fixed middle shelf (**10–33**). Make sure to put the toe-kick and apron in before you attach the second side. Clamp the carcass together with bar clamps and let the glue set.

Rabbet and Dado Joints

Using rabbets and dadoes is a traditional way to construct freestanding cabinets (**10–34** and **10–35**). Note that there is a separate Bill of Materials for this. The parts that fit into the joints need to be longer than those used with dowels or plate joinery. These joints are not self-locking, so you will need to reinforce them with finish nails or screws.

You can make the rabbets and dadoes using any of the methods described in chapter 4. When the parts are large and hard to handle, a router and a guide work well for making the joints (**10–36**). If the parts are smaller, you can make the joints on a table saw.

Exposed Joinery

Exposed dovetails and mortise-and-tenon joints can be used to add interest to traditional and contemporary designs (**10–37**). You can cut the joints by hand or use the adjustable dovetail jig described in chapter 4. This jig also has an accessory mortise-and-tenon attachment that works well for this

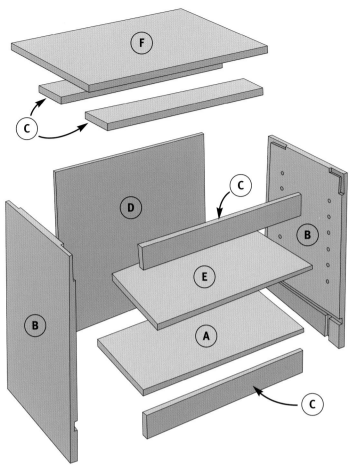

10–34. *Exploded view of a base module using rabbets and dadoes.*

10–36. *You can make the rabbets and dadoes using any of the methods described in chapter 4. Here, I'm using a router and a guide.*

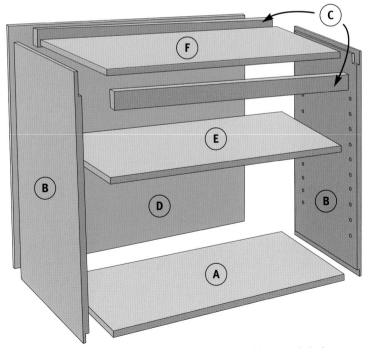

10–35. *Exploded view of a shelf module using rabbets and dadoes.*

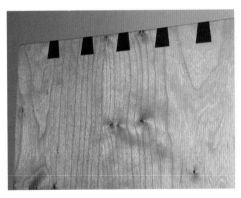

10–37. *Exposed dovetails and mortise-and-tenon joints can be used to add interest to traditional and contemporary designs.*

10–38. Using a router and a jig will produce mortises with rounded corners.

application. The jig will produce mortise-and-tenon joints with rounded corners (**10–38**). This looks good in a contemporary design, but is out of place in a traditional design. For a traditional look, you can square up the joints with a chisel.

The exploded view drawing (**10–39**) shows a shelf module that uses exposed dovetails and mortise-and-tenon joints. Note that the cleats use blind dowel joints. Even the doors are shown with through tenon joints, but you could eliminate the through tenons and make the doors using the router bits described in chapter 8. Be sure to use the Bill of Materials labeled "Exposed Joinery," because some of the parts need to be longer to allow for the through joints. The base modules use through mortise-and-tenon joints to attach the bottom and shelves. They also use blind dowel joints for the cleats (**10–40**). You may decide to eliminate the cleats and attach the top with dovetails.

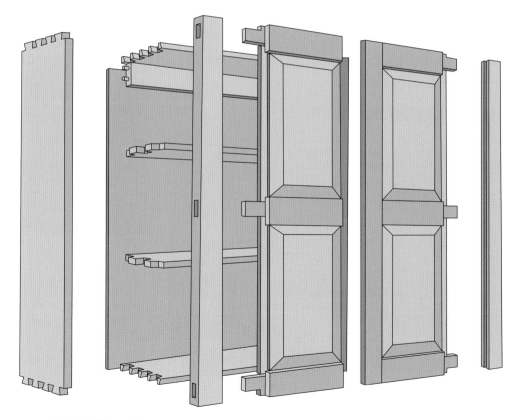

10–39. This exploded view shows a shelf module constructed using exposed joinery.

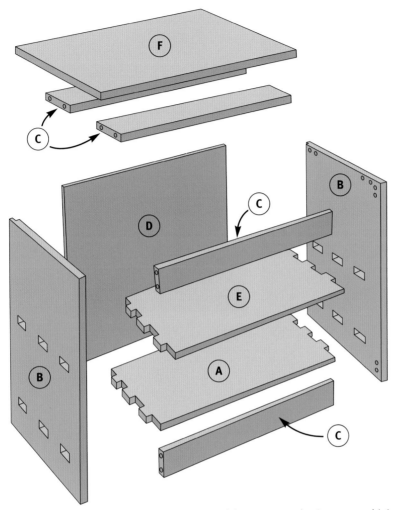

10–40. Exploded view showing a base module constructed using exposed joinery.

Cabinet Backs

BECAUSE THE SIDES ARE fully visible in a freestanding cabinet, the backs are placed in rabbets. The rabbets only need to be cut in the side pieces of the base modules. The back overlays the bottom shelf and the top cleats in the base modules. In the shelf module and the tall module, there is a rabbet for the back in the top as well as the sides. You can cut the rabbet using any technique described in chapter 4, but one of the best ways is to use a piloted rabbet bit in a router (**10–41**).

The backs can be made of any ¼-inch-thick material. When the back will be visible behind open shelves, use a material that will match the rest of the cabinet. If you are using melamine-covered particleboard, you can buy ¼-inch-thick particleboard covered with the same pattern. For solid lum-

10–41. The rabbet for the back can be made with a piloted rabbet bit in a router. (I've removed the bit from the router in this photo so that you can see it more clearly.)

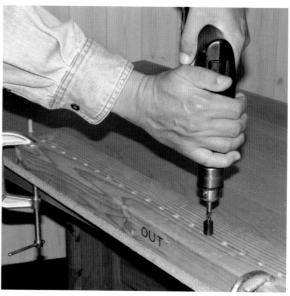

10–42. This cabinet uses a continuous series of holes for adjustable shelf pins.

10–43. This shop-made jig can be used to guide the drill to make shelf pin holes.

ber, you can use ¼-inch plywood with a face veneer of the same wood. For solid-lumber cabinets, you can also use ¼-inch-thick tongue-and-groove paneling. Prefinished wall paneling can also be used for the back.

Shelves

THE PLANS CALL FOR ADJUSTABLE SHELVES. You can use any of the methods described in chapter 7. In the drawings, I show a continuous series of holes drilled for adjustable shelf pins (**10–42**). Use drill guide to drill the shelf pin holes. You can use a commercial guide or make one from a piece of 2 x 4 as described in chapter 7 (**10–43**).

If you prefer, you can drill three holes spaced at intervals. This is a good method when the shelves are highly visible, as in the case of open book shelves. The three small holes are unobtrusive and provide sufficient adjustability for most uses. You can also use fixed shelves in dadoes or attached with dowels or biscuits. If you are using the exposed joinery, the shelves can be attached with mortise-and-tenon joints.

Doors

YOU CAN ADD DOORS to any of the modules. No modification to the module design is needed to add doors (**10–44**). Simply use full overlay doors with European hinges as described in chapter 8 (**10–45**). Drill a 35-mm hole in the door to accept the cup of the hinge. Attach the hinge to the door,

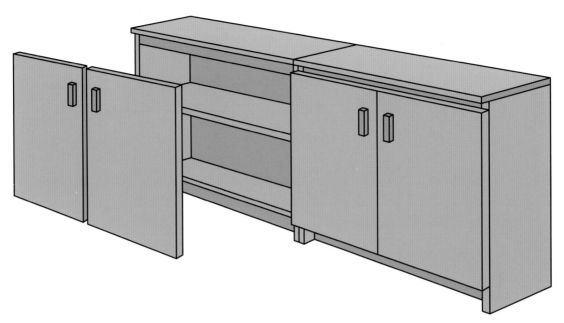

10–44. You can add doors to any of the modules. No modification to the module design is needed to add doors. Simply use full overlay doors with European hinges.

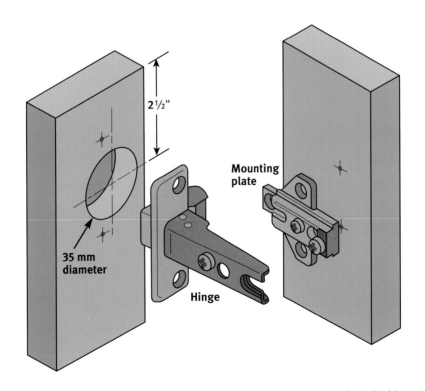

2½"

35 mm
diameter

**Mounting
plate**

Hinge

10–45. Drill 35-mm holes in the door, as shown here, to accommodate the hinge cup.

and then attach the base plate to the cabinet side. To install the doors, slide the hinge onto the base plate and tighten the screws (**10–46**). After the doors are in place, you can adjust the alignment with the adjustment screws on the hinge.

Drawers

YOU CAN ADD ONE OR MORE drawers to a base module. If you use the size given in the Bill of Materials, three equal-size drawers will fit in one module. You can vary the sizes to suit your design. Often the top drawer is smaller than the rest. The design calls for overlay drawer fronts. If you want the convenience of making all the drawer box parts the same size while having the look of different-size drawers, you can simply change the sizes of the overlay drawer fronts. The front of the drawer is as wide as the outside width of the cabinet, and it covers the front edges when it is closed (**10–47**). In this system, the maximum width for a drawer module is 18 inches.

Build overlay drawers following the instructions in chapter 9. You can use dowels or biscuits (**10–48**), rabbets and dadoes (**10–49**), or half-blind dovetails (**10–50**) when building the drawers. Use side-hung metal drawer slides to attach the drawers to the sides of the module. For the 15-inch-deep modules, use 14-inch-long drawer slides. Use 22-inch-long drawer slides for the 24-inch-deep modules.

When you use several drawers, no rail is needed between the drawers (**10–51**). If you want to include a drawer above a set of doors, you can add a rail, as shown in **10–52**. This rail will support the top of the doors when they are closed. If only one door is used with a smaller module, no rail is necessary.

10–46. Slide the hinge onto the base plate to install the doors.

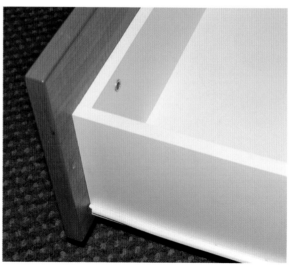

10–47. The front of the drawer is larger than the opening, and it covers the front edges of the cabinet.

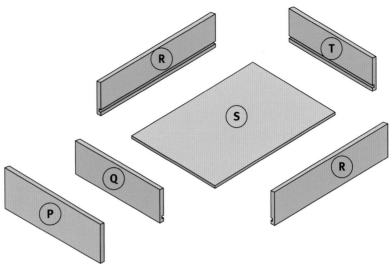

10–48. Drawer using dowel or biscuit joints (exploded view).

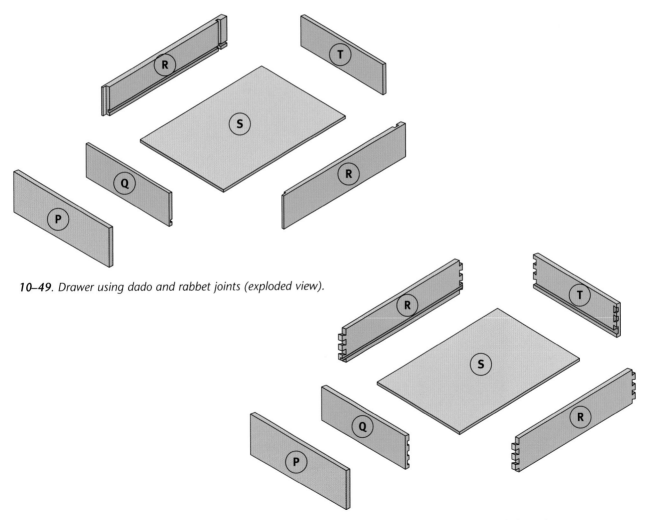

10–49. Drawer using dado and rabbet joints (exploded view).

10–50. Drawer using half blind dovetail joints (exploded view).

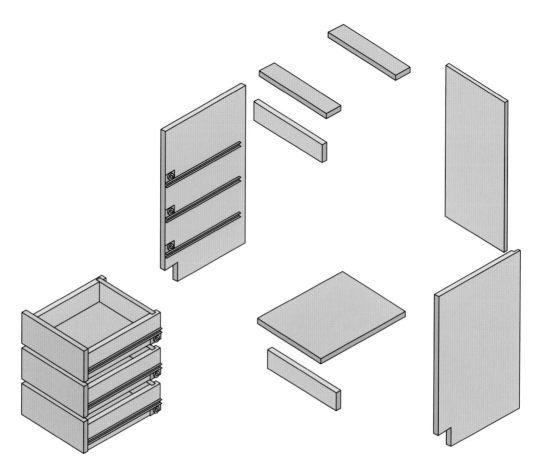

10–51. Use side-hung metal drawer slides to attach the drawers to the sides of the module. When you use several drawers, no rail is needed between the drawers.

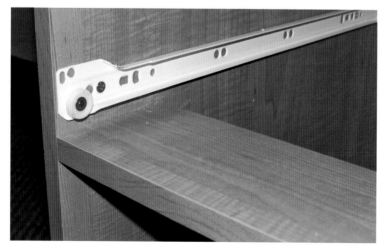

10–52. If you want to include a drawer above a set of doors, you can add a rail, as shown here. This rail will support the top of the doors when they are closed.

Bills of Materials for Various Cabinet Designs

Freestanding Modular Cabinets BILL OF MATERIALS		15-Inch-Deep Base Module (All Dimensions Actual, in Inches)	Dowel or Plate Joinery Refer to **Illus. 10–6** to **10–8** and **10–12**	
Part	**Description**	**Thickness**	**Size**	**Number Req'd**
A	bottom	¾	14¾ x (W*– 1½)	1
B	sides	¾	15 x 28¼	2
C	strips	¾	3¼ x (W*– 1½)	4
D	back	¼	25 x (W*–¾)	1
E	shelf	¾	14¾ x (W*– 1½)	varies
F	top	¾	15¾ x W*	1

*W = overall width of the module. It should not exceed 36 inches.
Note: Cut a ¼-inch x ⅜-inch rabbet for the back in the sides ("B").

Freestanding Modular Cabinets BILL OF MATERIALS		24-Inch-Deep Base Module (All Dimensions Actual, in Inches)	Dowel or Plate Joinery Refer to **Illus. 10–6** to **10–8** and **10–12**	
Part	**Description**	**Thickness**	**Size**	**Number Req'd**
A	bottom	¾	23¾ x (W*– 1½)	1
B	sides	¾	24 x 28¼	2
C	strips	¾	3¼ x (W*– 1½)	4
D	back	¼	25 x (W*–¾)	1
E	shelf	¾	23¾ x (W*– 1½)	varies
F	top	¾	24¾ x W*	1

*W = overall width of the module. It should not exceed 36 inches.
Note: Cut a ¼-inch x ⅜-inch rabbet for the back in the sides ("B").

Freestanding Modular Cabinets — 15-Inch-Deep Base Module — Rabbet and Dado Joinery

BILL OF MATERIALS — *(All Dimensions Actual, in Inches)* — *Refer to **Illus. 10–6, 10–12**, and **10–34***

Part	Description	Thickness	Size	Number Req'd
A	bottom	¾	14¾ x (W*– ¾)	1
B	sides	¾	15 x 28¼	2
C	strips	¾	3¼ x (W*– ¾)	4
D	back	¼	25 x (W*– ¾)	1
E	shelf	¾	14¾ x (W*– 1½)	varies
F	top	¾	15¾ x W*	1

*W = overall width of the module. It should not exceed 36 inches.
Note: Cut a ¼-inch x ⅜-inch rabbet for the back in the sides ("B").

Freestanding Modular Cabinets — 24-Inch-Deep Base Module — Rabbet and Dado Joinery

BILL OF MATERIALS — *(All Dimensions Actual, in Inches)* — *Refer to **Illus. 10–6, 10–12** and **10–34***

Part	Description	Thickness	Size	Number Req'd
A	bottom	¾	23¾ x (W*– ¾)	1
B	sides	¾	24 x 28¼	2
C	strips	¾	3¼ x (W*– ¾)	4
D	back	¼	25 x (W*– ¾)	1
E	shelf	¾	23¾ x (W*– 1½)	varies
F	top	¾	24¾ x W*	1

*W = overall width of the module. It should not exceed 36 inches.
Notes: Cut a ¼-inch x ⅜-inch rabbet for the back in the sides ("B").

Freestanding Modular Cabinets   24-Inch-Deep Base Module   Exposed Joinery

BILL OF MATERIALS   *(All Dimensions Actual, in Inches)*   Refer to **Illus. 10–6** to **10–12** and **10–40**

Part	Description	Thickness	Size	Number Req'd
A	bottom	¾	23¾ x W*	1
B	sides	¾	24 x 28¼	2
C	strips	¾	3¼ x (W*–1½)	4
D	back	¼	25 x (W*–¾)	1
E	shelf	¾	23¾ x W*	varies
F	top	¾	24¾ x W*	1

*W = overall width of the module. It should not exceed 36 inches.
Notes: 1) Strips ("C") attach with blind dowel joints. 2) The bottom ("A") and shelf ("E") use mortise-and-tenon joints. 3) **Note:** Cut a ¼-inch x ⅜-inch rabbet for the back in the sides ("B").

Freestanding Modular Cabinets   11-Inch-Deep Base Module   Dowel or Plate Joinery

BILL OF MATERIALS   *(All Dimensions Actual, in Inches)*   Refer to **Illus. 10–10** to **10–12**

Part	Description	Thickness	Size	Number Req'd
A	bottom	¾	10¾ x (W*–1½)	1
B	sides	¾	11 x 43	2
C	strips	¾	3¼ x (W*–1½)	4
D	back	¼	42⅝ x (W*–¾)	1
E	shelf	¾	10¾ x (W*–1½)	varies
F	top	¾	11 x (W*–1½)	1

*W = overall width of the module. It should not exceed 36 inches.
Note: Cut a ¼-inch x ⅜-inch rabbet for the back in the sides ("B") and the top ("F").

Freestanding Modular Cabinets   11-Inch-Deep Shelf Module   Rabbet and Dado Joinery

BILL OF MATERIALS   *(All Dimensions Actual, in Inches)*   *Refer to **Illus. 10–10** to **10–12** , **10–35***

Part	Description	Thickness	Size	Number Req'd
A	bottom	¾	10¾ x (W*– ¾)	1
B	sides	¾	11 x 43	2
C	strips	¾	3¼ x (W*– ¾)	4
D	back	¼	42⅝ x (W*– ¾)	1
E	shelf	¾	10¾ x (W*– 1½)	varies
F	top	¾	11 x (W*– ¾)	1

*W = overall width of the module. It should not exceed 36 inches.
Notes: 1) Cut a ¼-inch x ⅜-inch rabbet for the back in the sides ("B") and the top ("F"). 2) The bottom ("A") and the top ("F") fit into ¾-inch x ⅜-inch rabbets. 3) The size given for the shelf ("E") is for an adjustable shelf. If the shelf is fixed in a dado, the size is 10¾ x (W*–¾).

Freestanding Modular Cabinets   11-Inch-Deep Shelf Module   Exposed Joinery

BILL OF MATERIALS   *(All Dimensions Actual, in Inches)*   *Refer to **Illus. 10–10** to **10–12** , **10–39***

Part	Description	Thickness	Size	Number Req'd
A	bottom	¾	11 x W*	1
B	sides	¾	11 x 43	2
C	strips	¾	3¼ x (W*– 1½)	4
D	back	¼	42¼ x (W*– ¾)	1
E	shelf	¾	10¾ x W*	varies
F	top	¾	11 x W*	1

*W = overall width of the module. It should not exceed 36 inches.
Notes: 1) Cut a ¼-inch x ⅜-inch rabbet for the back in the sides ("B") and the top ("F"). 2) The size given for the shelf ("E") is for a fixed shelf using mortise-and-tenon joints. If the shelf is adjustable, then the size is 10¾ x (W*–1½). 3) Strips ("C") attach with blind dowel joints. 4) The bottom ("A") and top ("F") use dovetail joints.

Freestanding Modular Cabinets — 15-Inch-Deep Tall Module — Dowel or Plate Joinery

BILL OF MATERIALS — *(All Dimensions Actual, in Inches)* — *Refer to Illus. 10–13*

Part	Description	Thickness	Size	Number Req'd
A	bottom	¾	14¾ x (W*–1½)	1
B	sides	¾	15 x 72	2
C	strips	¾	3¼ x (W*–1½)	4
D	back	¼	68⅜ x (W*–¾)	1
E	shelf	¾	14¾ x (W*–1½)	varies
F	top	¾	15 x (W*–1½)	1

*W = overall width of the module. It should not exceed 36 inches.
Note: Cut a ¼-inch x ⅜-inch rabbet for the back in the sides ("B") and the top ("F").

Freestanding Modular Cabinets — 15-Inch-Deep Tall Module — Rabbet and Dado Joinery

BILL OF MATERIALS — *(All Dimensions Actual, in Inches)* — *Refer to Illus. 10–13*

Part	Description	Thickness	Size	Number Req'd
A	bottom	¾	14¾ x (W*–¾)	1
B	sides	¾	15 x 72	2
C	strips	¾	3¼ x (W*–¾)	4
D	back	¼	68⅜ x (W*–¾)	1
E	shelf	¾	14¾ x (W*–1½)	varies
F	top	¾	15 x (W*–¾)	1

*W = overall width of the module. It should not exceed 36 inches.
Notes: 1) Cut a ¼-inch x ⅜-inch rabbet for the back in the sides ("B") and the top ("F"). 2) The top ("F") fits into a ¾-inch x ⅜-inch rabbet cut in the sides. 3) The bottom ("A") fits in a ¾-inch x ⅜-inch dado cut in the sides ("B").

Freestanding Modular Cabinets — 15-Inch-Deep Tall Module — Exposed Joinery

BILL OF MATERIALS   *(All Dimensions Actual, in Inches)*   Refer to **Illus. 10–13**

Part	Description	Thickness	Size	Number Req'd
A	bottom	¾	14¾ x W*	1
B	sides	¾	15 x 72	2
C	strips	¾	3¼ x (W*–1½)	4
D	back	¼	68⅜ x (W*–¾)	1
E	shelf	¾	14¾ x W*	varies
F	top	¾	15 x W*	1

*W = overall width of the module. It should not exceed 36 inches.

Notes: 1) Cut a ¼-inch x ⅜-inch rabbet for the back in the sides ("B") and the top ("F"). 2) The size given for the shelf ("E") is for a fixed shelf using mortise-and-tenon joints. The center shelf must be fixed. If other shelves are adjustable, then the size is 14¾ x (W*–1½). 3) The strips ("C") attach with blind dowel joints. 4) The bottom ("A") uses mortise-and-tenon joints. 5) The top ("F") uses dovetail joints.

Freestanding Modular Cabinets — 24-Inch-Deep Tall Module — Dowel or Plate Joinery

BILL OF MATERIALS   *(All Dimensions Actual, in Inches)*   Refer to **Illus. 10–13**

Part	Description	Thickness	Size	Number Req'd
A	bottom	¾	23¾ x (W*–1½)	1
B	sides	¾	24 x 72	2
C	strips	¾	3¼ x (W*–1½)	4
D	back	¼	68⅜ x (W*–¾)	1
E	shelf	¾	23¾ x (W*–1½)	varies
F	top	¾	24 x (W*–1½)	1

*W = overall width of the module. It should not exceed 36 inches.

Note: Cut a ¼-inch x ⅜-inch rabbet for the back in the sides ("B") and the top ("F").

Freestanding Modular Cabinets 24-Inch-Deep Tall Module Rabbet and Dado Joinery

BILL OF MATERIALS

(All Dimensions Actual, in Inches) Refer to ***Illus. 10–13***

Part	Description	Thickness	Size	Number Req'd
A	bottom	¾	23¾ x (W*–¾)	1
B	sides	¾	24 x 72	2
C	strips	¾	3¼ x (W*–¾)	4
D	back	¼	68⅜ x (W*–¾)	1
E	shelf	¾	23¾ x (W*–1½)	varies
F	top	¾	24 x (W*–¾)	1

*W = overall width of the module. It should not exceed 36 inches.
Notes: 1) Cut a ¼-inch x ⅜-inch rabbet for the back in the sides ("B") and the top ("F"). 2) The top ("F") fits into a ¾-inch x ⅜-inch rabbet cut in the sides. 3) The bottom ("A") fits in a ¾-inch x ⅜-inch dado cut in the sides ("B").

Freestanding Modular Cabinets 24-Inch-Deep Tall Module Exposed Joinery

BILL OF MATERIALS

(All Dimensions Actual, in Inches) Refer to ***Illus. 10–13***

Part	Description	Thickness	Size	Number Req'd
A	bottom	¾	23¾ x W*	1
B	sides	¾	24 x 72	2
C	strips	¾	3¼ x (W*–1½)	4
D	back	¼	68⅜ x (W*–¾)	1
E	shelf	¾	23¾ x W*	varies
F	top	¾	24 x W*	1

*W = overall width of the module. It should not exceed 36 inches.
Notes: 1) Cut a ¼-inch x ⅜-inch rabbet for the back in the sides ("B") and the top ("F"). 2) The size given for the shelf ("E") is for a fixed shelf using mortise-and-tenon joints. The center shelf must be fixed. If other shelves are adjustable, then the size is 23¾ x (W*–1½). 3) The strips ("C") attach with blind dowel joints. 4) The bottom ("A") uses mortise-and-tenon joints. 5) The top ("F") uses dovetail joints.

Freestanding Modular Cabinets — Drawer for 15-Inch-Deep Modules — Dowel or Plate Joinery

BILL OF MATERIALS   *(All Dimensions Actual, in Inches)*   *Refer to **Illus. 10–48** and **10–51***

Part	Description	Thickness	Size	Number Req'd
P	false front	¾	7¾ x W*	1
Q	front	½	6 x (W*–3½)	1
R	side	½	6 x 14	2
S	bottom	¼	13½ x (W*–3)	1
T	back	½	6 x (W*–3½)	1

*W = overall width of the module. It should not exceed 18 inches.
Notes: 1) Sizes are for use with 14-inch metal side slides requiring ½-inch clearance. 2) Adjust the position of the false front ("P") to provide proper clearance between drawers. The top drawer should overlap the apron 1¾ inches. The bottom drawer should overlap the bottom shelf ¾ inch. 3) The bottom ("S") fits on a ¼-inch x ¼-inch groove ⅜ inch up from the bottom edge.

Freestanding Modular Cabinets — Drawer for 24-Inch-Deep Modules — Dowel or Plate Joinery

BILL OF MATERIALS   *(All Dimensions Actual, in Inches)*   *Refer to **Illus. 10–48** and **10–51***

Part	Description	Thickness	Size	Number Req'd
P	false front	¾	7¾ x W*	1
Q	front	½	6 x (W*–3½)	1
R	side	½	6 x 22	2
S	bottom	¼	21½ x (W*–3)	1
T	back	½	6 x (W*–3½)	1

*W = overall width of the module. It should not exceed 18 inches.
Notes: 1) Sizes are for use with 14-inch metal side slides requiring ½-inch clearance. 2) Adjust the position of the false front ("P") to provide proper clearance between drawers. The top drawer should overlap the apron 1¾ inches. The bottom drawer should overlap the bottom shelf ¾ inch. 3) The bottom ("S") fits on a ¼-inch x ¼-inch groove ⅜ inch up from the bottom edge.

Freestanding Modular Cabinets

Drawer for 15-Inch-Deep Modules

Rabbet and Dado Joinery

BILL OF MATERIALS

(All Dimensions Actual, in Inches)

Refer to Illus. 10–49 and 10–51

Part	Description	Thickness	Size	Number Req'd
P	false front	¾	7¾ x W*	1
Q	front	½	6 x (W*–3)	1
R	side	½	6 x 14	2
S	bottom	¼	13¼ x (W*–3)	1
T	back	½	5⅜ x (W*–3½)	1

*W = overall width of the module. It should not exceed 18 inches.
Notes: 1) Sizes are for use with 14-inch metal side slides requiring ½-inch clearance. 2) Adjust the position of the false front ("P") to provide proper clearance between drawers. The top drawer should overlap the apron 1¾ inches. The bottom drawer should overlap the bottom shelf ¾ inch. 3) The bottom ("S") fits on a ¼-inch x ¼-inch groove ⅜ inch up from the bottom edge. There is no groove in back. 4) The front rabbet is ½ inch x ¼ inch. 5) The rear dado is ½ inch x ¼ inch positioned ½ inch in from the rear of the sides.

Freestanding Modular Cabinets

Drawer for 24-Inch-Deep Modules

Rabbet and Dado Joinery

BILL OF MATERIALS

(All Dimensions Actual, in Inches)

Refer to Illus. 10–49 and 10–51

Part	Description	Thickness	Size	Number Req'd
P	false front	¾	7¾ x W*	1
Q	front	½	6 x (W*–3)	1
R	side	½	6 x 22	2
S	bottom	¼	21¼ x (W*–3)	1
T	back	½	5⅜ x (W*–3½)	1

*W = overall width of the module. It should not exceed 18 inches.
Notes: 1) Sizes are for use with 22-inch metal side slides requiring ½-inch clearance. 2) Adjust the position of the false front ("P") to provide proper clearance between drawers. The top drawer should overlap the apron 1¾ inches. The bottom drawer should overlap the bottom shelf ¾ inch. 3) The bottom ("S") fits on a ¼-inch x ¼-inch groove ⅜ inch up from the bottom edge. There is no groove in back. 4) The front rabbet is ½ inch x ¼ inch. 5) The rear dado is ½ inch x ¼ inch positioned ½ inch in from the rear of the sides.

Freestanding Modular Cabinets   Drawer for 15-Inch-Deep Modules   Exposed Joinery

BILL OF MATERIALS   *(All Dimensions Actual, in Inches)*   *Refer to **Illus. 10–50** and **10–51***

Part	Description	Thickness	Size	Number Req'd
P	false front	¾	7 ¾ x W*	1
Q	front	½	6 x (W*–2 ½)	1
R	side	½	6 x 13 ¾	2
S	bottom	¼	13 ½ x (W*–3)	1
T	back	½	6 x (W*–2 ½)	1

*W = overall width of the module. It should not exceed 18 inches.
Notes: 1) Sizes are for use with 14-inch metal side slides requiring ½-inch clearance. 2) Adjust the position of the false front ("P") to provide proper clearance between drawers. The top drawer should overlap the apron 1¾ inches. The bottom drawer should overlap the bottom shelf ¾ inch. 3) The bottom ("S") fits on a ¼-inch x ¼-inch groove ⅜ inch up from the bottom edge. 4) Use half blind dovetails on all four corners.

Freestanding Modular Cabinets   Drawer for 24-Inch-Deep Modules   Exposed Joinery

BILL OF MATERIALS   *(All Dimensions Actual, in Inches)*   *Refer to **Illus. 10–50** and **10–51***

Part	Description	Thickness	Size	Number Req'd
P	false front	¾	7 ¾ x W*	1
Q	front	½	6 x (W*–2 ½)	1
R	side	½	6 x 21 ¾	2
S	bottom	¼	21 ½ x (W*–3)	1
T	back	½	6 x (W*–2 ½)	1

*W = overall width of the module. It should not exceed 18 inches.
Notes: 1) Sizes are for use with 24-inch metal side slides requiring ½-inch clearance. 2) Adjust the position of the false front ("P") to provide proper clearance between drawers. The top drawer should overlap the apron 1¾ inches. The bottom drawer should overlap the bottom shelf ¾ inch. 3) The bottom ("S") fits on a ¼-inch x ¼-inch groove ⅜ inch up from the bottom edge. 4) Use half blind dovetails on all four corners.

Freestanding Modular Cabinets   Base Module   Door Sizes

BILL OF MATERIALS   *(All Dimensions Actual, in Inches)*   *Refer to **Illus. 10–12, 10–44**, and **10–45***

Description	Thickness	Size	Number Req'd
Single door	¾	23 ½ x W*	1
Double door	¾	23 ½ x (½ W*–¹⁄₁₆)	2

*W = overall width of the module. For single-door modules, it should not exceed 18 inches. For double-door modules, it should not exceed 36 inches.

Note: *If you add doors to the bottom section of a tall module, make the door height 24¼ inches. If you want the doors to be the same height as surrounding base modules, add an apron to the bottom section to match the other base modules.*

⑪ Cabinets for Home Entertainment and Electronics

F LAT-PANEL TVS AND COMPUTER DISPLAYS have liberated home entertainment center and computer cabinet designs from the old bulky style needed by cathode ray tube (CRT) sets. The old CRT picture tube TVs and computer monitors required a cabinet that was unnaturally deep. Now using flat-panel TVs and monitors, you can design electronics cabinets that have more furniture-like dimensions.

11–1. This entertainment center can be built using the modular cabinet plans from chapter 10. It uses two base modules and two tall modules. A frieze box ties together the two outside tall modules and covers the area above the TV.

Modular Cabinets

THE MODULAR CABINETS described in chapter 10 will accommodate most electronic gear without changing the dimensions. For large components, use the 24-inch-deep modules. You can combine the modules in many ways to make cabinets suitable for entertainment centers (**11–1**), home theaters (**11–2**), computer desks (**11–3**), and audio components (**11–4**).

11–2. Here, two tall modules flank the screen of a home theater. Notice that the sides of the cabinets have been painted blue to avoid glare on the screen.

11–3. A computer desk can be made by adding a desktop to the modules.

11–4. A 24-inch-deep tall module makes a good cabinet for audio components.

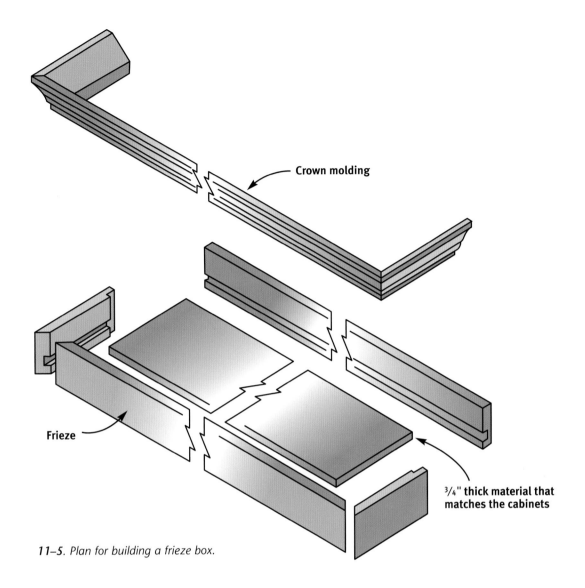

Crown molding

Frieze

¾" thick material that matches the cabinets

11–5. Plan for building a frieze box.

Frieze Box

To unify the modules in an entertainment center, you may want to incorporate a frieze box that covers the area over the TV. You can attach a cornice made from crown molding to the frieze. In **11–1**, a frieze box ties together the two outside tall modules and covers the area above the TV. **Illustration 11–5** is a plan for building the frieze. The bottom of the box is made from ¾-inch-thick material that matches the cabinets. It fits in a groove cut in the frieze sides. Adjust the length and width of the box to fit over the tops of the modules. When you assemble modules, attach the frieze box to the top of the tall modules with screws.

Although the basic modules can be used, you will need to modify them to allow for access, wiring and ventilation.

Access to the Back of the Components

Most of the connections for the components need to be made from the back. If the component is in a small cabinet with no access to the back, it can be a very frustrating situation when you try to make the connections. Ideally, you should be able to access the back of the components without removing them from the cabinet. One of the best methods is to include a door on the back of the cabinet (**11–6**). However, this works only in certain situations. If you used the cabinet as a room divider, for example, you would have free access to the back of the cabinet.

Sometimes the cabinet can be placed on the edge of a room to create a hallway effect. When there is a closet or hall on the other side of the wall, you can cut an opening through the wall and add a door. In most situations, a door on the back will be impractical, so you need to provide another way to access the back of the equipment. The simplest way is to make the shelves large enough so that you can turn the equipment around without removing it.

If the cabinet is small enough that you could move the fully loaded cabinet out from the wall when needed, you can cut openings in the back of the cabinet to provide access (**11–7**). Build the cabinet as usual, and then decide on the location of the necessary cutouts. Make the cutouts smaller than the external dimensions of the electronic component, so that when viewed from the front, the cutouts won't be visible. Use a jigsaw to make the cutouts.

Ventilation for Electronic Components

Electronic components require some ventilation to avoid overheating. Modern equipment produces much less heat than the older equipment, but it is still a good idea to provide some ventilation in a cabinet. The simplest

11–6. A door on the back of the cabinet will give you convenient access to the equipment wiring.

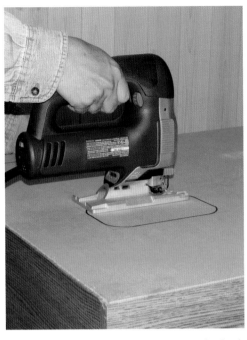

11–7. Use a jigsaw to make cutouts in the back of the cabinet.

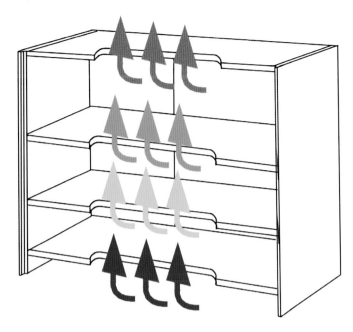

11–8. A ventilation chimney is a series of cutouts in the back of the shelves that provides an air path from the bottom of the cabinet to the top. Cool air (blue) is warmed by the equipment and rises; hot air (red) rises out of the top of the cabinet.

way is to use open shelves for the equipment, but often the design will include cabinet doors. Doors can improve the appearance of the cabinets, but they block most of the air flow to the components. Cutting access holes as described above can provide some ventilation. If you use access doors on the back of the cabinet, you could consider using louvered doors to provide ventilation.

When neither of these approaches will work, you can create a ventilation chimney at the back of the cabinet. This is simply a series of cutouts in the

11–9. You can cover the ventilation holes with a grill.

back of the shelves that provides an air path from the bottom of the cabinet to the top (11–8). This system uses the natural convection effect created when hot air rises. A cutout in the bottom of the cabinet allows cool air to flow in from the toe-kick area, and a cutout at the top allows the warm air to escape. When the top of the cabinet is above eye level, you can simply leave the ventilation holes open or cover them with a grill (11–9). When the top of a low cabinet will be visible, cut the ventilation hole in the back near the top.

11-10. A hole saw is a good tool for making wiring holes.

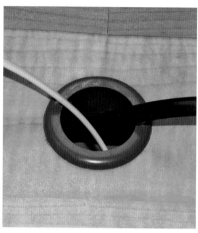

11-11. When the hole needs a finished look, you can add a grommet.

Wiring

The third concern when making cabinets for electronics is how to route the wiring. Some of the access and ventilation techniques described above also provide wiring areas. But sometimes you will need to run wires in other areas. You can simply cut holes in the shelves or the back of the cabinet in inconspicuous areas. A hole saw works well for this (**11-10**). Sometimes you must provide a wiring hole in a visible location. In this case, you can buy a wiring grommet that will give the hole a more finished look (**11-11**). Some grommets include a cover that allows you to cover most of the hole after you have the wires in place.

Doors and Remote Control Use

IF YOU WANT TO CONTROL devices behind cabinet doors with a remote control, you will need to provide a way for the infrared (IR) signals from the remote to get to the sensors on the device. One way is to use glass doors (**11-12**). Another possibility is to use a metal grill instead of glass (**11-13**). This also solves the ventilation problem.

You can buy the grill from woodworking-supply companies. It installs in a rabbet in the door like a glass door. The metal grill is also useful when you want to place speakers behind doors.

Another way to allow sound out of a cabinet is to install speaker grill cloth in the door opening (**11-14**). If you want to use solid doors, you can still control the devices if you buy an IR repeater. This is a device that has a small probe that you can mount in a hole somewhere on the front of the cabinet in an inconspicuous spot. The probe connects to the repeater box, and small emitters attach to the IR sensors on the devices (**11-15**). When you aim a remote at the probe, the signal is sent inside the cabinet to the electronic devices.

11–12. Glass doors allow the IR signals from a remote control to get to the device inside the cabinet.

11–13. A metal grill also allows IR signals into the cabinet. It also provides ventilation for the equipment and allows you to place speakers behind the door.

11–14. The lower doors of this cabinet have speaker grill cloth installed in the opening. This allows you to place speakers in the cabinet.

11–15. This IR emitter passes the IR signal from a probe outside the cabinet to the equipment inside. It attaches to the sensor with double sided tape.

Pocket Doors

POCKET DOORS ARE USEFUL on electronics cabinets, because they look like normal doors when closed, but they can slide completely inside the cabinet when open. You can use them to hide TVs and computer monitors when they are not in use, yet they provide unrestricted viewing when they are open.

Pocket doors require a special track hinge system (**11–16**). You can buy the tracks from most woodworking-supply companies. The track will come with specific instructions. You will need to buy the track before you build the cabinets and doors because each track has specific size requirements. The only drawback to this type of door is that the cabinet must be deeper than the door width for the doors to slide completely inside the cabinet.

TV Lift

A TV LIFT CAN ALLOW YOU to conceal a TV in a low cabinet and raise it to a comfortable viewing height when needed (**11–17**). Buy the lift components before building the cabinet because there will be specific requirements for the lift.

Illustration 11–18 shows a general plan for a cabinet used with a lift. The front doors are entirely decorative; they are attached to the solid front of the cabinet with screws from the rear. The back of the cabinet is made from ¾-inch-thick material to provide added strength. The top of the cabinet attaches to the lift. When the lift is activated, it raises the top and reveals the TV.

Computer Desks

DESKS CAN BE MADE WITH TWO base modules and a top that covers both modules and the kneehole. You can also attach the desktop to the side of a tall module on one or both ends. The desk shown in **11–3** uses a base module at one end and attaches to the side of a tall module at the other. Attach a cleat to the side of the tall module with screws, and then attach the top to the cleat. The chair braces described in chapter 5 work well for this.

In most cases, you should use 24-inch-deep modules for making desks. A desktop is normally between 5 and 6 feet long, but you can make it as long or short as you want. The kneehole should be between 24 and 30 inches. As an example, you could make a 5-foot desk using two 16-inch-wide base modules. This would leave a 28-inch-wide kneehole.

11–16. A pocket door slides into the cabinet when you open it. A special track is necessary to provide the sliding action.

11–17. A TV lift allows you to conceal a TV in a low cabinet and raise it to a comfortable viewing height when needed.

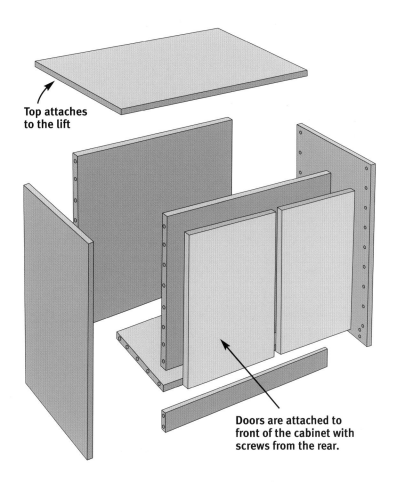

Top attaches to the lift

Doors are attached to front of the cabinet with screws from the rear.

11–18. Exploded view of a cabinet designed for a TV lift.

11–19. This desk uses a ready-made countertop as the desktop.

The desktop can be made from the same ¾-inch-thick material as the modules, or you can cover it with something more durable. Plastic laminate works well on desktops. You can also use a ready-made countertop as a desktop (**11–19**). There is more information about countertops in the next chapter.

The desktop can be the same width as the modules, or you can overhang the modules by up to 2 inches. You may want to attach an apron to the desktop. The apron strengthens the top and makes it more visually appealing. The apron should be 1½ to 2½ inches wide. You can attach it with dowels or biscuits, but pocket-hole screws are especially good for this application (**11–20**). Space the fasteners 6 inches apart.

If the desk will be placed against a wall, you can leave the module backs unfinished; if the desk will be placed so that the backs of the modules will be visible, cover the backs of the modules and the kneehole with a single piece of ¾-inch-thick material that matches the rest of the module. In this case, you won't need to use the ¼-inch backs for the modules and you won't need to make the rabbets for the back. Attach the back with the knock-down fittings described in chapter 5 (**11–21**). You can also use pocket-hole screws drilled inside the modules or chair braces.

Computer keyboards can be placed on a slide-out tray that fits under a desktop. This places the keyboard at a comfortable height and allows you to store it out of sight when it is not needed. You can buy ready-made keyboard trays that include all of the hardware, or you can build the tray from wood and add drawer slides (**11–22**).

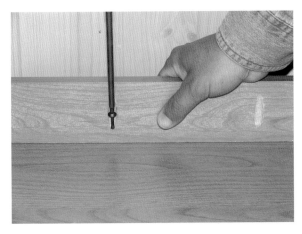

11–20. Using pocket-hole screws to attach an apron to a desktop.

11–21. Cover the backs of the desk modules and the kneehole with a single piece of ¾-inch-thick material that matches the rest of the module. You can use knock-down fittings to attach the back.

11–22. Computer keyboards can be placed on a slide out tray that fits under a desktop. This keyboard tray consists of a ¾-inch-thick board with drawer slides attaching it to side boards that hang from the desktop. If the kneehole is small, you can eliminate the side boards and attach the drawer slide directly to the side of the modules.

⑫ Built-In Cabinets

I N KITCHENS, BUILT-IN CABINETS are a necessity (**12–1**), but built-in cabinets can save space and add style in any room. Built-in bathroom vanities hide plumbing under the sink and add storage space as well (**12–2**). For some types of built-in cabinets, it is just a matter of building a freestanding cabinet as described in chapter 10 to the correct size and attaching it to the wall. For example, a tall module with drawers makes a good closet organizer (**12–3**). A built-in bookcase can be made from a tall module that is sized to fit in an alcove in a wall (**12–4**). Other construction techniques are used for more extensive built-in cabinets. Any cabinets that will be wall-hung should be built following the plans given later in this chapter. The freestanding modules are not designed to be wall-hung without floor contact.

12–1. Built-in kitchen cabinets are a necessity in a modern kitchen. Plans for the cabinets shown here are presented later in this chapter.

12–2. This bathroom vanity can be built following the plans in this chapter.

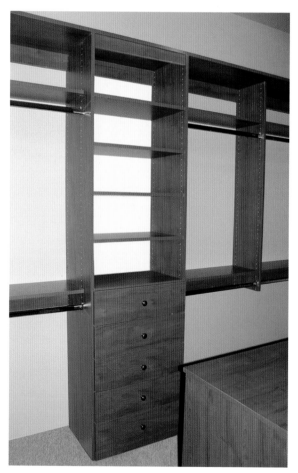

12–3. A cabinet in a closet can help to organize clutter. You can make one like this using the a tall module plan shown in Chapter 10.

12–4. An open cabinet can provide an attractive display area. This cabinet can be made by adjusting the size of a tall module (described in Chapter 10) to fit in an alcove.

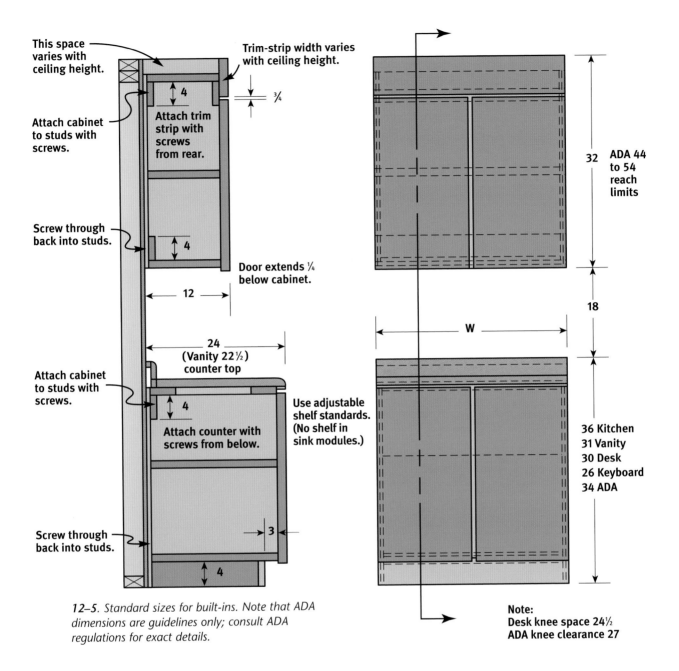

This space varies with ceiling height.

Trim-strip width varies with ceiling height.

Attach cabinet to studs with screws.

4

Attach trim strip with screws from rear.

¾

Screw through back into studs.

4

Door extends ¼ below cabinet.

12

24 (Vanity 22½) counter top

Attach cabinet to studs with screws.

4

Attach counter with screws from below.

Use adjustable shelf standards. (No shelf in sink modules.)

Screw through back into studs.

3

4

32   ADA 44 to 54 reach limits

18

W

36 Kitchen
31 Vanity
30 Desk
26 Keyboard
34 ADA

12–5. Standard sizes for built-ins. Note that ADA dimensions are guidelines only; consult ADA regulations for exact details.

Note:
Desk knee space 24½
ADA knee clearance 27

Standard Sizes of Cabinets

OVER THE YEARS, SOME STANDARD dimensions have developed for built-in cabinets. Since a built-in cabinet becomes a permanent fixture of the house, it is a good idea to follow the standard dimensions whenever possible. If there is a possibility that the cabinets will be used by someone with a disability, they should be built to ADA (Americans with Disabilities Act) standards. **Illustration 12–5** compares standard and ADA dimensions.

The standard working counter height is 36 inches. This height is to the top surface of the counter, so be sure to allow for the thickness of the counter when you build base cabinets. Bathroom vanities are usually 31 inches from the floor to the countertop. The standard counter width is 22½ to 24 inches. Desks and eating areas that will be used with standard chairs should be 30 inches to the countertop. Areas for computer keyboards should be 26 inches high. A good height for a TV shelf is approximately 24 inches, but this is determined more by personal preference.

Wall-hung cabinets are usually 12 to 14 inches wide. Generally, 72 to 80 inches is the maximum height for the top shelf. On an overhead cabinet, the distance between the countertop and the bottom should be at least 18 inches. Overhead cabinets mounted over a refrigerator are usually at least 72 inches above the floor (**12–6**). The minimum width to allow for a refrigerator or range is 31 inches, but large units may require wider openings.

Built-in bookcases vary in width from 8 to 12 inches. The wider size is preferable because it can handle most sizes of books. If possible, you should use adjustable shelves. If you use fixed shelves, at least one should be spaced wider than 12½ inches to accommodate large books. The other shelves can be spaced 10 inches apart to accommodate most books. When you place a closed cabinet below open bookshelves, the lower section should be 30 or 36 inches high. If a cabinet incorporates a bench seat, the seat should be 17 inches high.

12–6. Refrigerators need proper ventilation to operate efficiently. When building cabinets over a refrigerator, allow at least 6 inches between the bottom of the cabinet and the top of the refrigerator.

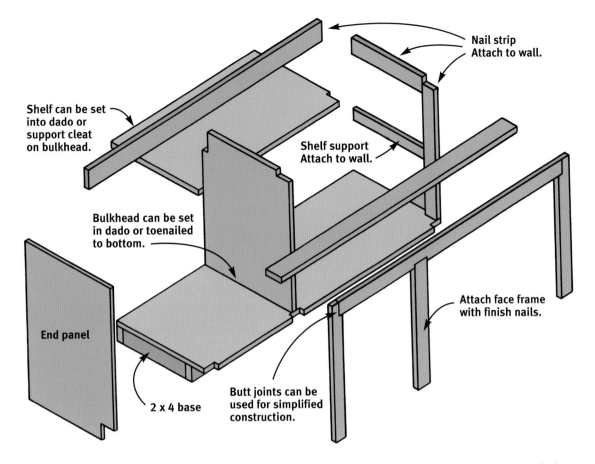

Shelf can be set into dado or support cleat on bulkhead.

Nail strip Attach to wall.

Shelf support Attach to wall.

Bulkhead can be set in dado or toenailed to bottom.

Attach face frame with finish nails.

End panel

2 x 4 base

Butt joints can be used for simplified construction.

12–7. Built-in-place cabinets can use walls for support. You attach the cabinet parts to nailing strips, which are attached to the wall.

Construction Techniques

BUILT-INS CAN BE BUILT in place or built in the shop and moved later. The construction practices are similar to those used with freestanding cabinets, but generally involve less complicated joinery. The carcasses are usually made from plywood or particleboard, so dimensional stability is not a problem. When face frames are used, they are usually made from solid hardwood. You can make the doors and drawer fronts from either solid lumber or manufactured materials.

Building Cabinets in Place

In the first half of the twentieth century, practically all kitchen cabinets were built in place. Although this method is not used very frequently today, you may still have occasion to use it. You can use two different methods for building cabinets in place. One way involves case construction. You build the cabinet basically as a freestanding unit, and then attach it to the walls, just to hold it in place. The other method involves skeleton-frame construction and uses the walls as structural members of the cabinet (**12–7**).

In most cases, the first method is best, because you don't have to compensate for out-of-square walls and you have a totally enclosed cabinet that will keep dust, insects, and rodents out better. The second method is less expensive, because you don't have to purchase materials to cover areas that are connected to walls.

Joinery in built-in-place cabinets is usually kept very simple. The cabinet gets a lot of its strength from the walls. Butt joints reinforced with nails are frequently used. The stiles and rails in face frames are usually butted or mitered at the corners and attached to the cabinet with finish nails through the face.

Prebuilding Cabinets

Today, practically all built-in cabinets are built off-site. With prebuilding, you spend less time at the actual site and the site stays cleaner. And by building the cabinets in a shop, you have more equipment available than you would have at the site. Prebuilt cabinets can be one-piece or modular. When a cabinet is very large, it is difficult to transport and install; when this is the case, you should make the cabinet in smaller sections, called modules, and then assemble the modules in place.

Prebuilt cabinets need to be stronger than built-in-place units because they have to withstand the stress of being moved and they can't rely on walls for strength. Case construction is almost always used. Many different forms of joinery can be used, including European assembly screws, dowels, and biscuits. If face frames are used, they can be dowelled or assembled using pocket-hole screws. The major limiting factor on the size of a prebuilt cabinet is the size of the smallest door opening it must pass through. If the cabinet needs to be larger than the door, you must build it in modules and then assemble it in place.

Modular Construction

MODULES CAN BE ANY SIZE. You should choose an inconspicuous place to join the modules. The best place is the point where the hinge sides of two doors meet. For kitchen and bathroom cabinets, the industry has loosely adopted some sizes that you can combine in different arrangements to fit most applications (12–8). A sink or cooking-top module is 36 inches wide, a drawer unit is 15 or 18 inches wide, and a single cabinet is 15 or 18 inches wide. Two-door modules can be 24, 30, or 36 inches wide. Under-the-counter modules are 24 inches deep, and overhead modules are 12 to 14 inches deep.

If the cabinets have to fit into an existing alcove, usually you will need to install a filler strip at the corners. To avoid this, you can vary the module

12–8. These cabinets are assembled from standard-size modules.

sizes to fit the opening. When the cabinets don't have to fit an alcove, the standard module sizes are very convenient.

Each module is a complete cabinet with sides and a back. Under-the-counter cabinets usually don't have a solid top; instead, a 4-inch-wide cleat joins the sides at the front and back. These cleats hold the module together and act as a mounting surface for the actual countertop, which you apply in one piece after installing the modules. The base and toe-kick can be integral with each module, or you can build a separate base that will support all of the modules (**12–9**). A separate base makes it easier to accommodate for variations in the floor and to line up the modules.

12–9. If you use a separate base or European cabinet legs, the sides won't extend all the way to the floor. The end of the base or the toe-kick trim will be visible.

A standard height for a toe-kick is 4 inches; rip the base material to this dimension. Place cross members in the base at each joint between modules. This will support the cabinets by the side pieces taking the strain off the bottom joints. If you install the base before the finished flooring, you can cove the flooring up the base or apply the same molding used around the floor to the base.

Many cabinet makers prefer to use European cabinet legs instead of a base. (See chapter 6.) The legs can be adjusted to compensate for irregularities in the floor, and they keep the cabinet sides off the floor, where they might be damaged by water.

Include two attaching cleats at the back of each module. The cleats should 4 inches wide and ¾ inch thick. You use the attaching cleats to secure the cabinet to the wall, so they should be firmly attached to the cabinet. When you use face frames, they should extend ¼ inch past the side of the cabinet. This gives you some room to fit and trim the modules.

When cabinets on adjacent walls meet at a corner, you can use special corner modules (**12–10**). In base cabinets, the module may incorporate a lazy Susan (**12–11**). If you plan on using a lazy Susan, be sure to buy the hardware before starting on the corner module, because different manufacturers recommend various construction techniques. Sometimes the corner in overhead cabinets will be blocked out and standard modules will be used.

Later in this chapter, you will find a set of plans and step-by-step directions for building modular cabinets.

Installing Cabinets

To install cabinets, you need to know something about the way walls are framed (**12–12**). Since cabinets can carry very heavy loads, they should only be attached to studs. Hollow wall fasteners are usually not adequate for this job.

Wall studs are almost always placed on 16-inch centers; this means that once you have found one stud, you can usually find another that is 16 inches away on either side of it. Some buildings are built with the studs on 24-inch centers, but this is rare. The only exception to the 16-inch rule is around openings such as windows and doors and at corners. In these cases, you will still find studs 16 inches apart, but there may be others that are less than 16 inches apart in between. If the wall has been constructed correctly, there will always be a stud at the corner.

There is usually a double plate at the top of a wall and a single plate at the bottom. This means that you can find solid backing along the entire wall approximately 2 inches below the ceiling and about 1 inch above the floor. These measurements take into account the average thickness of the floor and ceiling materials.

The best way to find a stud is with an electronic stud finder (**12–13**). To use the stud finder, simply pass it back and forth over the surface of the wall; when a light flashes, you have found a stud. After you have marked the stud locations on the wall, transfer the measurements to the cabinets. Drill holes for the mounting screws in the cleats before you lift the cabinets. Drill at

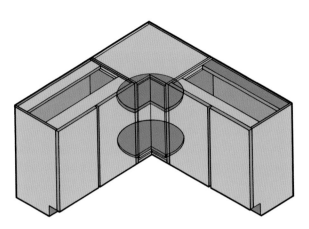

12–10. This shows how you can assemble three under-the-counter modules at a corner. The corner module contains a lazy Susan.

12–11. You can include a lazy Susan in a corner module to make more efficient use of the space.

12–13. An electronic stud finder will indicate when it is directly over a stud.

12–12. Before the drywall goes up, you can see that walls are usually framed with 2 x 4s on 16-inch centers. When you are installing cabinets, these studs are hidden, so you will need to find them to attach cabinets to the wall.

least two screw holes at each stud location in the top cleat. One screw at each stud location is all that is needed in the bottom cleat.

Install the overhead modules first. The easiest way to line up wall-hung cabinets is by temporarily nailing to the wall a strip (called a *ledger strip*) that the bottom-rear edge of the modules can rest on; however, this will leave visible holes in the wall, so it isn't always the best method. It's usually a good idea to have someone to help you when you are installing overhead cabinets. To lessen the weight of the modules, remove the doors before installation.

Standard height for the ledger strip is 54 inches from the floor. The short cabinets that go over refrigerators should be mounted 70 inches from the floor. Build a brace from 2 x 4s this same height to place under the front edge of the module during installation. To install the cabinets, place the rear edge on the ledger strip and put the brace under the module.

Put the first module in position and check it for plumb with a level. If the wall is not plumb, you may need to place shims behind the cabinet to adjust it (**12–14**). Screw it to the studs. In the upper attaching cleat, use two screws in a vertical line on each stud. For normal walls with ½-inch drywall over wood studs, use 2½-inch #10 sheet-metal screws. (Do not use drywall screws; they are not strong enough.)

Put the next cabinet in position. Have someone help you hold the module in position, and connect the two modules together before attaching the second one to the wall. Clamp the modules together, and then use wood screws to attach the modules to each other. Finally, you should secure the bottom of the cabinets to the wall by driving screws through the bottom cleat.

12–14. Use a level to check the cabinet for plumb, using shims if necessary. Notice the ledger strip below the cabinet. This helps support the cabinets during installation.

Next, install the under-the-counter modules. If you are using a separate base for under-the-counter cabinets, start by building the base out of ¾-inch-thick material that is 4 inches wide. Place a cross member where the sides of each module will meet so that there will be solid support for each module. Check the base for level in both length and width. You will probably need to make some adjustments because floors are seldom exactly level. Use cedar shims wedged between the floor and the base to make minor adjustments; major adjustments may require strips of plywood. When the base is level, nail the back of it to the wall and toenail the front to the floor.

Place the modules in their approximate position; if you plan on using filler strips at the corners, arrange the modules so that the strips come out even. If you use modules with an integral base, you must level each cabinet separately, making sure that the tops all line up. If necessary, place a filler strip where the next module will attach; then clamp the modules together and drive screws through the sides to attach them. When the modules in one section have been assembled, attach them to the wall by screwing through the attaching cleat into the studs. After that, attach the modules to the base or floor.

Scribing

When stiles or filler strips meet walls, you usually will need to trim them to fit the irregularities of the walls. This process is called *scribing*.

To scribe a cabinet to a wall, place the cabinet in the correct position and make sure it is level. Push the cabinet as tight as possible against the wall without moving it from a level position. Usually one corner will hit the wall and there will be a gap at the other end. If the gap is less than ⅛ inch, you only need to make a mark for the cut with a pencil. Lay the pencil against the wall so that the point is on the part to be trimmed and the body of the pencil is flat against the wall. Slide the pencil along the wall to duplicate the contour of the wall on the cabinet.

For larger gaps, you can place a piece of thin scrap between the pencil and the wall or you can use a scriber. A *scriber* is very similar to a drawing compass. It holds a pencil in one leg and has a point on the other. The difference between the two is that the scriber doesn't have any projections on the side of the leg, so it can rest flat against a wall. Start at the widest part of the gap, and place the leg with the metal point flat against the wall. Adjust the scriber so that the point of the pencil is just touching the edge of the cabinet or trim piece. Now run the scriber all along the wall to duplicate its contour on the cabinet (**12–15**).

In most cases, the wall will be fairly straight, but out of plumb; this results in a uniformly tapering cut on the cabinet. Probably the easiest way to make this type of cut is with a block plane. If you are scribing to a very irregular wall, such as one made of brick or stone, the wall contour will be very complex; when this is the case, use a jigsaw to trim the part.

12–15. A scriber helps to mark the area that must be trimmed to make a cabinet fit against an irregular wall. In this case, a filler strip is being scribed to fit against a stone wall.

Soffits

Overhead cabinets may not always extend to the ceiling. There are several ways to handle the space between the top of the cabinet and the ceiling. The space may simply be left open. If you want to enclose the space, you can build a drop ceiling, or soffit, out of 2-x-4 framing and cover it with drywall. This method is commonly used in new construction and when extensive remodeling is being done (**12–16**).

A somewhat less complex method involves building a 1-x-2 framework between the cabinet and the ceiling and covering it with ¼-inch plywood that matches the cabinet. Use a molding to conceal the joint between the cabinets and the ¼-inch plywood. When the space to be enclosed is not too tall, you can simply attach a ¾-inch-thick filler strip to the top of the cabinet.

Countertops

YOU CAN USE MANY DIFFERENT materials for countertops. Stone and solid-surface countertops are popular but they should be installed by professionals (**12–17**). You can do all of the cabinet installation and then hire a professional to install these products. For do-it-yourself installation, the two most popular choices are plastic laminates and ceramic tile.

You apply ceramic tile after assembling the cabinets, which makes it easy to attach the countertops. The top is usually made from ¾-inch-thick plywood. Apply several beads of panel adhesive to the mounting strips in the cabinet and put the top in place. Since you apply the tile later, you can simply attach the top with screws driven down from the top. Before you install the tiles, apply a base of cement backer board. The tile supplier will have specific directions and recommendations for types of adhesive and grout. You can cover the front edge with special edge tiles, as has been done on the cabinets in **12–18**, or you can apply a hardwood strip to the front of the counter.

You can build your own plastic laminate countertops. If you will be applying a self edge, the overhanging front lip is usually thickened by

12–16. The area above these cabinets is enclosed by a soffit.

12–17. Stone countertops are popular, but they require professional installation.

attaching a ¾-inch-thick strip under the top. Instead of a self edge, you can attach a strip of hardwood to the front of the countertop. Fill any holes or voids in the top before applying the plastic laminate.

If you use a backsplash of plastic laminate, apply it before installing the countertop. The easiest way to install a plastic laminate backsplash is by making it several inches oversized and gluing it to the wall before installing any of the cabinets. You can use a special molding where the counter joins the back-splash that has a slot to accept the laminate, or you can scribe the top to fit closely and later cover the joint with a small bead of caulking. Make any cutouts in the particleboard top before installing the laminate, but wait to make the cutouts in the plastic laminate until after you have installed it. A router

12–18. Ceramic tile can be installed by do-it-yourselfers. This countertop uses special edge tiles that cover the front edge, so no additional trim is needed.

with a laminate-trimming bit will follow the cutout in the particleboard; drill an entrance hole in the waste area to get the bit in position. For more details on applying plastic laminates, refer back to chapter 1.

Post-formed plastic laminate counters are also available. This type of counter has the plastic laminate already bonded to a particleboard core. The laminate has been heat-bent into a shape that provides a continuous front edge and often also includes a backsplash in a single seamless piece (**12–19**). This type of counter is usually order-cut to length. When the counter has a corner in it, the joint is usually factory-cut. Before attaching the counter to the cabinets, temporarily position it to see if scribing is necessary. The backsplash incorporates a scribing strip in its construction, so you can scribe it to fit tightly against the wall.

Since the plastic laminate is already applied to the top, all fasteners must be installed from inside the cabinets. Use panel adhesive on the mounting strips, and make sure that the screws won't break the surface of the laminate. Corner joints come from the factory prepared to take a special type of fastener that clamps them tightly together.

When an end of the counter will show, end-cap kits are provided by the factory. They include a precut cap and filler strips (**12–20**). Glue and nail the filler strip along the underside of the counter and between the backsplash and the wall so that there is solid backing for the end cap. The cap will usually be coated beforehand with heat-activated adhesive. Place the cap in position and heat it with a clothes iron. Since the end cap is precut to the approximate outline of the counter, only a small amount of trimming with a file is usually necessary. If you need to do a lot of trimming, you can use a router with a laminate-trimming bit.

12–20. Precut end caps are available for use with post-formed countertops. The kit shown here includes the necessary filler strips, nails, and the end caps. I've turned one end cap over in this photo so that you can see the hot-melt adhesive on the back.

12–19. Post-formed plastic laminate is heat-bent into a shape. This one includes a backsplash in a single seamless piece.

12–21. Flat-panel doors give these cabinets a contemporary look.

12–22. Raised panels give these cabinets a traditional look.

Modular Built-In Plans and Directions

THIS SECTION CONTAINS a complete set of plans for an entire system of modular cabinets. Using this set of plans, you can build several styles of cabinets. This system's versatility is due to the fact that full overlay doors and drawer fronts are used. This means that the style of the cabinet can be changed simply by altering the doors and drawer fronts. Construction is simplified because no face frames are used. Using concealed European hinges permits this type of construction. You can choose to use flat-panel doors (12–21), raised-panel doors (12–22), or simple slab doors (12–23). In any case, all of the construction will be the same, except for the doors and drawer fronts.

To make the plans as versatile as possible, only the dimensions that are the same for all module sizes are printed on the drawings. The various Bills of Materials give specific dimensions for each part. This system contains modules that you can use for kitchens, bathrooms, and other applications. The modules can be built in standard widths such as 15, 18, 24, 30, and 36 inches, but to make the plans as versatile as possible I will list the sizes with the variable "W" to indicate the width of the cabinet. This way, you can make custom-size

12–23. Slab doors are used on these utility cabinets for a garage, but they can also be used in contemporary cabinets. The look depends on the material you choose for the door.

cabinets to fit your application. Under-the-counter modules are 36 inches high for kitchens and 31 inches high for bathrooms. Overhead cabinets are 32 inches high for most applications and 16 inches high for over refrigerators, range hoods, and so forth.

The Bills of Materials and the step-by-step directions refer to the parts by the letters shown on the exploded-view plans.

These modules are designed to be built from particleboard or plywood. If you use particleboard, use the melamine-covered variety for all parts that show. Doors and drawer fronts can be made from solid lumber.

Use the built-in planer in the appendix to help you lay out the design and decide on the modules that will be necessary. Using the appropriate Bill of Materials, make a list of all the parts that you will need. Cut out all of the parts at once, and cut all the joints requiring a particular setup at the same time.

Doors, Drawer Fronts, and Trim

Construction techniques for doors and drawers will be the same no matter which joinery method you choose for the carcass. You are not limited to the three styles shown; almost any type of door or drawer front can be used with this system. For a country look, make cleated doors. If you don't want to go to the trouble of making genuine panel doors, you can use applied moldings with the slab doors to create a traditional look. Even glazed doors can be used with this system.

The doors use European-type hinges that require a 35-mm-diameter flat-bottomed recess in the back of the door. (See chapter 8.) First attach the hinges to the doors, and then attach the mounting plates to the sides of the modules. Wait until the modules are installed before you attach the doors. The hinges have three independent adjustments to square the door on the cabinet; raise or lower the door and adjust the clearance between doors. Once you have installed all of the doors, use the adjustments to line them up.

Slab Doors

This style, shown in **12–23**, is the simplest to make. You can use ¾-inch-thick hardwood-veneered plywood or melamine-covered particleboard. You can use any edge treatment discussed in chapter 1, but edge banding is recommended. Grain direction and figure matching are optional and depend on personal taste.

Panel Doors

Panel doors are more complicated to make than slab doors, but they can greatly enhance the look of the cabinets. The door fronts are made using panel construction techniques. (See chapter 8.) The doors in **12–22** were

12–24. Even if you choose panel doors, you can still use flat-faced drawers, as shown here.

made using the set of matched router bits discussed in chapter 8. They cut the edge on the raised panel and that cut the sticking and coped joints. You can purchase these bits from several of the mail-order woodworking-supply companies if you can't find them locally.

Any of the other methods for making panel doors discussed in chapters 6 and 8 can be used. The router-bit set will produce a coped joint that is strong enough for most applications. The door size listed in the Bill of Materials is the finished size of the door; refer to chapter 8 to determine the size of the individual parts of the panel door.

Drawer Fronts

There are two options for drawer fronts: You can simply use solid wood (**12–24**), or you can make a raised panel using the same procedure used to make the doors (**12–25**).

After the modules are installed, place the drawers in their runners and then attach the drawer fronts. Use 1¼-inch screws to attach the drawer fronts. Align each front with the preceding one before attaching them. The sizes listed in the Bill of Materials for the

12–25. If you want the drawer fronts to match the panel doors exactly, you can make small panels using the same procedure used to make the doors. Attach the panel fronts to the drawer box with screws from the rear. Make sure that the screws are driven into the outer fame, not the panel.

drawer fronts allow for an overhanging countertop and ⅛-inch gaps between drawers. If you use a different type of countertop, you can make all of the drawer fronts larger or smaller or simply make the top or bottom one larger to compensate for the difference.

End Caps

The exposed ends of the carcasses can be covered with end caps to make them match the doors (**12–26**). You build end caps the same way as doors. They are applied to the exposed ends of modules after installation. Use screws driven from inside the cabinet into the backs of the end caps to hold them in place.

Cornice

After the doors are in place, you can install a trim strip or cornice at the top. If you want the cabinets to reach to the ceiling, you can cover the gap with a trim strip. The width of the trim strip depends on the ceiling height; for an 8-foot ceiling, the strip will be approximately 8 inches. Scribe the strip so that it fits the ceiling and has an even reveal along the top edge of the doors. Attach the trim from behind with 1¼-inch screws through the front filler of the modules.

If you want a cornice, apply a piece of crown molding at the top (**12–27**). Follow the directions

12–26. The exposed ends of the carcasses can be covered with end caps to make them match the doors. You build end caps the same way as doors. They are applied to the exposed ends of modules after installation. Use screws driven from inside the cabinet into the backs of the end caps to hold them in place. Make sure that the screws are driven into the outer fame, not the panel.

12–27. You can attach a crown molding to the top of the cabinets to form a cornice.

given in chapter 6. The molding can be attached with screws driven from behind or with finish nails. A nail gun works well for this. You can drive a few nails from the front to hold the molding in position and then drive the rest of the nails from the rear where they won't be visible.

Toe-Kick

You can make the toe-kick to match the cabinets, or there are several ways you can cover the toe-kick. Carpet or vinyl flooring can be coved up the walls and over the toe-kick. If you have used wood or tile molding on the walls, you can apply it to the toe-kick, or you can apply a rubber base to the toe-kick.

Drawers

You can use any of the techniques for making drawers described earlier in this book, but in this section I will show you a new method that uses pocket-hole screws (**12–28**):

1. Cut out the parts. You can use plywood, particleboard, or solid lumber. The drawers in the illustrations are made from ½-inch-thick melamine-covered particleboard, and the edges are covered with matching edge banding.

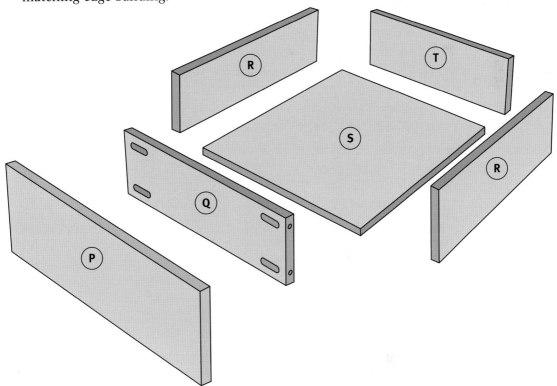

12–28. This exploded view shows the parts of a drawer using pocket-hole joinery.

12–29. Drill the pocket holes on the outside of the box where they won't be visible.

2. Drill pocket holes. The front and back of the drawer box (part Q) are attached to the sides with pocket-hole screws. The pocket holes are drilled on the outside of the box so that they won't be visible (**12–29**). The false front (part P) will hide the pocket holes on the front, and the back ones won't be visible when the drawer is in the cabinet. For drawers 6 inches deep and smaller, use two screws for each joint. For larger drawers, space the screws 64 mm apart.

3. Assemble the box. Clamp the joints together and drive the screws into the pocket using a power drill.

4. Attach the bottom. The bottom of this type of drawer is made from the same ½-inch melamine-covered particleboard as the rest of the drawer box. It is not set in a groove; instead, it is simply attached to the bottom with screws. Use the same screws that you use for pocket-hole joinery. Drill a pilot hole and countersink for the screws. You can use the same drill bit that you use to drill the pocket holes, but these holes need to be straight. Use the drill guide described for European assembly screws to guide the drill as you make the pilot holes in the bottom (**12–30**). Position the wooden fence so that the

12–30. Use a drill guide to make the pilot holes in the drawer bottom.

screws will be centered in the ½-inch-thick sides. You could also use a drill press for this operation. Space the screws 37 mm in from the corners and no more than 128 mm apart around the perimeter of the bottom.

Before you attach the bottom, measure diagonals and square the drawer. Then attach the bottom by driving the screws with a power drill.

5. Install slides. The drawers are designed for a drawer slide that attaches to the side and has a lip that wraps around the bottom of the drawer. When this slide is installed, it will completely hide the exposed edge of the bottom and provide support for the drawer bottom (**12–31**).

6. Install the false front. Place the drawer box in the cabinet and hold the false front in place. Mark the location when you are satisfied with the front position. Now remove the drawer and drill pilot holes for four screws that will attach the false front. Drive in the screws, and the drawer is complete.

12–31. When this slide is installed, it will completely hide the exposed edge of the bottom.

Carcass Construction

THROUGHOUT THIS BOOK, you have learned several methods of construction; the carcasses for these built-in cabinets can be built using three of those methods. Most commercial shops use either dowel construction or European assembly screws. Biscuit joinery is another method that is popular with do-it-yourselfers. European assembly screws are the newest innovation in cabinetmaking. They simplify construction considerably and they are one of the strongest methods. Since the European assembly screw method is the newest, easiest, and strongest technique, I will present it first and then I will cover the other methods.

Step-by-Step Directions

The basic dimensions are the same for all of the built-in cabinets described in this chapter (12–5). The first three steps are the same for all methods:

1. Cut out the parts. A table saw will make cutting out the parts faster, especially if it has a fence extension so that you can set the fence to make all of the cuts. However, if you are working alone, it can be difficult to handle a full-size sheet of material. Even if you will be using a table saw to cut most of the smaller parts, an aluminum saw guide and a portable circular saw are probably the best way to make the initial cuts from a full sheet (12–32). Since none of the carcass will show from the outside of the cabinet, you can use white-melamine-covered particleboard for all of the carcass parts.

2. Apply edge banding. The front edges of the carcass will be visible when the doors are open, so you should cover them with edge banding. In this case, it is easiest to apply the edge banding before assembly (12–33).

3. Shelf and drawer hardware. You can use any type of adjustable shelf standard with this system. The cabinets in the illustrations use a continuous series of holes drilled for adjustable shelf pins. Use a drill guide to drill the shelf pin holes. You can use a commercial guide or make one from a piece of 2 x 4 as described in chapter 7 (12–34).

It is easer to install the drawer slide before you assemble the cabinet, so attach the drawer slide to the cabinet side at this stage.

12–32. An aluminum saw guide and a portable circular saw are probably the best way to make the initial cuts from a full sheet.

12–33. Use white plastic edge banding to match the white-melamine-covered particleboard. Here, I'm using an iron to apply edge banding with pre-applied hot-melt adhesive.

12–34. Use a drill guide to drill the shelf pin holes.

European Assembly Screws

Most of the outside surfaces of a built-in cabinet module are hidden, so this is a perfect place to use European assembly screws. The few exposed ends will be covered with decorative panels after installation to hide the screw heads. The cabinets are assembled without glue. All of the strength comes from the screws. This makes assembly easier because there is no squeezed-out glue to clean up. The only clamps you will need are to hold parts together as you drive in the screws.

In this design, the backs are made from ¾-inch-thick material, and they are attached with screws. This eliminates the need for separate attaching cleats. Attaching screws can be driven directly through the back into the wall studs. These modules are designed to use a separate base or European cabinet legs. The plastic legs keep the particleboard away from any water that may be on the floor and simplify construction and installation. Because these cabinets use a separate base, the construction process is almost identical for base cabinets and overhead cabinets. The only difference is in the top construction. **Illustration 12–35** is an exploded view of a base cabinet using

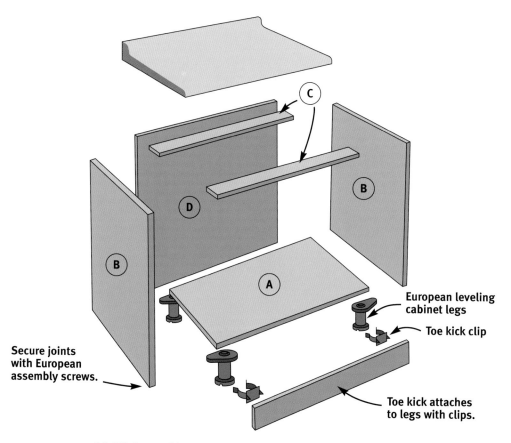

12–35. Base cabinet using European assembly screws (exploded view).

this type of construction, and **12–36** shows an overhead cabinet.

Here are the steps for making built-in cabinets using European assembly screws:

1. Cut out the parts.

2. Apply edge banding.

3. Install shelf and drawer hardware.

4. Drill pilot holes and drive screws in the corner joints. European assembly screws require a pilot hole to be drilled in both mating parts. The important thing is to ensure that the pilot holes are straight and centered on the edge

Secure joints with European assembly screws.

12–36. Overhead cabinet using European assembly screws (exploded view).

of the board. Because of the large diameter of the screws, the joint will be weakened if the holes are off-center. If the hole is not straight, the screw may break out of the joint when you drive it in. To drill the holes correctly, use a drill guide, as described in chapter 6. Attach a wooden fence that is 256 mm long to the base of the guide. The holes should be 37mm in from the edges and 128 mm on center.

When you attach the wooden fence to the drill guide, center it in relation to the drill bit. That will make the ends of the fence 128 mm from the center of the drill bit. Also draw a line on the fence 37 mm from the center of the drill bit. When you drill the first hole, align the 37 mm line with the edge of the board as you hold the fence flat against the end. This will position the first hole in 37 mm from the edge.

After the first hole is drilled, reposition the guide so that the end of the fence is aligned with the center of the first hole and drill the next hole. Continue in this manner until you get close to the other edge; then use the 37-mm mark to drill the last hole.

Start by placing one side and the bottom together. Use bar clamps to hold the parts in position while you drill the pilot holes (**12–37**). Next, use a drill to drive

12–37. Use a drill guide when drilling the pilot holes for the European assembly screws.

the screws. Once the screws are in, you can remove the bar clamps and move to the next joint.

If you are making an overhead cabinet, the top and bottom are the same. For a base cabinet, two cleats are placed at the top. These will be used to attach the countertop after the modules are installed.

5. Install the back. Once the sides are joined to the top and bottom, you can install the back. In this design, the back is made from the same ¾-inch-thick material as the rest of the carcass. The back completely overlays the cabinet edges. This will leave the edges of the back exposed, but this is not a problem because the edges will be hidden once the modules are installed. Square up the carcass before you drill the pilot holes for the back. Measure the diagonals and use a bar clamp if necessary to pull the carcass into square (**12–38**).

Now drill the pilot holes for the screws following the same procedure as you used above. Once you drive in the screws, the carcass is done (**12–39**).

6. Build a base or attach the legs. The base modules need a separate base or legs. You can cut the parts beforehand, but wait to assemble the base or install the legs until you are on-site and ready to install the cabinets. This makes it easier to get the cabinets in the building, and you can customize the base to compensate for irregularities in the floor. The base is made from ¾-inch-thick material that is ripped to 4 inches wide. You can use material that matches the cabinets or choose something that matches the floor or moldings in the room. If the base will get wet, avoid using particleboard. Plywood or solid lumber is more water-resistant.

In **12–40**, I show a miter joint at the front corner. This gives the base a clean look when the corner is visible. If the corner won't be visible, you can use a butt joint. Make sure to place a cross member at the joint between each module. This supports the sides of the cabinet.

Before you place the modules on the base, make any adjustments necessary to make the base level. Drive pocket screws through the base into the floor to keep the base stationary.

Instead of a base, you can use European leveling cabinet legs. These are plastic legs that can be adjusted to level the cabinets (**12–41**). Use four legs on cabinets up to 30 inches wide; use six legs for 36-inch cabinets. Corner cabinets may require eight legs. If you can't find these legs locally, look on the Internet. Most mail-order woodworking-supply companies sell them. When you install the legs, make sure that the side support is positioned so

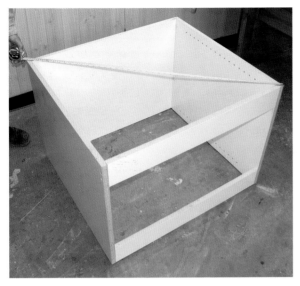

12–38. Square up the carcass before you drill the pilot holes for the back. Measure the diagonals and use a bar clamp if necessary to pull the carcass into square.

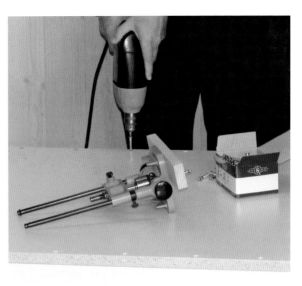

12–39. Driving the screws to hold the back in place.

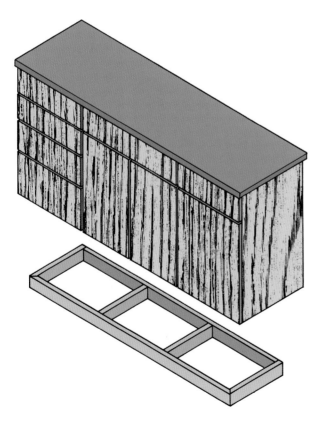

12–40. Base for European assembly screw modules.

12–41. European leveling cabinet legs have a separate mounting plate. Attach them with screws before you install the cabinets. Insert the legs and place the cabinets.

that it will support the side of the cabinet. This will take some of the strain off the bottom joint of the module. The legs come preset to 4 inches, so you only need to adjust them if the floor is not level.

For utility cabinets like the garage cabinet shown in **12–23**, you can leave the legs exposed. For a more finished look, cover the legs with a toe-kick board. The legs come with clips that attach to the back of the toe-kick board. After the modules are installed, simply snap the toe-kick board in place (**12–42**).

Dowel Joinery

This next design is more traditional. The sides extend below the bottom shelf to form a base, and the toe-kick is part of the cabinet. The back is made from ¼-inch material, and attaching cleats are used to attach the cabinet to the wall (**12–43** and **12–44**). Many commercial shops use a similar design. Of course, a commercial shop will use a boring machine to drill the dowel holes, but you can achieve the same results using a dowelling jig.

12–42. The legs come with clips that attach to the back of the toe-kick board. After the modules are installed, simply snap the toe-kick board in place. (I have turned a cabinet upside down to take this picture, but you would usually attach the toe-kick after the cabinets are in place and leveled.)

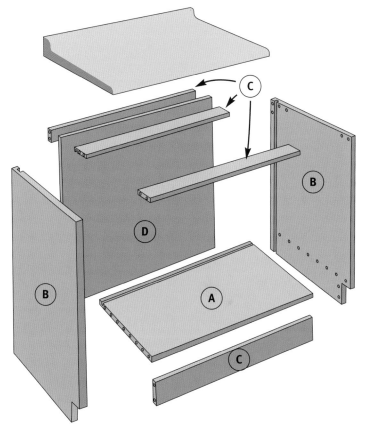

12–43. Base cabinet using dowel joints or biscuits, exploded view.

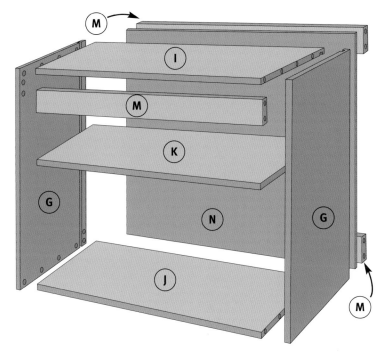

12–44. Overhead cabinet using dowel joints or biscuits (exploded view).

12–45. Cutting the groove for the back using a router with a clamp on aluminum guide.

Here are the steps for making built-in cabinets using dowel joinery:

1. Cut out the parts.

2. Apply edge banding.

3. Install the shelf and drawer hardware.

4. Cut a groove for the back. In this design, the back hides the attaching cleats. To accomplish this, place the back in a groove that is ¾ inch in from the back of the cabinet. For overhead cabinets, cut the groove in the top, bottom, and both sides. For base cabinets, cut the groove in the bottom, both sides, and the rear top cleat. You can cut the groove on a table saw with a dado blade set to ¼ inch or use a ¼-inch bit in the router. Guide the router with a clamp-on aluminum guide (**12–45**).

12–46. Using a jigsaw to cut the toe-kick notch.

5. Cut the toe-kick notch. If you are making a base cabinet, you can use a circular saw to cut the toe-kick notch, but you won't be able to cut all the way to the corner. Use a handsaw or a jigsaw to complete the cut. You can alternately use a jigsaw to make the entire cut (**12–46**).

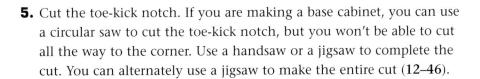

6. Drill the dowel holes. Refer to the directions given in chapters 6 and 10. Some joints are of the T type; chapter 10 gives instructions for this joint. As described in chapters 6 and 10, begin by marking the location of the parts and number the joints on both parts. Make an X on each part to indicate the front edge, and draw an arrow on the end of the shelf pointing toward the bottom. Label the horizontal parts "A" and the sides "B." Follow the instructions given in chapters 6 and 10 to drill the holes.

For overhead cabinets, use four dowels per joint, and use eight dowels per joint for base cabinets. The dowels should be spaced 16 mm in from the front and 16 mm from the front of the groove at the back; the rest of the dowels should be equally spaced no more than 75 mm on center. The simplest way to lay out the joints is to make a story stick that will be used as a guide for the other boards.

The only thing that is a little unusual is the setup for drilling the dowel holes for the attaching cleats. Because the cleats are narrower than the board they attach to, you will need to place a scrap of material that is the same thickness under the edge of the side board as you clamp on the dowelling jig. The spacer clamp can be clamped to this scrap (**12–47**). Clamp the cleat down to the bench so that it won't move when you change the jig to the other dowel position.

7. Assemble the cabinet. Assembly procedures are similar to those described in chapter 10. Make sure to put the toe-kick and cleats in before you attach the second side. If you are using melamine-covered particleboard, be sure to use melamine glue. Clamp the carcass together with bar clamps and let the glue set (**12–48**).

12–47. To drill the dowel holes for the attaching cleats, you will need to place a scrap of material that is the same thickness under the edge of the side board as you clamp on the dowelling jig. The spacer clamp can be clamped to this scrap.

12–48. Clamp the carcass together with bar clamps and let the glue set.

Plate Joinery

You can use plate joinery instead of dowels. The rest of the design remains essentially the same as used for the dowels above. Use the same plans shown in **12–43** and **12–44**.

Here are the steps for making built-in cabinets with plate joinery:

1. Cut out the parts.

2. Apply edge banding.

3. Shelf and drawer hardware.

4. Cut a groove for the back.

5. Cut the toe kick notch.

6. Cut the biscuit slots. The construction follows the same procedures described in chapter 6. Use the directions given there for T-type joints, to cut the slots in the bottom of the base. Use the large (#20) biscuits. Mark the biscuit locations on the edge of a story stick, hold the story stick in place, and transfer the marks. Mark the centerlines for the first and last biscuit 2 inches in from the edges. Space the rest of the biscuits equally. The biscuits should not be more than 4 inches apart on center. That will result in six biscuits per joint for a 24-inch-wide cabinet and three biscuits per joint for a 12-inch-wide cabinet (**12–49**).

7. Assemble the cabinet. Assembly procedures are similar to those described in chapter 6. Make sure to put the toe-kick and cleats in before you attach the second side. If you are using melamine-covered particleboard, be sure to use melamine glue. Clamp the carcass together with bar clamps and let the glue set.

12–49. If you use plate joinery, the centerline of the first and last biscuits should be 2 inches in from the edges. The rest of the biscuits should not be more than 4 inches apart on center.

Corner Modules

When two cabinets meet at a corner, a special module is required. The simplest type uses a modified two-door module with slab doors. **Illustration 12–50** shows how the modules are placed in the corner. If you don't need a filler strip, you can butt the cabinets directly against each other.

To modify the standard double-door module, attach the inactive door solidly to the carcass instead of hinging it. In some cases, it's better to have the active door open on the opposite side. To do this, it has to be hinged where the two doors meet. Install a 2-inch-wide filler behind the edge of the inactive door where the hinge can be attached. You can also use this method with overhead cabinets. If you use this type with a panel-door style, you will need to build a dummy panel door that will cover the exposed area instead of using the full-size inactive door.

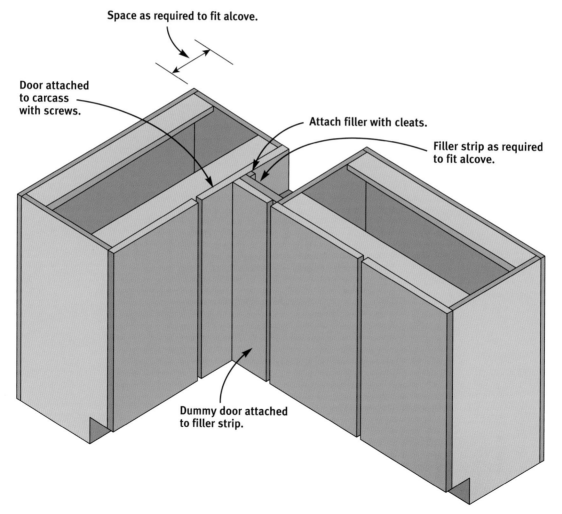

Space as required to fit alcove.

Door attached to carcass with screws.

Attach filler with cleats.

Filler strip as required to fit alcove.

Dummy door attached to filler strip.

12–50. This corner module uses a single door set diagonally across the corner.

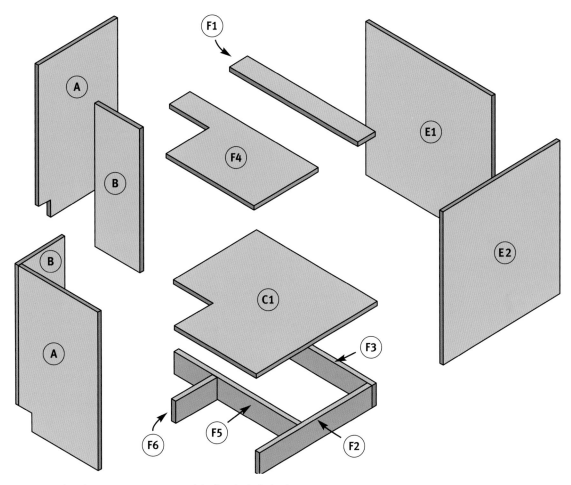

12–51. Under-the-counter corner module (exploded view).

A major advantage with this type of corner module is that you can adjust it to fit tightly in an alcove. The disadvantages are that the space in the corner is wasted and the part of the shelf behind the inactive door is hard to reach.

The type of corner module shown in **12–51** eliminates the disadvantages of the first type, but it can't be adjusted to the size of an alcove as easily. This type can be used with a lazy Susan, making it easy to reach all the items stored in the unit. Note that the plans shown here can be adapted to use European assembly screws, dowels, or biscuits.

The sides (part "A") are the same as those used in the other modules. The bottom (part "C1") and the front-counter mounting strip (part "F4") have the front corner cut out so that the front of the module will line up with both banks of cabinets. A nailing strip (part "F3") is used to reinforce the joint where the two backs (part "E") meet. The size given in the Bill of Materials for part "E" is for the longest side; since a butt joint is used at the

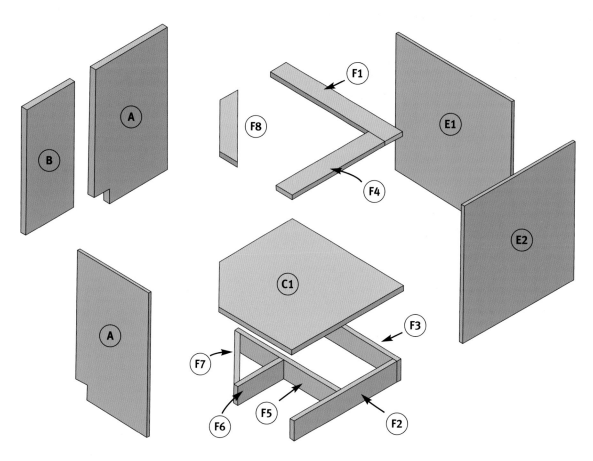

12–52. Under-the-counter diagonal corner module (exploded view).

rear corner, one of the backs must be trimmed ¼ inch. The long toe-kick (part "F5") extends the full width of the module, and the short toe-kick (part "F6") butts into it. Assembly is basically the same as for a standard module. The doors are hinged to the sides (part "A") and meet in the center; there should not be any overlap where the doors meet or else they won't work independently.

Another type of corner module is shown in **12–52** and **12–53**. In this module, a single door is used; it is set diagonally across the corner. This type offers a large interior that works well with a lazy Susan, but it won't work with the standard corner miter used on postformed counters. The countertop must follow the diagonal across the corner.

This module is built in much the same way as the one in **12–51**, except that some parts toward the front of the module must be cut at a 45-degree angle. The counter mounting strip (part "F8") is cut at a 45-degree angle on the ends to fit into the rabbet along the top of part "A." The bottom (part "C2") has the front corner cut off at a 45-degree angle. The toe-kick (part "F7") is cut at a 45-degree angle on both ends. You must use a special hinges for the door to function correctly. They mount just like standard European hinges, but they are designed to work with a door mounted at a 45-degree angle. They attach to the side of the cabinet as usual.

You can also use this type of corner module for overhead cabinets. Its construction is shown in **12–54**. The front filler strip (part "L1") is cut at a 45-degree angle on both ends and installed in the rabbet at the top of the side (part "G"). When installing these corner modules, it may be necessary to add a spacer between the corner module and the adjacent cabinet to get sufficient door clearance.

12–53. This corner module uses a single door set diagonally across the corner.

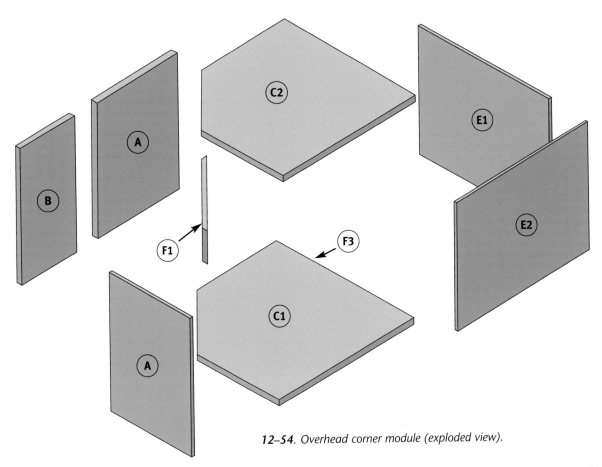

12–54. Overhead corner module (exploded view).

Appliance Garages

An appliance garage is a cabinet placed on the counter to hide small kitchen appliances when they are not in use. An appliance garage is attached directly to the countertop and has no bottom so that the appliances can slide over the countertop into the garage. When you use plastic laminate for the countertop, you should install the appliance garage after the laminate is in place; if you use ceramic tile, install the garage before the tile and cut the tile to fit around the sides of the garage.

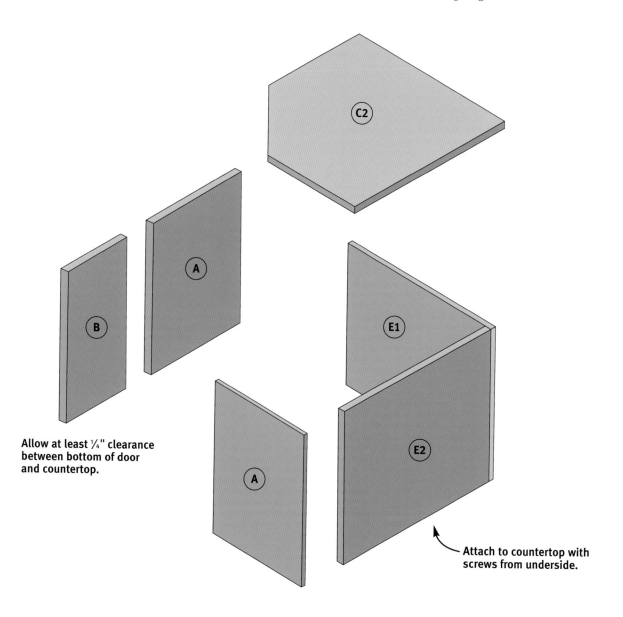

Allow at least ¼" clearance between bottom of door and countertop.

Attach to countertop with screws from underside.

12–55. Corner appliance garage (exploded view).

Corner Appliance Garage

The appliance garage shown in **12–55** fits in a corner. The two back pieces (parts "E1" and "E2") are made from ¾-inch-thick material to give strength to the carcass. After assembly, slide the appliance garage between the countertop and the bottom of the overhead cabinets. Attach the sides to the countertop with screws driven from the underside of the countertop. Attach the top of the garage to the underside of the overhead cabinets with screws through the top.

Roll-Top Appliance Garage

The tambour door is ideally suited for use on an appliance garage, because it rolls completely out of the way to allow easy access to the appliances. The roll-top appliance garage, shown in **12–56**, can be made in any width up to 36 inches. The plans show a shop-made track, but you could also use the commercial roller shade type of tambour door described in chapter 8.

Begin by making the sides (part "G2"). Cut a template for the tambour groove from ¼-inch hardboard. The template should be 9 inches wide and 16⅛ inches high. Round the two top corners to a 1½-inch radius. Clamp the template to the inside surface of the side (part "G2"). Space the template 1⅛ inches from each side and place the bottom of the template flush with the bottom of the side. Mount a template-following collar and a ¼-inch bit in a router. Then make a mark on the rear edge of the side 8 inches down from the top. This mark represents the end of the tambour groove.

Now set the router to make a ⅜-inch-deep cut; be sure to take into account the ¼-inch thickness of the template. Position the router so that the template-following collar is against the template at the bottom-front corner. Start the router and follow the template around to the mark at the rear. Repeat this process on the other side. Remember that the sides are handed; therefore, when they are placed together like the open covers of a book, the rear edges will be touching.

Next, cut the stopped rabbets at the top-front corner. To complete the sides, make the stopped dado at the rear.

The width of the tambour is ¾ inch less than the overall width of the appliance garage. The pull strip is ¾ inch thick and 1 inch wide. Cut a ¼-inch x ¼-inch rabbet on the front and back edges of both ends. This will leave a ¼-inch tongue on the end of the pull strip that will fit into the tambour groove. Rout finger pulls into the front of the pull strip. Next, cut 28 strips that are ¼ inch x ¾ inch to make the tambour. Refer to chapter 8 for complete details on tambour construction. The final finished height of the tambour, including the pull strip, should be 20 inches.

Assemble the unit by gluing the back into the dado and installing the two strips (part "L2") in the rabbets in the front corners of the sides. Slide the tambour into the groove from the opening at the bottom-front corner.

Attach the appliance garage to the countertop with screws through the countertop into the sides. Drive screws through the bottom of the overhead cabinets into the sides and front strip (part "L2").

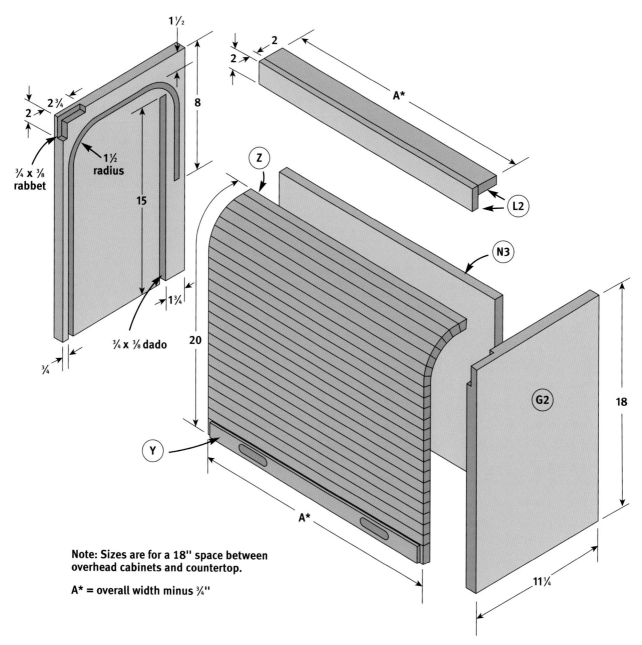

12–56. Roll-top appliance garage (exploded view).

Bills of Materials for Modular Cabinets

Built-In Modular Cabinets BILL OF MATERIALS	Kitchen Base Module (All Dimensions Actual, in Inches)		European Assembly Screw Joinery Refer to *Illus.* 12–5 and 12–35	
Part	**Description**	**Thickness**	**Size**	**Number Req'd**
A	bottom	¾	22½ x (W*–1½)	1
B	sides	¾	22½ x 31¼	2
C	cleats	¾	4 x (W*–1½)	2
D	back	¾	31¼ x W*	1
E	shelf	¾	22½ x (W*–1½)	varies
G	single door	¾	31½ x W*	1
F	double door	¾	31½ x ½ W*	2

*W = overall width of the module. It should not exceed 36 inches.
Notes: 1) Single-door modules should not exceed 24 inches wide.
2) Doors extend ¼ inch below the bottom shelf.
3) If countertop has an overhanging front lip, subtract lip measurement from door height.

Built-In Modular Cabinets

Vanity Base Module

European Assembly Screw Joinery

BILL OF MATERIALS

(All Dimensions Actual, in Inches)

*Refer to **Illus. 12–5** and **12–35***

Part	Description	Thickness	Size	Number Req'd
A	bottom	¾	21 x (W*–1½)	1
B	sides	¾	21 x 26¼	2
C	cleats	¾	4 x (W*–1½)	2
D	back	¾	26¼ x W*	1
E	shelf	¾	21 x (W*–1½)	varies
G1	single door	¾	26½ x W*	1
G2	double door	¾	26½ x ½ W*	2

*W = overall width of the module. It should not exceed 36 inches.
Notes: 1) Single door modules should not exceed 24 inches wide.
2) Doors extend ¼ inch below bottom shelf.
3) If countertop has an overhanging front lip, subtract the lip measurement from the door height.

Built-In Modular Cabinets

Overhead Long Module

European Assembly Screw Joinery

BILL OF MATERIALS

(All Dimensions Actual, in Inches)

*Refer to **Illus. 12–5** and **12–36***

Part	Description	Thickness	Size	Number Req'd
G	sides	¾	10½ x 32	2
I	top	¾	10½ x (W*–1½)	1
J	bottom	¾	10½ x (W*–1½)	1
K	shelf	¾	10½ x (W*–1½)	varies
M	cleats	¾	4 x (W*–1½)	1
N	back	¾	32 x W*	1
F1	single door	¾	28¼ x W*	1
F2	double door	¾	28¼ x ½ W*	2

*W = overall width of the module. It should not exceed 36 inches.
Notes: 1) Single-door modules should not exceed 24 inches wide.
2) Doors extend ¼ inch below the bottom shelf.

Built-In Modular Cabinets — Overhead Short Module — European Assembly Screw Joinery

BILL OF MATERIALS   *(All Dimensions Actual, in Inches)*   *Refer to **Illus. 12–5** and **12–36***

Part	Description	Thickness	Size	Number Req'd
G	sides	¾	10½ x 16	2
I	top	¾	10½ x (W*–1½)	1
J	bottom	¾	10½ x (W*–1½)	1
K	shelf	¾	10½ x (W*–1½)	varies
M	cleats	¾	4 x (W*–1½)	1
N	back	¾	16 x W*	1
F1	single door	¾	12¼ x W*	1
F2	double door	¾	12¼ x ½ W*	2

*W = overall width of the module. It should not exceed 36 inches.
Notes: 1) Single door modules should not exceed 24 inches wide.
2) Doors extend ¼ inch below bottom shelf.

Built-In Modular Cabinets — Kitchen Base Module — Dowel or Plate Joinery

BILL OF MATERIALS   *(All Dimensions Actual, in Inches)*   *Refer to **Illus. 12–5** and **12–43***

Part	Description	Thickness	Size	Number Req'd
A	bottom	¾	23¼ x (W*–1½)	1
B	sides	¾	23¼ x 35¼	2
C	cleats and toe-kick	¾	4 x (W*–1½)	4
D	back	¼	30½ x (W–¾)	1
E	shelf	¾	22¼ x (W*–1½)	varies
G	single door	¾	31½ x W*	1
F	double door	¾	31½ x ½ W*	2

*W = overall width of the module. It should not exceed 36 inches.
Notes: 1) Single door modules should not exceed 24 inches wide.
2) Doors extend ¼ inch below the bottom shelf.
3) If the countertop has an overhanging front lip, subtract the lip measurement from the door height.

Built-In Modular Cabinets

Vanity Base Module

Dowel or Plate Joinery

BILL OF MATERIALS

(All Dimensions Actual, in Inches)

Refer to Illus. **12–5** *and* **12–43**

Part	Description	Thickness	Size	Number Req'd
A	bottom	¾	21¾ x (W*–1½)	1
B	sides	¾	21¾ x 30¼	2
C	cleats and toe-kick	¾	4 x (W*–1½)	4
D	back	¼	25½ x (W*–¾)	1
E	shelf	¾	20¾ x (W*–1½)	varies
F1	single door	¾	26½ x W*	1
F2	double door	¾	26½ x ½ W*	2

W = overall width of the module. It should not exceed 36 inches.
Notes: *1) Single-door modules should not exceed 24 inches wide.*
2) Doors extend ¼ inch below bottom shelf.
3) If the countertop has an overhanging front lip, subtract the lip measurement from the door height.

Built-In Modular Cabinets

Overhead Long Module

Dowel or Plate Joinery

BILL OF MATERIALS

(All Dimensions Actual, in Inches)

Refer to Illus. **12–5** *and* **12–44**

Part	Description	Thickness	Size	Number Req'd
G	sides	¾	11¼ x 32	2
I	top	¾	11¼ x (W*–1½)	1
J	bottom	¾	11¼ x (W*–1½)	1
K	shelf	¾	10¼ x (W*–1½)	varies
M	cleats	¾	4 x (W*–1½)	3
N	back	¼	31¼ x (W*–¾)	1
F1	single door	¾	28¼ x W*	1
F2	double door	¾	28¼ x ½ W*	2

W = overall width of the module. It should not exceed 36 inches.
Notes: *1) Single-door modules should not exceed 24 inches wide.*
2) Doors extend ¼ inch below bottom shelf.

Built-In Modular Cabinets

BILL OF MATERIALS

Overhead Short Module

(All Dimensions Actual, in Inches)

Dowel or Plate Joinery

Refer to **Illus. 12–5** and **12–44**

Part	Description	Thickness	Size	Number Req'd
G	sides	¾	11¼ x 16	2
I	top	¾	11¼ x (W*–1½)	1
J	bottom	¾	11¼ x (W*–1½)	1
K	shelf	¾	10¼ x (W*–1½)	varies
M	cleats	¾	4 x (W*–1½)	3
N	back	¼	15¼ x (W*–¾)	1
F1	single door	¾	12¼ x W*	1
F2	double door	¾	12¼ x ½ W*	2

*W = overall width of the module. It should not exceed 36 inches.
Notes: 1) Single-door modules should not exceed 24 inches wide.
2) Doors extend ¼ inch below the bottom shelf.

Built-In Modular Cabinets

BILL OF MATERIALS

Kitchen Top Drawer (4 Inches)

(All Dimensions Actual, in Inches)

Pocket-Hole Joinery

Refer to **Illus. 12–8**

Part	Description	Thickness	Size	Number Req'd
P	false front	¾	6 x W*	1
Q	front	½	3½ x (W*–3½)	1
R	side	½	3½ x 20	2
S	bottom	½	20 x (W*–2½)	1
T	back	½	3½ x (W*–3½)	1

*W = overall width of the module. It should not exceed 24 inches.
Notes: 1) Sizes are for use with 20-inch-long metal drawer slides that support the drawer bottom and require ½-inch side clearance. 2) Adjust size of part "P" to provide proper clearance between drawers. 3) Kitchen modules require one 4-inch drawer, two 6-inch drawers, and one 8-inch drawer.

Built-In Modular Cabinets

BILL OF MATERIALS

Kitchen Middle Drawer (6 Inches)
(All Dimensions Actual, in Inches)

Pocket-Hole Joinery
*Refer to **Illus. 12–28***

Part	Description	Thickness	Size	Number Req'd
P	false front	¾	7 x W*	1
Q	front	½	5½ x (W*–3½)	1
R	side	½	5½ x 20	2
S	bottom	½	20 x (W*–2½)	1
T	back	½	5½ x (W*–3½)	1

*W = overall width of the module. It should not exceed 24 inches.
Notes: 1) Sizes are for use with 20-inch-long metal drawer slides that support the drawer bottom and require ½-inch side clearance. 2) Adjust size of part "P" to provide proper clearance between drawers. 3) Kitchen modules require one 4-inch drawer, two 6-inch drawers, and one 8-inch drawer.

Built-In Modular Cabinets

BILL OF MATERIALS

Kitchen Bottom Drawer (6 Inches)
(All Dimensions Actual, in Inches)

Pocket-Hole Joinery
*Refer to **Illus. 12–28***

Part	Description	Thickness	Size	Number Req'd
P	false front	¾	10 x W*	1
Q	front	½	7½ x (W*–3½)	1
R	side	½	7½ x 20	2
S	bottom	½	20 x (W*–2½)	1
T	back	½	7½ x (W*–3½)	1

*W = overall width of the module. It should not exceed 24 inches.
Notes: 1) Sizes are for use with 20-inch-long metal drawer slides that support the drawer bottom and require ½-inch side clearance. 2) Adjust the size of part "P" to provide proper clearance between drawers. 3) Kitchen modules require one 4-inch drawer, two 6-inch drawers, and one 8-inch drawer.

Built-In Modular Cabinets

BILL OF MATERIALS

Vanity Top Drawer (4 Inches)

(All Dimensions Actual, in Inches)

Pocket-Hole Joinery

*Refer to **Illus. 12–28***

Part	Description	Thickness	Size	Number Req'd
P	false front	¾	6 x W*	1
Q	front	½	3 ½ x (W*–3 ½)	1
R	side	½	3 ½ x 18	2
S	bottom	½	18 x (W*–2 ½)	1
T	back	½	3 ½ x (W*–3 ½)	1

*W = overall width of the module. It should not exceed 24 inches.
Notes: 1) Sizes are for use with 18-inch-long metal drawer slides that support the drawer bottom and require ½-inch side clearance. 2) Adjust the size of part "P" to provide proper clearance between drawers. 3) Vanity modules require one 4-inch drawer, one 6-inch drawer, and one 8-inch drawer.

Built-In Modular Cabinets

BILL OF MATERIALS

Vanity Middle Drawer (6 Inches)

(All Dimensions Actual, in Inches)

Pocket-Hole Joinery

*Refer to **Illus. 12–28***

Part	Description	Thickness	Size	Number Req'd
P	false front	¾	8 x W*	1
Q	front	½	5 ½ x (W*–3 ½)	1
R	side	½	5 ½ x 18	2
S	bottom	½	18 x (W*–2 ½)	1
T	back	½	5 ½ x (W*–3 ½)	1

*W = overall width of the module. It should not exceed 24 inches.
Notes: 1) Sizes are for use with 18-inch-long metal drawer slides that support the drawer bottom and require ½-inch side clearance. 2) Adjust the size of part "P" to provide proper clearance between drawers. 3) Vanity modules require one 4-inch drawer, two 6-inch drawers, and one 8-inch drawer.

Built-In Modular Cabinets

BILL OF MATERIALS

Vanity Bottom Drawer (8 Inches)

(All Dimensions Actual, in Inches)

Pocket-Hole Joinery

*Refer to **Illus. 12–28***

Part	Description	Thickness	Size	Number Req'd
P	false front	¾	11 x W*	1
Q	front	½	7½ x (W*– 3½)	1
R	side	½	7½ x 18	2
S	bottom	½	18 x (W*– 2½)	1
T	back	½	7½ x (W*– 3½)	1

*W = overall width of the module. It should not exceed 24 inches.
Notes: 1) Sizes are for use with 18-inch-long metal drawer slides that support the drawer bottom and require ½-inch side clearance. 2) Adjust the size of part "P" to provide proper clearance between drawers. 3) Vanity modules require one 4-inch drawer, one 6-inch drawer, and one 8-inch drawer.

Built-In Modular Cabinets

BILL OF MATERIALS

Vanity Two-Door Base Corner Module

(All Dimensions Actual, in Inches)

*Refer to **Illus. 12–51***

Part	Description	Thickness	Size	Number Req'd
A	sides	¾	21¾ x 30¼	2
B	doors	¾	26¼ x 12	2
C1	bottom	¾	32¼ x 32¼	1
E1	back	¾	26¼ x 33	1
E2	back	¾	26¼ x 32¼	1
F1	strip	¾	4 x 32¼	1
F2	strip	¾	4 x 32¼	1
F3	strip	¾	4 x 33	1
F4	strip	¾	15¼ x 32¼	1
F5	strip	¾	4 x 32¼	1
F6	strip	¾	4 x 14¼	1

Notes: 1) The sides are handed. Make one left side and one right side. 2) To lay out the notch in the front corner of the bottom ("C1"), measure 21½ inches from the rear, along the edges that attach to the sides. Use the notch in "C1" to lay out "F4." 3) The door sizes are full-size; if the countertop has an overhanging lip, adjust the door size.

Built-In Modular Cabinets

Kitchen Two-Door Base Corner Module

BILL OF MATERIALS

(All Dimensions Actual, in Inches)   *Refer to* **Illus. 12–51**

Part	Description	Thickness	Size	Number Req'd
A	sides	¾	35¼ x 23¼	2
B	doors	¾	31¼ x 12	2
C1	bottom	¾	33¾ x 33¾	1
E1	back	¾	31¼ x 34½	1
E2	back	¾	31¼ x 33¾	1
F1	strip	¾	4 x 33¾	1
F2	strip	¾	4 x 33¾	1
F3	strip	¾	4 x 34½	1
F4	strip	¾	15¼ x 33¾	1
F5	strip	¾	4 x 33¾	1
F6	strip	¾	4 x 14¼	1

Notes: *1) Sides are handed. Make one left side and one right side. 2) To lay out the notch in the front corner of the bottom ("C1"), measure 21½ inches from the rear, along the edges that attach to the sides. Use the notch in "C1" to lay out "F4." 3) Door sizes are full-size; if the countertop has an overhanging lip, adjust the door size.*

Kitchen Single-Door Base Corner Module

(All Dimensions Actual, in Inches)   *Refer to* **Illus. 12–52**

Part	Description	Thickness	Size	Number Req'd
A	sides	¾	35¼ x 23¼	2
B	door	¾	31¼ x 16	1
C1	bottom	¾	33¾ x 33¾	1
E1	back	¾	31¼ x 34½	1
E2	back	¾	31¼ x 33¾	1
F1	strip	¾	4 x 33¾	1
F2	strip	¾	4 x 33¾	1
F3	strip	¾	4 x 34½	1
F4	strip	¾	4 x 29¾	1
F5	strip	¾	4 x 33¾	1
F6	strip	¾	4 x 15½	1
F7	strip	¾	4 x 22	1
F8	strip	¾	4 x 30	1

Notes: *1) Use hinges designed for 45-degree doors with a 110-degree opening. 2) To lay out the angle on the front corner of the bottom ("C1"), measure 23¼ inches from the rear, along the edges that attach to the sides. 3) Door sizes are full-size; if the countertop has an overhanging lip, adjust the door size.*

Built-In Modular Cabinets

Vanity Single-Door Base Corner Module

(All Dimensions Actual, in Inches)   Refer to *Illus. 12–52*

Part	Description	Thickness	Size	Number Req'd
A	sides	¾	21¾ x 30¼	2
B	door	¾	26¼ x 16	1
C1	bottom	¾	32¼ x 32¼	1
E1	back	¾	26¼ x 33	1
E2	back	¾	26¼ x 32¼	1
F1	strip	¾	4 x 32¼	1
F2	strip	¾	4 x 32¼	1
F3	strip	¾	4 x 33	1
F4	strip	¾	4 x 28¼	1
F5	strip	¾	4 x 32¼	1
F6	strip	¾	4 x 15½	1
F7	strip	¾	4 x 22	1
F8	strip	¾	4 x 30	1

Notes: 1) Use hinges designed for 45-degree doors with a 110-degree opening. 2) To lay out the angle on the front corner of the bottom ("C1"), measure 21¾ inches from the rear, along the edges that attach to the sides. 3) Door sizes are full-size; if the countertop has an overhanging lip, adjust the door size.

Built-In Modular Cabinets — Single-Door Overhead Long Corner Module

BILL OF MATERIALS

(All Dimensions Actual, in Inches)   *Refer to* **Illus. 12–54**

Part	Description	Thickness	Size	Number Req'd
A	sides	¾	32 x 11¼	2
B	door	¾	28¼ x 16	1
C1	bottom	¾	21¾ x 21¾	1
C2	top	¾	21¾ x 21¾	1
E1	back	¾	32 x 22½	1
E2	back	¾	32 x 21¾	1
F1	strip	¾	4 x 17½	1

Notes: 1) Use hinges designed for 45-degree doors with a 110-degree opening.
2) To lay out the angle on the front corner of the bottom ("C1") and the top ("C2,") measure 11¼ inches from the rear, along the edges that attach to the sides.

Built-In Modular Cabinets — Single-Door Overhead Short Corner Module

BILL OF MATERIALS

(All Dimensions Actual, in Inches)   *Refer to* **Illus. 12–54**

Part	Description	Thickness	Size	Number Req'd
A	sides	¾	16 x 11¼	2
B	door	¾	12¼ x 16	1
C1	bottom	¾	21¾ x 21¾	1
C2	top	¾	21¾ x 21¾	1
E1	back	¾	16 x 22½	1
E2	back	¾	16 x 21¾	1
F1	strip	¾	4 x 17½	1

Notes: 1) Use hinges designed for 45-degree doors with a 110-degree opening.
2) To lay out the angle on the front corner of the bottom ("C1") and the top ("C2"), measure 11¼ inches from the rear, along edges that attach to the sides.

Built-In Modular Cabinets — Corner Appliance Garage

(All Dimensions Actual, in Inches)   *Refer to Illus. 12–55*

Part	Description	Thickness	Size	Number Req'd
A	sides	¾	18 x 11¼	2
B	door	¾	17¾ x 16	1
C2	top	¾	21¾ x 21¾	1
E1	back	¾	16 x 22½	1
E2	back	¾	16 x 21¾	1

Notes: 1) *Use hinges designed for 45-degree doors with a 110-degree opening.*
2) *To lay out the angle on the front corner of the top ("C2"), measure 11¼ inches from the rear, along the edges that attach to the sides.*
3) *Sizes are to fit 18-inch spacing between the countertop and the overhead cabinets.*

Built-In Modular Cabinets — Roll-Top Appliance Garage

(All Dimensions Actual, in Inches)   *Refer to Illus. 12–56*

Part	Description	Thickness	Size	Number Req'd
G2	sides	¾	18 x 11¼	2
L2	strips	¾ SL	2 x (W*–¾)	2
N3	back	¾	15 x (W–¾)	1
Y	pull strip	¾ SL	1 x (W*–¾)	1
Z	tambour strips	¼ SL	¾ x (W*–¾)	28

W = overall width of the module. It should not exceed 36 inches.
Material Key: *SL = solid lumber*

Notes: 1) *The sides are handed. Make one left side and one right side.*
2) *Sizes are to fit 18-inch spacing between the countertop and the overhead cabinets.*

Appendix

Built-In Planner

THIS PLANNER IS DESIGNED to help you visualize how a completed built-in cabinet installation will look and to give you the opportunity to try various layouts on paper. It is specifically designed for use with the modular cabinet system described in chapter 12, but it will be helpful in the planning of any built-in cabinet installation.

You can buy CAD software that will generate perspective drawings of kitchen cabinets, and if you plan on making many cabinets I suggest that you use CAD software. However, if you will only be making a few cabinets, this planner will prove useful.

You can use the planner to produce three types of plans: a front elevation that depicts one wall, an oblique projection that adds a three-dimensional quality to one wall, or a modified oblique view that depicts up to three walls in a single view.

The first step in planning the installation is to decide on the basic layout. If you are designing a kitchen, it would be a good idea to consult a book on kitchen design for information on traffic flow, work areas, and appliance layout. To determine the basic layout for any modular cabinet system, accurately measure the area that is available for the cabinets. Make a rough sketch, showing the dimensions and indicating the possible positions for appliances. Once you have this information, you can begin to put the planner to use.

Using the Planner

The planner consists of a layout grid and a set of scale drawings of the various sizes of the cabinet modules described in chapter 12. There is also a set of drawings of a few common appliances.

The first step in using the planner is to make a front elevation of each wall. Since you will probably need more copies of the cabinet modules than the amount included in this book, it's a good idea to make several photocopies of the pages you will need; also, make as many copies of the layout grid as you will need to complete the set of plans. The layout grid is large enough to handle most average-size installations; however, if you are planning a very large installation, you may need to tape two copies of the layout grid together.

Use the measurements you indicated on your rough sketch to draw an outline of the first wall on the layout grid. The layout grid is divided into small squares; each square equals 6 inches. At this point, use only the vertical and horizontal lines and ignore the diagonal lines. There is a scale at the bottom of the page. Cut it out and use it to measure the outline of the wall. This scale operates in the same way as the architect's scale described in chapter 2.

Next, cut out the front elevations of the appliances that you intend to place on that wall. Lay them on the layout grid and try them in various locations until you are satisfied. With the appliances in position, you can now determine the size of the cabinet modules that you can use. The purpose of the appliance drawings is to indicate the usual clearance allowed in a cabinet installation for a particular appliance. If you plan on using especially large appliances, such as a side-by-side refrigerator/ freezer, be sure to check on the actual size of the appliance. If you are using smaller appliances, it is usually a good idea to allow the normal clearance anyway so that you can change to full-size appliances at a later date.

Use the scale provided to measure the distance between the appliances; then look over the different-size modules shown on the front elevation illustration and decide on a combination that will fit. You may want to move an appliance one way or another to make the modules come out even. Now cut out the modules you have chosen and lay them on the layout grid. At this point, you can look at your design and decide if it is correct; you may want to move things around until you are more satisfied.

If the cabinets must fit tightly between two walls, it is unlikely that the standard-module sizes will come out even. Chapter 12 describes how to use filler strips or corner modules to adjust the size. On the planner, try to arrange the modules so that the size of the filler strips is as small as possible; then cut the picture of a larger-size module to the appropriate size and place it where the filler should go.

When you are satisfied with the layout, you can make it permanent by gluing the cutouts to the layout grid. A glue stick works well. **Illustration A–1** shows what a completed front elevation looks like. If this installation consists of more than one wall, make a front elevation for each wall.

After making the front elevations, you can use the planner to add a three-dimensional quality that will give you a better idea of how the completed installation will look. If only one wall is involved, you can make an oblique projection of a single wall, as shown in **A–2**. This is not the usual type of oblique projection that's described in chapter 2, but it gives you the impression of standing off to the side of the cabinets looking down the length of the room.

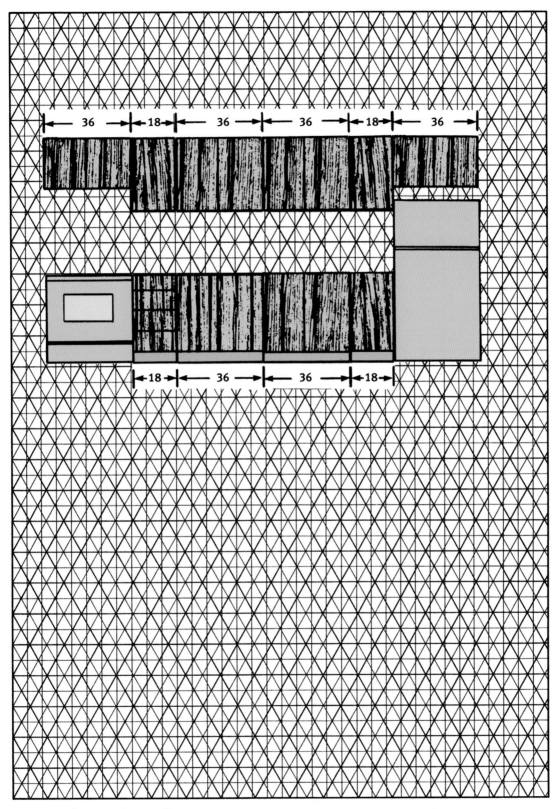

A–1. Front elevation of one wall.

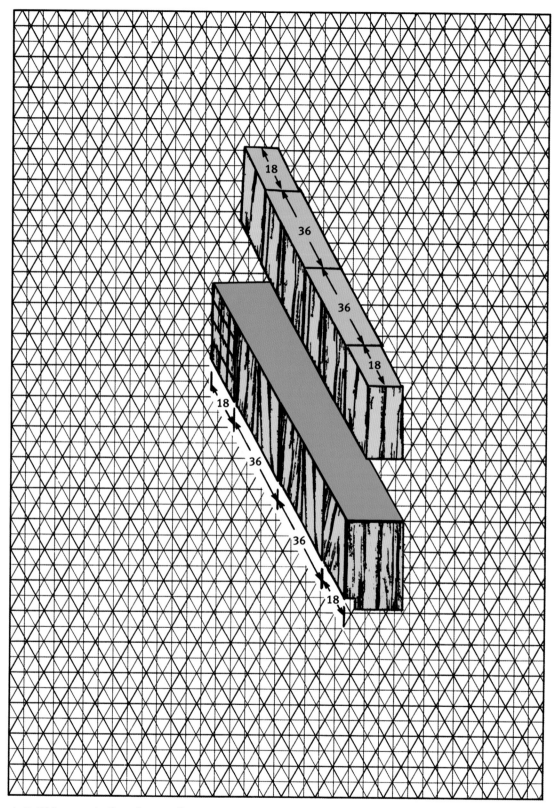

A–2. Oblique projection of one wall.

To make this view, decide whether you want it to be on the right or left side of the page. The cutouts on the oblique illustrations are labeled "left" and "right." Cut out the same-size appliances and cabinet modules from the oblique illustrations that you used in the front elevation. Arrange them on the layout grid the same way you did for the front elevation—only this time, align them with the diagonal lines. Cut out the sides from the front elevation illustration to fill in the ends of the cabinets.

This planner is especially useful for installations that involve more than one wall. In most types of drawings, you can't see the front surface of three walls in a single view, but this planner uses a modified type of oblique drawing that is similar to a perspective drawing. The drawings are not true perspective drawings, since all of the modules appear the same size instead of getting smaller as the distance from the viewpoint increases. This means that the completed drawing won't have the depth of a perspective drawing, but it will still give you a fairly good idea of what the completed room will look like. This is a major advantage because it is much easier to change a feature you don't like while it is on paper than it is to change it after the cabinets are installed.

Illustration A–3 shows a complete plan, including all three walls of the installation. To make a plan like this one, start with the longest wall. Make a front elevation of this wall the same way as described earlier, except use the appliances and sink modules that include a top view. Next, cut out a strip of countertop and place it along the top of the under-the-counter cabinets. Where the cabinets join at a corner, use one of the special corner cutouts.

One point to keep in mind when designing cabinets that meet at a corner is that the under-the-counter cabinets extend out from the wall farther than the overhead cabinets. This can affect the way the fronts of the upper and lower cabinets line up. If you want the doors on the upper cabinets to line up with the doors on the lower cabinets, you will have to add an additional cabinet or spacer at the ends of the overhead cabinets to compensate for the difference in the projection from the wall between the upper and lower cabinets.

After the corners are in place, use the oblique cutouts to make the other two walls in the same manner as described earlier for an oblique drawing of a single wall. Use the cutouts labeled "left" on the left side of the page and those labeled "right" on the right side of the page.

If you are satisfied with the layout you have produced, the final step is to make a full-size story stick. For small installations, the story stick can be a long scrap of plywood. For larger installations, place masking tape on the floor of the room parallel to the walls that will receive the

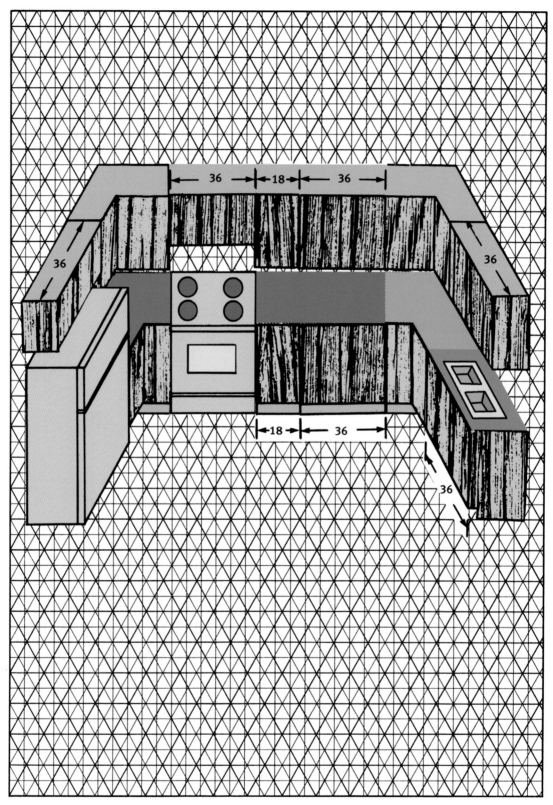

A–3. Complete three-wall view.

cabinets, or place the masking tape on the floor of your shop. Make marks on the stick or tape that indicate the exact length of one wall. Refer to the front elevation for that wall. and make marks for the exact sizes of each module or appliance.

When you have marked all of the modules on the story stick, you can measure directly from the end of the last module to the wall mark to get the exact size of the filler or non-standard-size module needed to fit the available space. The story stick also lets you double-check your layout at full scale so that you can see exactly how far a walk it will be from the sink to the refrigerator.

If everything works out on the story stick, make a list of all of the modules you need and then go to chapter 12 for instructions on building them.

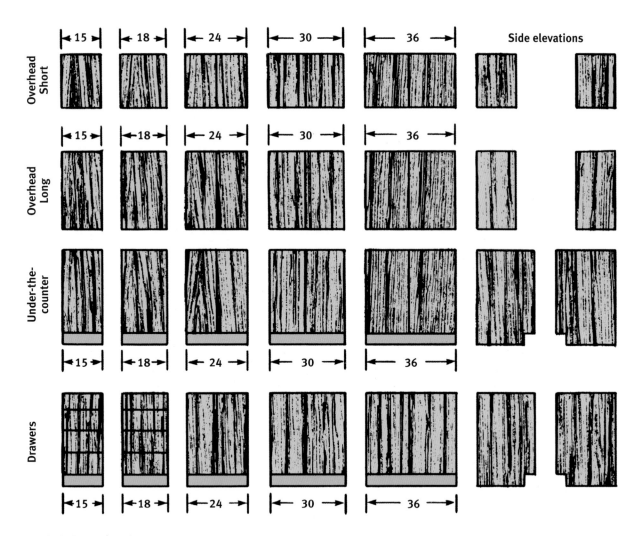

A–4. Front elevations.

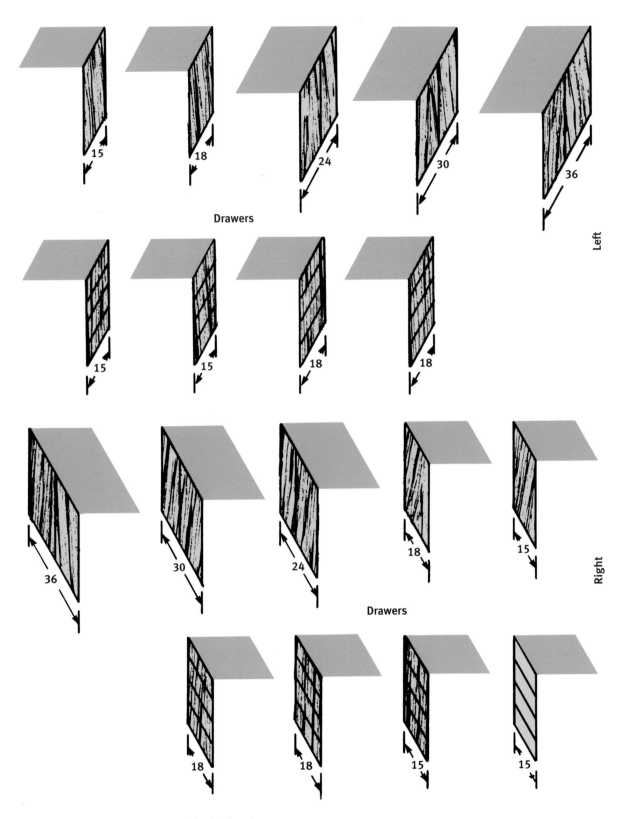

Drawers

15 18 24 30 36

Left

15 15 18 18

36 30 24 18 15

Right

Drawers

18 18 15 15

A–5. Under-the-counter modules (oblique).

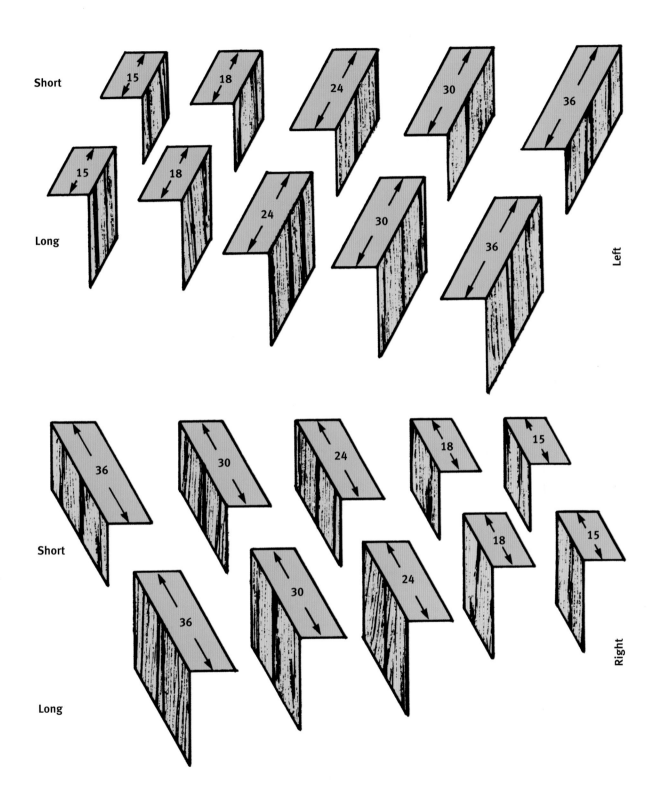

Short

Long

Left

15 18 24 30 36

15 18 24 30 36

Short

Long

Right

36 30 24 18 15

36 30 24 18 15

A–6. Overhead modules (oblique).

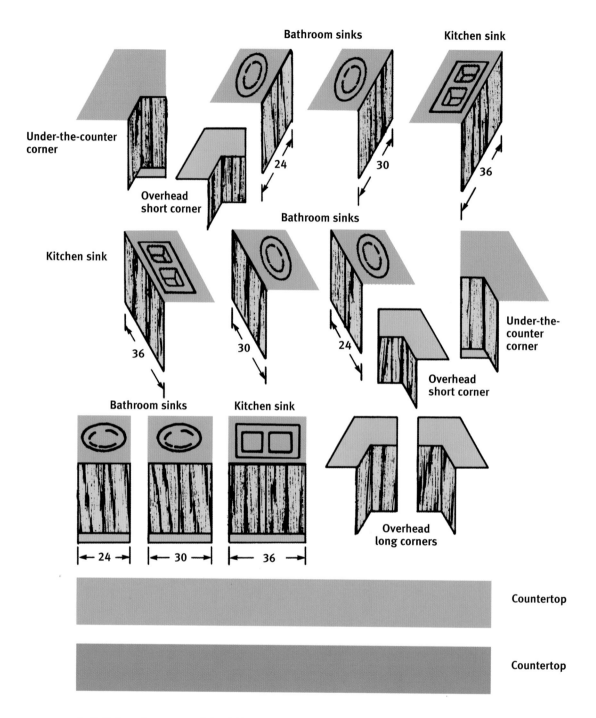

Bathroom sinks

Kitchen sink

Under-the-counter corner

Overhead short corner

24

30

36

Kitchen sink

Bathroom sinks

Under-the-counter corner

Overhead short corner

36

30

24

Bathroom sinks

Kitchen sink

Overhead long corners

24

30

36

Countertop

Countertop

A–7. Sink and corner modules (oblique).

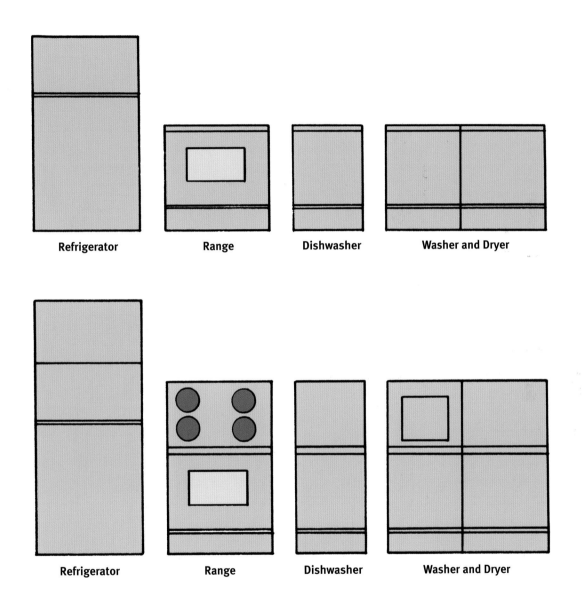

Refrigerator **Range** **Dishwasher** **Washer and Dryer**

Refrigerator **Range** **Dishwasher** **Washer and Dryer**

A–8. Appliances (front elevation).

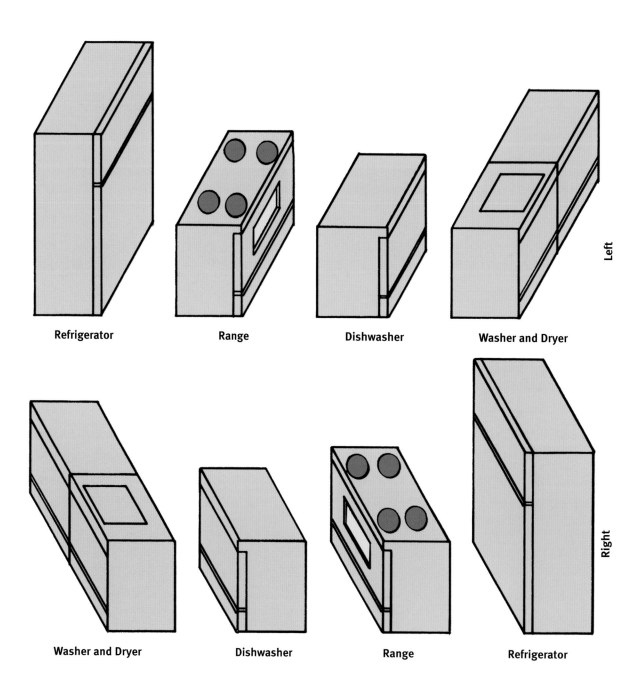

Refrigerator   **Range**   **Dishwasher**   **Washer and Dryer**

Left

Washer and Dryer   **Dishwasher**   **Range**   **Refrigerator**

Right

A–9. Appliances (oblique).

A–10. Built-in planner layout grid.

About the Author

SAM ALLEN HAS MORE THAN 35 YEARS of woodworking experience. He began building custom cabinets for friends and relatives while he was still in high school. In his senior year, he was chosen to represent his school in a statewide industrial arts competition. He earned money for college by building cabinets for a local unfinished furniture store.

After graduating from Brigham Young University with a Bachelor of Science degree in Industrial Education, Sam worked as a carpenter and cabinetmaker, gaining experience in both custom and mass-production cabinetmaking techniques.

Sam's appreciation of hand-tool techniques and antique reproductions began with his study of the cabinets and furniture produced by the early settlers of his native state of Utah. The dry climate of Utah tends to exaggerate problems caused by wood movement; this has led Sam to extensively study and experiment with techniques that will minimize these problems.

Sam Allen is a widely published freelance writer. He is the author of more than 10 woodworking books, including *Wood Finisher's Handbook* and *Making Workbenches: Planning, Building, Outfitting.* He has written scores of articles for magazines such as *Popular Mechanics, The Wood-Worker's Journal, Fine Woodworking,* and *Popular Woodworker.*

METRIC EQUIVALENTS

INCHES TO MILLIMETERS AND CENTIMETERS
MM = millimeters CM = centimeters

Inches	MM	CM	Inches	CM	Inches	CM
⅛	3	0.3	9	22.9	30	76.2
¼	6	0.6	10	25.4	31	78.7
⅜	10	1.0	11	27.9	32	81.3
½	13	1.3	12	30.5	33	83.8
⅝	16	1.6	13	33.0	34	86.4
¾	19	1.9	14	35.6	35	88.9
⅞	22	2.2	15	38.1	36	91.4
1	25	2.5	16	40.6	37	94.0
1¼	32	3.2	17	43.2	38	96.5
1½	38	3.8	18	45.7	39	99.1
1¾	44	4.4	19	48.3	40	101.6
2	51	5.1	20	50.8	41	104.1
2½	64	6.4	21	53.3	42	106.7
3	76	7.6	22	55.9	43	109.2
3½	89	8.9	23	58.4	44	111.8
4	102	10.2	24	61.0	45	114.3
4½	114	11.4	25	63.5	46	116.8
5	127	12.7	26	66.0	47	119.4
6	152	15.2	27	68.6	48	121.9
7	178	17.8	28	71.1	49	124.5
8	203	20.3	29	73.7	50	127.0

Index